Solution-Focused Cognitive and Systemic Therapy

Solution-Focused Cognitive and Systemic Therapy: The Bruges Model is the first book in English to lay out the Bruges Model, a meta-model that incorporates solution-focused therapy in an analysis of the therapeutic alliance and common factors that account for the majority of the efficacy of any therapeutic endeavor. This book is divided into three parts, covering each of the common factors: client factors, therapist and relationship factors, and placebo factors. Each part summarizes the state of our theoretical knowledge, then dives into specific clinical and educational applications in specific populations and contexts.

Luc Isebaert, MD, is the director of Korzybski International and head of the teaching staff of the Korzybski Institutes of Bruges, Paris, and the Netherlands. He is the developer of the Bruges Model.

Solution-Focused Cognitive and Systemic Therapy

The Bruges Model

Luc Isebaert

Routledge
Taylor & Francis Group

NEW YORK AND LONDON

First published 2017
by Routledge
711 Third Avenue, New York, NY 10017

and by Routledge
2 Park Square, Milton Park, Abingdon, Oxon, OX14 4RN

Routledge is an imprint of the Taylor & Francis Group, an informa business

© 2017 Luc Isebaert

First published in French by Éditions érès as *Alliance thérapeutique et therapies
brèves: Le modèle de Bruges*

© 2015 Luc Isebaert

Library of Congress Cataloging-in-Publication Data
A catalog record has been requested for this book

ISBN: 978-1-138-67767-8 (hbk)
ISBN: 978-1-138-67768-5 (pbk)
ISBN: 978-1-315-55941-4 (ebk)

Typeset in Baskerville
by Apex CoVantage, LLC

To the memory of Steve de Shazer, and to the memory of Roland Kuhn

Contents

PART III
Placebo Factors   155

Foreword

> To exchange one orthodoxy for another is not necessarily an advance. The enemy is the gramophone mind, whether or not one agrees with the record that is being played at the moment.
>
> George Orwell

Solution-Focused Brief Therapy (SFBT; de Shazer, 1985, 1994), like much of family therapy, emerged from a climate of theoretical and practical skepticism and intense interest in the mechanisms of therapeutic change. There was a growing disillusionment with psychodynamic therapy, and out of this dissatisfaction emerged a desire to find new ways of doing therapy in a less time-consuming manner. This search eventually evolved into a cadre of brief, systemic, contextual approaches that despite divergent influences had common themes: (1) a shift from the individual to relationship, interaction, and context; (2) a shift toward active, responsive intervention; (3) a shift toward client-specific versus theory-specific intervention; and (4) a gradual movement toward therapy as an evolving, co-constructed conversation.

It is worth taking note of the persons and ideas that inspired much of the work described in this book. The Bateson project's double-bind theory of schizophrenia (Bateson, Jackson, Haley, & Weakland, 1956) suggested that the communication of people considered schizophrenic "made sense" in the context of multiply conflicting and paradoxical injunctions prevalent in the person's significant social system, the family. The Bateson project contributed the cornerstone to a burgeoning brief-therapy movement—that problems can be understood in the context of communicative interaction in significant relationships.

Jay Haley and John Weakland's prolific study of Milton Erickson's work spawned strategic brief therapy (Haley, 1973) and significantly influenced both the interactional approach of the Mental Research Institute (MRI; Watzlawick, Weakland, & Fisch, 1974) and SFBT (de Shazer, 1982). First among these influences was Erickson's insistence that therapists should tailor their approach to fit the client's unique worldview, expectations, and preferred method of working. Second, rather than approaching psychological distress as deficit, Erickson highlighted the client's abundant storehouse of resources, challenging therapists to pursue and magnify resources rather than disabilities. Third, Erickson demonstrated that change can happen quickly and often in dramatic, unexpected ways.

SFBT, arguably the most influential of the brief approaches emerging from that era of ideas and innovation, continues to evolve, as evidenced by the Bruges Model, Solution-Focused Cognitive and Systemic Therapy (SFCST) (Isebaert, 2004). Inherent in SFCST is the fundamental faith that clients can and will realign the parts of their lives that are distressing, given the powerful context of a relationship that respects and follows clients' leads (even when their lead is for therapists to lead). It takes seriously research that, over and over, places clients as the prime movers in therapy and the therapeutic alliance as the fuel for that movement—the client is the heart and the alliance is soul of therapeutic change (Duncan, 2010a). Although the word *research* may evoke visions of pencil-necked geeks with no lived connection to the therapy experience, SFCST practitioners may be interested to discover that research adamantly supports it. That is the topic of this book.

This story illustrates the sentiments that many practitioners, perhaps most solution-focused ones, feel about research: Two researchers were attending their annual conference. Although enjoying the proceedings, they decided to find some diversion to combat the tedium of sitting all day and absorbing vast amounts of information. They settled on a hot-air balloon ride and were quite enjoying themselves until a mysterious fog rolled in. Hopelessly lost, they drifted for hours until finally a clearing in the fog appeared and they saw a man standing in an open field. Joyfully, they yelled down at the man: "Where are we?" The man looked at them, and then down at the ground, before turning a full 360 degrees to survey his surroundings. Finally, after scratching his beard and what seemed to be several moments of facial contortions reflecting deep concentration, the man looked up and said, "You are above my farm."

The first researcher looked at the second researcher and said, "That man is a researcher—he is a scientist!" To which the second researcher replied, "Are you crazy, man? He is a simple farmer!" "No," answered the first researcher emphatically, "that man is a researcher and there are three facts that support my assertion: First what he said was absolutely 100% accurate; second, he systematically addressed our question through an examination of all of the empirical evidence at his disposal, and then carefully deliberated before delivering his conclusion; and third, what he told us is absolutely useless to our predicament."

The research presented in this book, hopefully, will be useful to your predicament. After a discussion of the most replicated finding of the therapy literature—the "Dodo Verdict"—this chapter describes the common factors of change and their perfect fit with SFCST. This chapter also suggests that SFCST therapists can enhance their positive outcomes by piggybacking on their use of scaling questions with more formal feedback measures about the benefit and fit of services.

The Dodo Verdict: The Differential Effectiveness of Competing Therapies

Plus ça change, plus c'est la même chose.

Alphonse Karr

In the children's classic tale *Alice in Wonderland* (1865/1962), Lewis Carroll wrote of a race intended to help dry the animals that were soaked by Alice's homesick tears. The animals ran off helter skelter in different directions, and the race was soon stopped after all were exhausted. The animals demanded that the dodo bird proclaim a winner of the race, until at last he exclaimed the now-famous verdict, "Everybody has won, and all must have prizes." An inspection of Saul Rosenzweig's prophetic 1936 article, "Implicit Common Factors in Diverse Forms of Psychotherapy," reveals the quote by the dodo bird used as an epigraph (see the original article and an interview with Rosenzweig in Duncan, 2010b). The dodo's pronouncement was cleverly invoked to describe the equivalence of effectiveness among the psychotherapies of Rosenzweig's day; it has since become a metaphor for the amazingly consistent finding that all approaches work about equally well. The 1936 article was remarkably clairvoyant; Luborsky et al. (1975) empirically confirmed Rosenzweig's crystal ball assessment of psychotherapy some forty years earlier.

The Dodo Verdict remains the best description of the data—the most replicated finding in the psychological literature—encompassing a broad array of research designs, problems, populations, and clinical settings. The more things change, the more they remain the same: A recent study in the UK (Stiles, Barkham, Twigg, Mellor-Clark, & Cooper, 2006) comparing cognitive behavioral therapy (CBT), psychodynamic therapy (PDT), and person-centered therapy (PCT) as routinely practiced once again found no differences among the investigated approaches.

Perhaps a more controversial illustration is provided by the treatments for the diagnosis du jour, Post-Traumatic Stress Disorder (PTSD). CBT has been demonstrated to be effective and is widely believed to be the treatment of choice, but several approaches with diverse rationales and methods have also been shown to be effective: eye-movement desensitization and reprocessing, cognitive therapy without exposure, hypnotherapy, psychodynamic therapy, and present-centered therapy. A recent meta-analysis comparing these treatments found all of them about equally effective (Benish, Imel, & Wampold, 2007). What is remarkable here is the diversity of methods that achieve about the same results. Two of the treatments—cognitive therapy without exposure and present-centered therapy—were designed to exclude any therapeutic actions that might involve exposure (clients were not allowed to discuss their traumas because that invoked imaginal exposure). Despite the presumed extraordinary benefits of exposure for PTSD, the two treatments without it, or in which it was incidental (PDT), were just as effective (Benish et al., 2007). This study confirms that the competition among the more than 250 therapeutic school remains little more than the competition among aspirin, Advil, and Tylenol. All of them relieve pain and work better than no treatment at all. As the dodo wisely judged, all deserve prizes because none stands above the rest.

Unfortunately, the mountain of evidence that researchers have amassed has had little impact on the graduate or post-graduate training of mental health professionals, or sadly, on professional attitudes. We spend thousands of dollars on workshops, conferences, and books to learn highly publicized methods of treatment. Unfortunately, instead of feeling hopeful or validated, we often wind up feeling demoralized. Why isn't this powerful sword slaying the dragon of my client's misery? The answer all too often is to blame ourselves: We are just not measuring up. The Holy Grail seems just out of reach.

Don't get me wrong. There is nothing wrong with models and techniques, especially ones, like SFCST, that enhance or empower the effects of the factors that account for change—but becoming beholden to *one* or believing that salvation will come from them is folly. They are indeed false gods. First, given the robust findings supporting the Dodo Verdict, it is important to keep in mind that even the much-ballyhooed models—often called "empirically supported" or "validated" or "evidence based"—have only shown themselves to be better than sham treatments or no treatment at all, which is not exactly news to write home to Mom about. Think about it. What if one of your friends went out on a date with a new person, and when you asked about the guy, your friend replied, "He was better than nothing—he was better than watching TV or washing my hair." (Or, if your friend was a researcher: "he was *significantly* better, at a 95% confidence level, than watching TV or washing my hair"). How impressed would you be?

Second, the idea that change primarily emanates from the model or techniques you wield is a siren call destined to smash you against the jagged rocks of ineffective therapy. That therapists might possess the psychological equivalent of a "pill" for emotional distress resonates strongly with many, and is nothing if not seductive as it plays upon our desires to be helpful. A treatment for a specific "disorder," from this perspective, is like a silver bullet, potent and transferable from research setting to clinical practice. Any therapist need only load the silver bullet into any psychotherapy revolver and shoot the psychic werewolf stalking the client. In a most unfortunate interpretation, clients are reduced to a diagnosis and therapists defined by a treatment technology—both interchangeable and insignificant to the procedure at hand. This "product" view of psychotherapy is most empirically vacuous because the treatment itself accounts for so little of outcome variance, while the client and the therapist—and their relationship—account for so much more.

In truth, we are easily smitten by the lure of flashy techniques. Amid explanations and remedies aplenty, therapists courageously continue the search for designer explanations and brand name miracles; they remain disconnected from the power for change that resides in the pairing of two unique persons, the application of strategies that resonate with both, and the impact of a quality partnership. This, of course, doesn't mean that SFCST or any technique is unimportant but rather that it is delivered among a constellation of other factors that are often taken for granted. The Dodo Verdict is not a criticism of solution-focused models or any others but rather simply draws our attention to the common factors of change.

This Is What Works—the Common Factors: Do More of It!

> What . . . accounts for the result that apparently diverse forms of psychotherapy prove successful in similar cases? Or if they are only apparently diverse, what do these therapies actually have in common that makes them equally success-ful? . . . it is justifiable to wonder . . . whether the factors that actually are in operation in several different therapies may not have much more in common than have the factors alleged to be operating.
>
> Saul Rosenzweig

Rosenzweig (1936) not only predicted 70-plus years of data, but he also pre-sented the classic argument, still used today, for a common-factors perspective—namely, because all approaches appear equal in effectiveness, there must be pantheoretical factors in operation that overshadow any perceived or presumed differences among approaches. In short, he discussed the factors common to therapy as an *explanation* for the comparable outcomes of varied approaches. Writing in the *American Journal of Orthopsychiatry*, Rosenzweig observed that no form of psychotherapy or healing is without cures to its credit. Concluding that success is therefore not a reliable guide to the validity of a theory, he suggested that some potent implicit common factors, perhaps more important than the methods purposely employed, explained the uniformity of success of seem-ingly diverse methods. Rosenzweig (1936) summarized these common factors in addition to the therapeutic relationship:

> (1) the operation of implicit, unverbalized factors, such as catharsis, and the yet undefined effect of the personality of the good therapist; (2) the formal consistency of the therapeutic ideology as a basis for reintegration; (3) the alternative formulation of psychological events and the interdependence of personality organization as concepts which reduce the effectual importance of mooted differences between one form of psychotherapy and another.
>
> (p. 415)

If Rosenzweig wrote the first notes of the call to the common factors, Johns Hopkins University's Jerome Frank composed an entire symphony. Jerome Frank (1973) proposed:

> two apparently very different psychotherapies, such as psychoanalysis and systematic desensitization, might be analogous to penicillin and digitalis—totally different pharmacological agents suitable for totally different

conditions. On the other hand, the active ingredient of both may be the same, analogous to two compounds marketed under different names, both of which contain aspirin. I believe the second alternative is closer to the mark.

(pp. 313–314)

Frank's contributions continue to ring true with modern common-factors theorists. His 1961 book, *Persuasion and Healing*, was the first entirely devoted to the commonalities cutting across approaches. He incorporates much of Rosenzweig's brief proposal, but articulates a far more expanded theoretical and empirical context, especially regarding the profound effects of expectation and placebo in healing endeavors. In this and later editions (Frank, 1973; Frank & Frank, 1991), Frank placed therapy within the larger family of projects designed to bring about healing. He (joined by his daughter, Julia, in the last edition) looked for the threads linking such different activities as traditional psychotherapy, group and family therapies, inpatient treatment, drug therapy, medicine, religiomagical healing in non-industrialized societies, cults, and revivals.

In his analysis, Frank (1973) identified four features shared by all effective therapies: (1) an emotionally charged, confiding relationship with a helping person; (2) a healing setting; (3) a rationale, conceptual scheme, or myth that provides a plausible explanation for the client's symptoms and prescribes a ritual or procedure for resolving them; and (4) a ritual or procedure that requires the active participation of both client and therapist and that is believed by both to be the means of restoring the client's health. Frank's work is particularly helpful, as noted later, in understanding the role of model and technique as the vehicle for delivering the other factors.

Several others have identified these elements found in all therapies, but Brigham Young University's Michael Lambert deserves special mention. After an extensive analysis of decades of outcome research, Lambert (1986) identified four factors—and their estimated percentages of outcome variance—as the principal elements accounting for improvement: client/extratherapeutic variables (40%); relationship factors (30%); placebo, hope, and expectancy (15%); and model/techniques (15%); see Figure 0.1. Although these elements were not derived from a statistical analysis, he suggested that they embody what studies indicated about treatment outcome. Lambert's portrayal of the common factors bravely differentiated factors according to their relative contribution to outcome, opening a new vista of understanding models and their proportional importance to success—a bold challenge to their revered status.

Inspired by Lambert's proposal, the integration movement, and our roots in Ericksonian, interactional, and solution focused therapies, my colleagues and I (Duncan, Hubble, & Miller, 1997; Duncan & Moynihan, 1994; Duncan, Solovey, & Rusk, 1992) proposed a "client directed" perspective to apply the common factors based on their differential impact on outcome. "Client directed" spoke to the power of extratherapeutic (or client) factors as well as the privilege that should be afforded to client ideas and theories, view of the alliance, and preferences about intervention; intervention effectiveness was

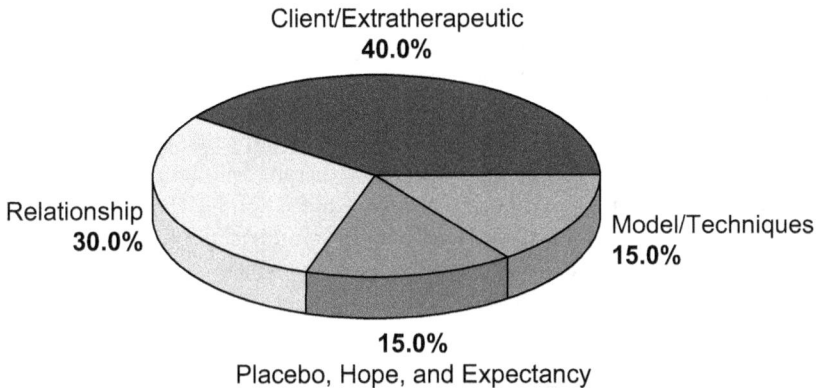

Figure 0.1 Lambert's Common Factors

Note: Adapted from Asay and Lambert (1999). The empirical case for the common factors in therapy: Quantitative findings. In: Hubble, M.A., Duncan, B.L., and Miller, S.D. (Eds.): *The heart and soul of change: What works in therapy* (pp. 33–56). American Psychological Association, Washington, DC.

described as dependent on rallying client resources and as a tangible expression of the quality of the alliance. Successful treatment, we argued, was a matter of tapping in to client resources and ensuring a positive experience of the alliance. To these two elements, based on several major findings of the process-outcome and expectancy literatures, a third aspect was added: namely, the client's ideas regarding the presenting problem, its causes, and potential remedies (what I termed the client's "theory of change"; Duncan et al., 1992). I have been writing about my attempts to operationalize the factors ever since (e.g., Duncan, 2010a; Duncan, Miller, Wampold, & Hubble, 2010; Sparks & Duncan, 2010). The common factors help us take a step back and get a big-picture view of what really works, suggesting that we spend our time in therapy commensurate to each element's differential impact on outcome.

   Recent findings from meta-analytic studies as well as more attention to therapist variance paint a more complicated but satisfying representation of the different factors, their effects, and their relationship to each other. The "pie chart" view of the common factors incorrectly implies that the proportion of outcome attributable to each is static and can be added up to 100% of therapy effects. This suggested that the factors were discrete elements and could be distilled into a treatment model, techniques created, and then these techniques administered to the client. Any such formulaic application across clients, however, merely leads to the creation of another model. On this point, the jury has deliberated and the verdict has been rendered: Whether common factors or not, model differences ultimately matter little in terms of outcome. In truth, the factors are interdependent, fluid, dynamic, and dependent on who the players are and what their interactions are like.

Five factors comprise this perspective—client, therapist, alliance, the model/technique delivered, and feedback—all interdependent and overlapping. Technique is the alliance in action, carrying an explanation for the client's difficulties and a remedy for them, an expression of the therapist's belief that the treatment could be helpful in hopes of engendering the same response in the client. Indeed, you cannot have an alliance without a treatment, an agreement between the client and therapist about how therapy will address the client's goals. Similarly, you cannot have a positive expectation for change without a credible way for both the client and therapist to understand how change can happen. The only way to know whether the common factors are in operation is to obtain real-time client feedback about the benefit and fit of services.

Extratherapeutic/Client Factors

To understand the common factors, it is first necessary to separate the variance due to psychotherapy from that attributed to extratherapeutic factors, those variables incidental to the treatment model, idiosyncratic to the specific client, and part of the client's life circumstances that aid in recovery despite participation in therapy (Asay & Lambert, 1999)—everything about the client that has nothing to do with us.

Figure 0.2 offers my thinking about the factors, trying to make sense of their different but overlapping proportions of the variance of change. The proportion

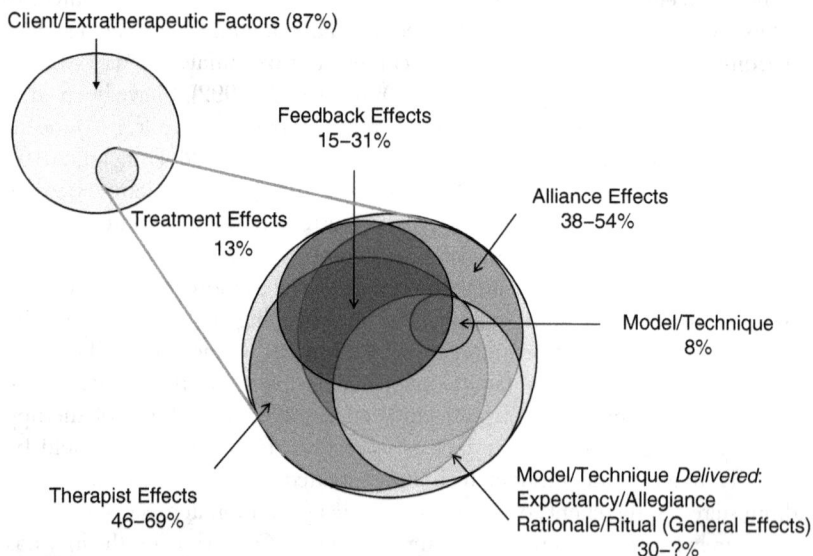

Client/Extratherapeutic Factors (87%)

Feedback Effects
15–31%

Alliance Effects
38–54%

Treatment Effects
13%

Model/Technique
8%

Therapist Effects
46–69%

Model/Technique *Delivered*:
Expectancy/Allegiance
Rationale/Ritual (General Effects)
30–?%

Figure 0.2 The Evolution of Common Factors With the Proposed Feedback Factor

Note: Adapted from Duncan, B.L. (2010). *On becoming a better therapist*. American Psychological Association, Washington, DC.

of outcome attributable to client/extratherapeutic factors is represented by the circle on the left. The variance accounted for by treatment is depicted by the small circle nested within client/extratherapeutic factors (on the lower right side). Even a casual inspection reveals the disproportionate influence of what the client brings to therapy. Client/extratherapeutic factors, including unexplained and error variance, account for 87% of the variance of change, leaving 13% of the variance accounted for by psychotherapy (Wampold, 2001). These extratherapeutic aspects consist of client strengths, struggles, motivation, distress, relational support, change itself, and even chance events. Examples such as persistence, faith, a supportive grandmother, membership in a religious community, divorce, a sense of personal responsibility, a new job, a good day at the track, a crisis successfully managed all may be included. These elements are the most powerful of the common factors in therapy: The client is the engine of change (Bohart & Tallman, 2010).

The impact of extratherapeutic factors on outcome makes even more curious the adoption of pathological descriptions of clients. Duncan and Miller (2000b) debunk the cult of client incompetence and expose the field's hidden assumptions—the heroic psychotherapist galloping in on the white stallion of theoretical clarity brandishing a sword of empirically supported treatments to rescue the helplessly disordered patient terrorized by the psychic dragon of mental illness—and call for a "recasting" of the therapeutic drama to assign clients their rightful heroic roles in change.

Lambert, Garfield, and Bergin (2004) note:

> it is the client more than the therapist who implements the change process . . . we need to reform our thinking about the efficacy of psychotherapy. Clients are not inert objects or diagnostic categories on whom techniques are administered. They are not dependent variables on which independent variables operate . . . people are agentive beings who are effective forces in the complex of causal events.
>
> (p. 814)

In the absence of compelling evidence for any specific variables that cut across clients to predict outcome or account for unexplained variance, this most potent source remains largely uncharted. Client factors cannot be generalized because they differ with each client. These unpredictable differences can emerge only one client at a time, one alliance at a time, one therapist at a time, and one treatment at a time.

We do know something for sure: If we don't recruit these idiosyncratic contributions to outcome in service of client goals, we are inclined to fail. Indeed, in a comprehensive review of 50 years of literature for the fifth edition of the *Bergin and Garfield's Handbook of Psychotherapy and Behavior Change*, Orlinsky, Rønnestad, and Willutzki (2004) indicate, "the quality of the patient's participation . . . [emerges] as the *most* important determinant of outcome" (p. 324; emphasis added).

Rallying clients and their resources to the cause of change is perhaps what SFCST does best, intentionally combing the client's experience in search of existing strengths and solutions. Looking at exceptions or situations when the problem doesn't occur shines a spotlight on client resources, illuminating possibilities for solution. Attending to client factors is the sine qua non of solution-focused practice; enlisting, recruiting, or harvesting client resources and participation are part and parcel of solution-focused work (Murphy, 2008). Outcome research encourages us to view clients as vital partners in the counseling process and aligns directly with solution-focused practice. Interestingly, as we will see, this focus is one of the distinguishing factors of better therapists.

Figure 0.2 also illustrates the second step in understanding the common factors. The second, larger circle in the center depicts the overlapping elements that form the 13% of variance attributable to treatment. Visually, the relationship among the common factors (as opposed to a static pie chart depicting discreet elements adding to a total of 100%) is more accurately represented with a Venn diagram, using overlapping circles and shading to demonstrate mutual and interdependent action. The factors, in effect, act in concert and cannot be separated into disembodied parts (Duncan et al, 1992).

To exemplify the various factors and their attending portions of the variance, the tried-and-true Treatment of Depression Collaborative Research Program (TDCRP) (Elkin et al., 1989) will be enlisted. The TDCRP randomly assigned 250 depressed participants to four different conditions: CBT, interpersonal therapy (IPT), antidepressants plus clinical management (Innovative Medicines Initiative, or IMI), and placebo pill plus clinical management. The four conditions achieved about the same results, although both IPT and IMI surpassed placebo (but not the other treatments) on the recovery criterion (yet another example of the Dodo Verdict). Although the TDCRP is now more than 20 years old, the data continue to be analyzed and relevant, as we will see.

Therapist Effects

> Since no one method of therapy has a monopoly on all the good therapists, another potentially common factor is available to help account for the equal success of avowedly different methods.
>
> Saul Rosenzweig

Therapist factors represent the amount of variance attributable not to the model wielded, but rather to *whom* the therapist is. Variability among therapists continues to be the rule rather than the exception (Beutler et al., 2004). Traditionally, much of the research on therapist variance has been on discrete variables such interpersonal skills, awareness, and so on. Teyber and McClure (2000), however, rightfully assert that such a focus may detract from the more important influences of therapist, intervention, and client fit—on the outcomes of specific therapists matched with specific clients. Indeed, therapist factors have emerged as potent and predictive aspects of therapeutic services, accounting for more of the variance of outcome than any treatment provided, second only to what the client brings. Wampold (2005) comments:

> the variance of outcomes due to therapists (8% to 9%) is larger than the variability among treatments (0%–1%), the alliance (5%), and the superiority of an EST to a placebo treatment (0%–4%), making it the most robust predictor of any factor studied.

(p. 204)

Depending on the study, estimates indicate that between 6% (Crits-Christoph et al., 1991; Anker, Owen, Duncan, & Sparks, 2010; Wampold & Brown, 2005) and 9% (Project MATCH Research Group, 1998) of the variance in outcomes is attributable to therapist effects. Putting this into perspective, the amount of variance attributed to therapist factors is about six to nine times more than that of model differences; or, of the variance attributed to treatment (13%), therapist factors account for from 46 to 69%.[1] In the TDCRP, 8% of the overall variance (or 61% of the variance attributed to treatment) in the outcomes within each treatment was due to therapists (Kim, Wampold, & Bolt, 2006). The psychiatrists in the study highlight this finding: The clients receiving sugar pills from the top third most-effective psychiatrists did better than the clients taking antidepressants from the bottom third least-effective psychiatrists. Even with medication, it matters who is delivering it.

What accounts for the variability? Although we know for sure that some therapists are better than others, there is not a lot of research about what distinguishes the best from the rest—but there is one good possibility and one no-brainer. Gassman and Grawe (2006) conducted minute-by-minute analyses of 120 sessions involving 30 clients treated for a range of psychological problems. They found that unsuccessful therapists focused on problems while neglecting client strengths. When the unsuccessful therapists did focus on clients' strengths, they did so more at the end of a therapy session. Successful therapists focused on their clients' strengths from the very start. They immediate activated client resources to address client problems.

The no-brainer is that the most definitive thing we know about what makes some therapists better than others is their ability to secure a good alliance across a variety of client presentations and personalities. Two recent studies (Baldwin, Wampold, & Imel, 2007; Anker et al., 2010) found that therapists who generally form better alliances also had better outcomes. Baldwin et al. (2007) dispelled common folklore by demonstrating that good alliances were more of a function of what therapists brought to the table than clients: Therapists adept at alliances were able to transcend the type of client while other less-effective therapists were not. In fact, Owen and colleagues found that the alliance accounted for all of the variance among therapists, after considering gender, discipline, and even specific experience (with couples therapy). Such findings suggest that the alliance may represent the best arena for influencing therapist effects.

These two areas—what Gassman and Grawe called *resource activation,* and securing strong alliances with more clients—likely represent the best ways to create positive outcomes, regardless of therapist orientation. Once again, SFCST appears to have a leg up, as a further examination of the alliance will reveal.

The Alliance

> Observers seem intuitively to sense the characteristics of the good therapist time and again . . . sometimes being so impressed as almost to believe that the personality of the therapist would be **sufficient** [emphasis added] in itself, apart everything else, to account for the cure of many a patient by a sort of catalytic effect.
>
> Saul Rosenzweig

The next class of factors represents a wide range of relationship-mediated variables found among therapies, no matter the therapist's theoretical persuasion. Therapist-provided variables, especially the core conditions popularized by Rogers (1957), have not only been empirically supported, but are also remarkably consistent in client reports of successful therapy (Norcross & Lambert, 2005). Researchers repeatedly find that a positive alliance—an interpersonal partnership between the client and therapist to achieve the client's goals (Bordin, 1979)—is one of the best predictors of outcome (Horvath & Bedi, 2002; Horvath & Symonds, 1991; Martin, Garske, & Davis, 2000). The amount of variance attributed to the alliance ranges from 5% to 7% of overall variance or 38–54% of the variance accounted for by treatment. Simply put, the alliance accounts for five to seven times the amount of variance of outcome as model and technique. There are more than 1,000 process-outcome findings that support the association between a strong alliance and positive outcome (Orlinsky et al., 2004).

Despite this, however, naysayers will dismiss the alliance by saying the research is only correlational. This is like saying that smoking cigarettes is only correlated with lung cancer! Even more damning, they say, is that we don't know which comes first, client experience of a strong alliance or client report of change or benefit—the classic chicken or the egg question. Our recent alliance study of 500 clients (Anker, Owen, Duncan, & Sparks, 2010) directly addressed this question. The alliance significantly predicted outcome over and above substantial early change, demonstrating that the alliance is not merely an artifact of client improvement but rather a force to be reckoned with in and of itself.

Finally, Krupnick et al. (1996) analyzed data from the TDCRP and found that while the alliance, from the client's perspective, was predictive of success for all conditions, the treatment model was not. Mean alliance scores explained up to 21% of the variance, while treatment differences accounted for approximately 0% of outcome variance (Wampold, 2001). Keep in mind that treatment accounts for, on average, 13% of the variance. The alliance in the TDCRP explained more of the variance by itself, illustrating how the percentages are not fixed and depend on the particular context of client, therapist, alliance, and treatment model.

The alliance as classically defined by Bordin (1979) includes the relational bond between the therapist and client as well as their agreement about the goals and task of therapy. Although much ignored, it is a fact that the alliance is our most powerful ally and represents the most influence we can have over outcome. SFCST inherently brings significant attention to the alliance in several ways and does not give the alliance short shrift. This can be challenging for all therapists: The alliance is not sexy in comparison to promises of "miracle cures" and "outcomes light years ahead" that often permeate the therapy field. But the alliance is not the anesthesia before surgery—it's not the stuff you do until you get to the real therapy. We do not offer Rogerian reflections to lull clients into complacency so we can stick the real intervention to them! The alliance is probably best conceptualized as an all-encompassing framework for psychotherapy; it transcends any specific therapist behavior and is a property of all aspects of providing services (Hatcher & Barends, 2006). The alliance is evident in anything and everything you do to engage the client in purposive work, from offering an explanation or technique to scheduling the next appointment. You have to *earn* the alliance; it's not given to you. You have to put yourself out there with every person, every interaction, and every session. This is a daunting task.

A review of the research (Norcross, 2010) in the second edition of *The Heart and Soul of Change* (Duncan et al., 2010) confirms what you already know. Regarding empathy, a meta-analysis of 47 studies found an effect size (ES) of .32. To put this in perspective, the ES of model and technique differences is only .20. So your client's perception of empathy is more powerful than any technique you can ever wield. With respect to positive regard, when clients rate outcome, 88% of studies find a significant relationship between client experience of positive regard and a successful conclusion of therapy. Carl Rogers was on to something!

SFCST embraces relational concepts such as empathy and positive regard via attention to validating clients as well as a concerted effort to highlight what's right with clients as opposed to what's wrong with them, to see them as fully capable of resolving any problems. Perhaps where solution-focused practices have been in the forefront of securing good alliances, however, has been with the attention to agreement with the client about the goals and the tasks of therapy—what you are going to work on and how you are going to do it. Tenaciously following client goals and mining solutions from client experience all but guarantees the required agreement about the goals and tasks of therapy.

In an important way, the alliance is dependent on the delivery of some particular treatment: a framework for understanding and solving the problem. On one hand, there can be no alliance without treatment. On the other hand, technique is only as effective as its delivery system: the client-therapist relationship. If technique fails to engage the client in purposive work, it is not working properly and a change is needed. If the search for exceptions or a strength-based perspective does not inspire the client's participation, for example, then, as good as those ideas are, they are not useful with this client. Here is where the variety of models and techniques pays off.

While there is no differential efficacy among approaches in general, there is differential efficacy among approaches with the client in your office *now*. The question is: Does the approach resonate or not? Does its application help or hinder the alliance? Is it something that both you and the client can get behind? Your alliance skills are truly at play here—your interpersonal ability to explore the client's ideas, discuss options, collaboratively form a plan, and negotiate any changes when benefit to the client is not forthcoming. Technique, its selection and application, in other words, are instances of the alliance in action.

The issue of resonance and the agreement about tasks—finding a framework for therapy that both you and the client can believe in—is why it makes a lot of sense to ask clients about their ideas about how to proceed, or at the very least getting client approval of any intervention plan. Traditionally, such a process has not been the case; the search has been for interventions that promote change by validating the therapist's favored theory. Serving the alliance requires taking a different angle—the search for ideas that promote change by validating the client's view of what is helpful—the *client's theory of change* (Duncan & Miller, 2000a; Duncan & Moynihan, 1994; Duncan et al., 1992). Not surprisingly, Frank and Frank (1991) said it best: "Ideally, therapists should select for each patient the therapy that accords, or can be brought to accord, with the patient's personal characteristics and view of the problem" (p. xv).

Recall again the TDCRP. Clients' perceptions of treatment fit or match with their beliefs about the origin of their depression and what would be helpful (psychotherapy or medication), contributed to early engagement, continuation in therapy, and the development of a positive alliance (Elkin et al., 1999).

Model/Technique Delivered[2]: Allegiance and Placebo (Expectancy) Factors

> Whether the therapist talks in terms of psychoanalysis or Christian Science is from this point of view relatively unimportant as compared with the formal consistency with which the doctrine employed is adhered to, for by virtue of this consistency the patient receives a schema for achieving some sort and degree of personality organization.
>
> Saul Rosenzweig

Model/technique factors are the beliefs and procedures unique to any given treatment. They offer an explanation for the client's difficulties and establish methods for resolving them. Because comparisons of therapy techniques have found little differential efficacy, they may all be understood as healing rituals—technically inert, but nonetheless powerful, organized methods for enhancing the effects of client expectations for change—the so-called and perhaps poorly named placebo factors. Whether soliciting exceptions, or instructing clients to lie on a couch, talk to an empty chair, or chart negative self-talk, mental health and substance abuse professionals are engaging in healing rituals.

These specific aspects (the impact of the differences among treatments) are very small, only about 1% of the overall variance or 8% of that attributable to treatment. But the *general effects* of delivering a treatment are far more potent. Most therapeutic methods or tactics share the common quality of preparing clients to take some action to help themselves. In particular, therapists expect their clients to do something different—to develop new understandings, feel different emotions, face fears, or alter or reinstate old patterns of behavior. In short, model and technique provide a structure and focus for both the client and therapist to navigate the waters of change.

As Jerome Frank (1973) seminally noted, all models include a rationale or myth, an explanation for the client's difficulties, and a procedure or ritual, strategies to follow for resolving them. Models achieve their effects in large part (if not completely) *through* the activation of placebo, hope, and expectancy, combined with the therapist's belief in (allegiance to) the treatment administered. As long as a treatment makes sense to, is accepted by, and fosters the active engagement of the client, the particular approach used is unimportant. Said another way, therapeutic techniques are placebo-delivery devices (Kirsch, 2005).

Robust expectancy effects appear to be the rule rather than the exception. Baskin, Tierney, Minami, and Wampold (2003) found a relationship between the structural equivalence of the placebo to the active treatment and the size of the difference between the placebo and that treatment. Structural equivalence included the length of the sessions and duration of treatment, the training of the therapists, and the lack of constraint of the conversation to neutral or non-problem topics. Comparisons between active treatments and placebos not structurally equivalent produced larger effects than comparisons between active treatments and structurally equivalent placebos—which produced negligible differences ($d = .15$), just shy of the differences typically found among treatment approaches ($d = .20$). Expectancy variables, therefore, loom large in treatment effects and are inextricably intertwined with the delivery and success of any intervention.

In both medicine and psychotherapy, when the placebo or technically inert condition is offered in a context that creates positive expectations, it reliably produces effects almost as large, or as large as the treatment itself (Wampold, Minami, Tierney, Baskin, & Bhati, 2005). Based on their meta-analysis, Wampold et al. conclude:

> the placebo effect is robust. With regard to placebo effects in medicine, when disorders were amenable to placebo treatments and the design of the study was sufficient to detect a placebo effect, the placebo effect was indeed present and approached the size of treatment effects. . . . In psychotherapy, it has been claimed that treatments produce effects that are

roughly twice as large as placebo effects. . . . However, when psychotherapy placebos are well designed, the placebo effect approaches the treatment effect.

(p. 850)

The TDCRP is again instructive. First, across all conditions, client expectation of improvement predicted outcome (Sotsky et al., 1991). Second, an inspection of the Beck Depression Inventory scores of those who completed the study (see Elkin et al., 1989) reveals that the placebo plus clinical management condition accounted for nearly 93% of the average response to the active treatments.

Allegiance and expectancy are two sides of the same coin—the belief by both the therapist and the client in the restorative power and credibility of the therapy's rationale and related rituals. The degree to which the therapist delivering the treatment believes the chosen therapy to be efficacious weighs in as a strong determinant of outcome in clinical trials. Meta-analytic investigations of allegiance have generally found effects ranging up to an ES of .65 (Wampold, 2001). Given that the upper bound for specific effects is estimated at .20, the therapist's attitude toward the therapy is critical to effective treatment. The therapist's allegiance to an approach contributes to the client coming to believe in a treatment as well. Expectancy and allegiance effects, therefore, are not thought to arise specifically from a given treatment procedure; they come from the hopeful expectations that accompany the use and implementation of the method.

To punctuate the point about the more powerful general effects, consider present-centered therapy mentioned earlier as a treatment that works for PTSD (see Wampold, 2007 for a full description). Researchers testing the efficacy of CBT for (PTSD) wanted a comparison group that contained curative factors shared by all treatments (warm empathic relationship) while excluding those believed unique to CBT (exposure). This control treatment, present-centered therapy (PRCT), contained no treatment rationale and no therapeutic actions. Moreover, to rule out any possibility of exposure, even covert in nature, clients were not allowed to talk about the traumatic events that had precipitated therapy. PRCT was, of course, found to be less effective than CBT—it wasn't really a treatment with professed "active" ingredients. However, when later a manual containing a rationale and condition-specific treatment actions was added to facilitate standardization in training and delivery, few differences in efficacy were found between PRCT and CBT in the treatment of PTSD (McDonagh et al., 2005). In fact, significantly fewer clients dropped out of PRCT than CBT. Thus, when PRCT was made to resemble a bona fide treatment (that is, it added placebo, expectancy, and allegiance variables), it was not only as effective but also more acceptable than CBT.

The act of administering treatment—the *model/technique delivered*—is the vehicle that carries allegiance and placebo effects in addition to the specific effects of the given approach.

It pays, therefore, to have several rationales and remedies at your disposal that you believe in, as well as believing in the possibility of the client's ideas about change. Placebo factors are also fueled by a therapist belief that change occurs naturally and almost universally—the human organism, shaped by millennia of evolution and survival, tends to heal and to find a way, even out of the heart of darkness (Sparks & Duncan, 2010).

Another strength of solution-focused approaches and yet another way that SFCST is congruent with common factors research is the attention given to the hope of a better future. Starting with the Miracle Question and a clear eye toward the future, SFCST encourages hope through compliments, presuppositional language, and ascribing gains to client efforts and actions. Each of these behaviors inspires the expectation that change is not only possible, it is inevitable—another basic assumption and profound contribution of a solution focused perspective.

Finally, it is important to note that suggesting specific effects are small in comparison to general effects, and that psychotherapy approaches achieve about the same results does not mean that solution-focused models and techniques are not important. It merely means these specific aspects of models are the vehicles that allow for resource activation and client engagement—the magnifying glass that harnesses the power of sunshine, focusing it into a single beam, and ignites change in the client's life. SFCST happens to be in concert, in both theory and practice, with those factors that are most important to outcomes. But the proof of the pudding is in the taste: While there is no differential efficacy on aggregate, there are approaches that are likely better or worse for the client in your office now. The only way to know that is by monitoring the outcome of your services. Before turning to the fifth common factor, a look at the state of affairs in psychotherapy will set the stage.

The Good, the Bad, and the Ugly of Psychotherapy

> The only man I know who behaves sensibly is my tailor; he takes my measurements anew each time he sees me. The rest go on with their old measurements and expect me to fit them.
>
> George Bernard Shaw

The good news is that the efficacy of psychotherapy is very good: The average treated person is better off than about 80% of the untreated sample (Duncan et al., 2010), translating to an effect size (ES) of about .80.[3] Moreover, these substantial benefits apparently extend from the laboratory to everyday practice. For example, the real world study mentioned earlier in the UK (Stiles et al., 2006) comparing CBT, PDT, and PCT as routinely practiced reported a pre–post ES of around 1.30. In short, there is a lot to feel proud about our profession: Psychotherapy works.

But there's more to the story. The bad news is twofold: First, dropouts are a significant problem in the delivery of mental health and substance abuse services, averaging at least 47% (Wierzbicki & Pekarik, 1993). When dropouts are considered, a hard rain falls on psychotherapy's efficacy parade, both in randomized clinical trials (RCT) and in clinical settings. Second, despite the fact that the general efficacy is consistently good, not everyone benefits. Hansen, Lambert, and Foreman (2002), using a national database of more than 6,000 clients, reported a sobering picture of routine clinical care in which only 20% of clients improved as compared to the 57–67% rates typical of RCTs. Whichever rate is accepted as more representative of actual practice; the fact remains that a substantial portion of clients go home without help.

After the good and the bad, here comes the ugly: Explaining part of the volatile results, variability among therapists is the rule rather than the exception. Not surprisingly, as noted earlier, some therapists are much better at securing positive results than others. In fact, therapist effectiveness ranges from 20% to 70%! Moreover, even very effective clinicians seem to be poor at identifying deteriorating clients. Hannan et al. (2005) compared therapist predictions of client deterioration to actuarial methods. Though therapists were aware of the study's purpose, familiar with the outcome measure used, and informed that the base rate was likely to be 8%, they accurately predicted deterioration in only one out of 550 cases; psychotherapists did not identify 39 out of the 40 clients who deteriorated. In contrast, the actuarial method correctly predicted 36 of the 40.

So despite the overall efficacy and effectiveness of psychotherapy, dropouts are a substantial problem; many clients do not benefit; and therapists vary significantly in effectiveness, and are poor judges of client deterioration. Most of us provide an invaluable service to our clients, but sadly most of us don't know how effective we really are: We don't know who will drop out or who will ultimately not benefit or even deteriorate. Do you know how effective you are? With dropouts considered, how many of your clients leave your office absent of benefit? Which clients in your practice now are at risk for dropout or negative outcome? What is the solution to these problems?

To the Rescue: Feedback and Practice-based Evidence

> However beautiful the strategy, you should occasionally look at the results.
>
> Sir Winston Churchill

There is a practical clinical solution to these everyday pitfalls called *practice-based evidence* (Barkham et al., 2001; Duncan, Miller, & Sparks, 2004). Howard, Moras, Brill, Martinovich, and Lutz (1996) were the first to advocate for the systematic evaluation of client response to treatment during the course of therapy and recommended such information be used to "determine the appropriateness of the current treatment . . . the need for further treatment . . . [and] prompt a clinical consultation for patients who [were] not progressing at expected rates" (Howard et al., 1996, p. 1063). When this occurs—when client feedback is systematically collected and used to tailor treatment—good things happen. For example, using the Outcome Questionnaire 45.2, feedback pioneer Michael Lambert has conducted five RCTs. All five demonstrated significant gains for feedback groups over treatment as usual (TAU) for clients at risk for a negative outcome. Of TAU at-risk cases, 22% reached reliable improvement and clinically significant change compared with 33% for feedback to therapist groups, 39% for feedback to therapists and clients, and 45% when feedback was supplemented with support tools such as measures of the alliance (Lambert, 2010). The addition of client feedback alone—without new techniques or models of treatment and leaving therapists to practice as they saw fit—enabled over two times the amount of at-risk clients to benefit from psychotherapy. Think of that advantage in your practice. Consider the pool of clients in your practice right now who are not benefiting. Systematic feedback could allow you to recapture good outcomes with many of those clients who would otherwise not benefit.

Continuous client feedback individualizes psychotherapy based on treatment response; provides an early warning system that identifies at-risk clients, thereby preventing dropouts and negative outcomes; and suggests a tried-and-true solution to the problem of therapist variability—namely that feedback necessarily improves performance.

Although there are several quality feedback systems available (see Lambert, 2010), the feedback process described here is the Partners for Change Outcome Management System (PCOMS) (Duncan, 2010a; Duncan et al., 2004; Miller, Duncan, Sorrell, & Brown, 2005). Much of this system's appeal rests on the brevity of the measures and therefore its feasibility for everyday use in the demanding schedules of front-line clinicians—it was developed with the in-the-trenches therapist in mind. The Outcome Rating Scale (ORS) and the Session Rating Scale (SRS) are both four-item measures designed to track outcome and the therapeutic alliance, respectively. PCOMS was based on Lambert's continuous assessment model using the Outcome Questionnaire 45.2 (Lambert et al., 1996), but there are differences beyond the measures. First, PCOMS is integrated into the ongoing psychotherapy process and routinely includes a transparent discussion of the feedback with the client (Duncan et al., 2004). Session-by-session interaction is focused by client feedback about the benefits or lack thereof of psychotherapy. Second, PCOMS assesses the therapeutic alliance every session and includes a discussion of any potential problems. Lambert's system includes alliance assessment only when there is a lack of progress.

Four studies have demonstrated the benefits of client feedback with the ORS and SRS. Miller, Duncan, Brown, Sorrell, and Chalk (2006) explored the impact of feedback in a large culturally diverse sample utilizing a telephonic employee assistance program (EAP). Although the study's quasi-experimental design qualifies the results, the use of outcome feedback doubled overall effectiveness and significantly increased retention. Three recent RCTs used PCOMS to investigate the effects of feedback versus TAU. First, in an independent investigation, Reese, Norsworthy, and Rowlands (2009) found that clients who attended therapy at a university counseling center or a graduate training clinic demonstrated significant treatment gains for feedback when compared to TAU. Second, our recent study in Norway (Anker, Duncan, & Sparks, 2009), the largest RCT of couples therapy ever done, found that feedback clients reached clinically significant change nearly four times more than non-feedback couples. The feedback condition maintained its advantage at a six-month follow-up and achieved a 46% lower separation/divorce rate. Feedback is a powerful phenomenon. It improved the outcomes of nine of ten therapists in this study. The third RCT (Reese, Toland, Sloan, & Norsworthy, 2010) replicated the Norway study with couples and found similar results.

An inspection of Figure 0.2 shows that feedback overlaps and affects all the factors—it is the tie that binds them together—allowing the other common factors to be delivered one client at a time. Soliciting systematic feedback is a living, ongoing process that engages clients in the collaborative monitoring of outcome, heightens hope for improvement, fits client preferences, maximizes therapist–client fit and client participation, and is itself a core feature of therapeutic change. It provides for a transparent interpersonal process that solicits the client's help in ensuring a positive outcome.

At first blush, feedback may seem like an odd addition to the list of factors that cut across all approaches (Duncan, 2010a; Sparks & Duncan, 2010). The process of attaining formal client feedback and using that input to tailor services, however, seems a worthy addition for several reasons. First, the effects of feedback are independent of the measures used—a variety of outcome instruments have demonstrated a positive impact on outcome. Second, systematic feedback improves outcome regardless of the specific process used, whether in collaboration with clients or merely giving the feedback to therapists—over the phone or face-to-face, paper and pencil administrations versus electronic formats matters not. Third, feedback increases client benefits across professional discipline, clinical setting, client population, as well as beginning or experienced therapists. Fourth, feedback significantly improves outcome regardless of the model practiced: The feedback process does not dictate what technique is utilized, but rather is a vehicle to modify any delivered treatment for client benefit. Fifth, attaining informal client feedback about the benefit and fit of services is common among psychotherapists. Any goal-directed, symptom-oriented, or other approach that openly discusses the outcome of services (e.g., scaling questions) is incorporating informal client feedback into the therapeutic mix. Feedback speaks to an interpersonal process of give and take between the clinician and client, and (at least to some extent) can be argued to be characteristic of many therapeutic encounters. Finally, the evidence regarding feedback continues to build. Feedback, then, similar to the history of the alliance, has been initially viewed as an important aspect of conducting effective psychotherapy, and is garnering a growing evidence base that supports a more formal understanding and systematic inclusion. Given its broad applicability, lack of theoretical baggage, and independence of a specific instrument or defined practice, feedback can be argued to be a factor that demonstrably contributes to outcome regardless of the theoretical predilection of the clinician.

SFCST is strongly behind the belief that clients are better positioned than anyone else to inform and evaluate the therapy process in ways that are most beneficial to them—the client is the ultimate authority on the usefulness of services. The ORS and SRS piggyback on this belief in a more formal way to provide immediate feedback on what is working and what is not. In keeping with the client-driven emphasis of SFBT (de Shazer et al., 2007), what follows describes two practical tools for accessing the client's perspective of the benefit and fit of services: the ORS (Miller, Duncan, Brown, Sparks, & Claud, 2003) and the SRS (Duncan, Miller, Sparks, Claud, Reynolds, Brown, & Johnson, 2003).

Common Factors: One Client at a Time

> At bottom every man [sic] knows well enough that he is a unique being, only once on this earth; and by no extraordinary chance will such a marvelously picturesque piece of diversity in unity as he is, ever be put together a second time.
> Friedrich Nietzsche

Common-factors research provides general guidance for enhancing those elements shown to be most influential in positive outcomes. The specifics, however, can be derived only from the client's response to any treatment delivered—the client's feedback regarding progress in therapy and the quality of the alliance. Therapists need not know what approach should be used with each "disorder," but rather whether the delivered approach is a good fit for and benefits the client. The systematic collection of feedback simply formalizes what most of us aspire to be: sensitive to client experiences and interested in results. That is what practice-based evidence intends to do—draw on the resources and ideas of clients and therapists while monitoring their impact on treatment benefit.

Acquiring formal feedback enables a transparent conversation unlike most of us has ever experienced. With a collaborative focus on the benefit and fit of psychotherapy, clients can teach us how to do more effective work, specifically, on a session by session, and even within-session basis. Beyond lessons about life or about the work of psychotherapy in general, a culture of continuous client feedback keeps our utmost attention on the here and now with *this* client in *this* session. Clients teach us with their responses—whether or not they are benefiting and whether or not our service is a good fit for them—as well as their reactions and reflections about the next step. In short, practice-based evidence enables your clients to teach you how to do better work, especially those who are not responding to your therapeutic business as usual.

It boils down to this: identifying clients who aren't responding to what you usually do that works and addressing the lack of progress in a positive, proactive way that keeps them engaged while you collaboratively seek new directions. To retain clients at risk for slipping through the proverbial crack, we need to embrace what we know about positive change in therapy. Time and again, from the pioneering work of Ken Howard (Howard, Kopta, Krause, & Orlinsky, 1986) to current sophisticated investigations using the latest statistical methods (Baldwin, Berkeljon, Atkins, Olsen, & Nielsen, 2009), studies reveal that the majority of clients experience change in the first seven visits. This means that clients who report little or no progress early on will likely show no improvement over the entire course of therapy, or will end up on the drop-out list—early change predicts engagement in therapy and a good outcome at termination (Brown, Dreis, & Nace, 1999). This doesn't mean that if a client reports early change, the problem is "cured" or completely resolved. Rather, it suggests that the client has a subjective sense that therapy has gotten under way and that he or she's on the right path. The research about early change is quite a gift; monitoring change provides a tangible way for us to identify folks who are not responding so that we can chart a new course.

Punctuating this point just when I thought the TDCRP data couldn't be ana-lyzed any more, a study by Lutz, Stulz, and Köck (2009) found three patterns of early response that predicted depression severity at treatment termination and follow-up. These findings further support that early change is an important factor for the prediction of short- and long-term outcome in psychotherapy.

A second robust predictor of positive change described earlier, solidly dem-onstrated by a large body of studies (Norcross, 2010), is that tried-and-true but taken for granted old friend, the therapeutic alliance. Clients who highly rate their partnership with their therapists are more apt to remain in therapy and benefit from it. Instead of regarding the first sessions as a warm-up period or a chance to try out the latest technique, we should direct special attention to engaging the client from the beginning of therapy.

Obtaining feedback provides invaluable data about the prospects for treat-ment success or failure. Specifically, it gives us information about the match among ourselves, our approach, and the client. The feedback process directly involves clients in monitoring progress toward their goals and how well the services they're receiving fit their needs. Asking them to participate in this way increases their sense of agency in any decisions about their care.

Recall that feedback doubles your effectiveness with those not responding to your therapy as usual. Think about this for a minute. Even if you are one of the most effective therapists now, for every cycle of ten clients you see, three will go home without benefit. Over the course of a year, for a therapist with a full caseload, this amounts to a lot of unhappy clients. You can recover a substan-tial portion of those folks that don't benefit by first identifying who they are, keeping them engaged, and tailoring your services accordingly.

Monitoring Outcome: The Outcome Rating Scale

> Feedback is the breakfast of champions.
>
> Ken Blanchard and Spencer Johnson

For a measure to be used on an everyday basis, it must not only be reliable and valid, but it must also be feasible: brief, easy, cheap, and immediately relevant to the work at hand. Dissatisfied with the complexity, length, and user-unfriendliness of existing outcome measures, my colleagues and I developed the ORS (Miller et al., 2003) and Child ORS (Duncan et al., 2006) as brief clinical alternatives. The ORS and all the measures discussed here are available for free download at www.heartandsoulofchange.com.

Figure 0.3 reveals that the ORS assesses four dimensions: (1) Individual—personal or symptomatic distress or well being, (2) Interpersonal—relational

Outcome Rating Scale (ORS)

Name_____ Age (Yrs):____ Sex: M / F
Session#____ Date:_____
Who is filling out this form? Please check one: Self_____ Other_____
If other, what is your relationshop to this person?_____

Looking back over the last week, including today, help us understand how you have been feeling by rating how well you have been doing in the following areas of your life, where marks to the left represent low levels and marks to the right indicate high levels. *If you are filling out this form for another person, please fill out according to how you think he or she is doing.*

Individually
(Personal well-being)

|---|

Interpersonally
(Family, close relationships)

|---|

Socially
(Work, school, friendships)

|---|

Overall
(General sense of well-being)

|---|

The Heart and Soul of Change Project

www.heartandsoulofchange.com

© 2000, Scott D. Miller and Barry L. Duncan

Figure 0.3 The Outcome Rating Scale. Download free working copies at www.heartandsoulofchange.com. Many translations are available.

distress or how well the client is getting along in intimate relationships, (3) Social—the client's view of satisfaction with work/school and relationships outside of the home, and (4) Overall—a big picture or general sense of well-being. Changes in these areas are widely considered to be valid indicators of successful outcome. The ORS simply translates these four dimensions into a visual analog format of four 10-cm lines, with instructions to place a mark on each line with low estimates to the left and high to the right. The four 10-cm lines add to a total score of 40. The score is simply the summation of the marks made by the client to the nearest millimeter on each of the four lines, measured by a centimeter ruler or available template. Because of its simplicity, ORS feedback is immediately available for use at the time the service is delivered. Rated at a seventh-grade reading level and translated into multiple languages, the ORS is easily understood by adults and adolescents from a variety of different cultures and enjoys rapid connection to clients' day-to-day lived experience.

Although we were hoping for the best regarding the reliability and validity of the ORS, we never dreamed in a million years that we could get the results that we got. Miller et al. (2003) reported that the internal consistency of the ORS was .93. Concurrent validity of the ORS has been demonstrated as adequate through correlates with the Outcome Questionnaire 45.2 ($r = .60$; Bringhurst, Watson, Miller, & Duncan, 2006; $r = .74$; Campbell & Hemsley, 2009; $r = .59$ Miller et al., 2003); it was also validated in Norwegian (Anker et al., 2009) and Dutch (Hafkenscheid, Duncan, & Miller, 2010). While one can never reduce items by that much and not lose some of the richness of the longer measures, the ORS more than accomplished our main goal: to give a reliable and valid measure to mental health and substance abuse professionals that they could actually use on a client by client basis. This simple measure allows everyone to know, and to react to, the client's view of whether the services being offered are helping. For more information about the psychometrics, visit www.heartand-soulofchange.com and download the articles referenced.

How did such a short measure perform so well psychometrically? As it turns out, all these instruments, regardless of what they purport to measure, assess the same thing: distress. So whether they are measuring anxiety, depression, interpersonal problems—and importantly, whether they are 64 or 45, or even 4 items—they all measure the client's subjective view of distress, what researchers call loading on the same factor. That is how we lucked out, and that's how a four-item measure can give you a reliable and valid indicator of client progress in therapy. You can use longer measures, but you don't have to.

The brevity of the ORS really makes a difference, because—as is news to no one on the front lines—the number of forms and other oversight procedures has exploded. Few have the time to devote to the repeated administration, scoring, and interpretation of lengthy measures, so feasibility is critical. Clients quickly tire of measures that lack obvious face validity, require more than a few minutes to complete, or appear to take away from time spent with the counselor. Low compliance rates are the most frequent result.

To be sure, because of its brevity, the ORS is weaker psychometrically and does not have the same breadth and depth of assessment as the longer scales. At the same time, a measure that goes unused is useless regardless of its strengths. In the real world of delivering services, finding the right outcome measure means striking a balance between the competing demands of validity, reliability, and feasibility. The development of the ORS and CORS reflects our attempt to find such a balance (Duncan et al., 2006; Miller et al., 2003).

Intimately related to feasibility is the issue of the immediacy and utility of the feedback—whether the measure has an intended *clinical* use to improve the effectiveness of rendered services. Most outcome measures were developed primarily as pre–post and/or periodic assessment devices. Such instruments provide an excellent way to measure program effectiveness but are not feasible to administer frequently, and therefore do not provide real-time feedback for immediate treatment modification before clients drop out or suffer a negative outcome. In short, they are not clinical tools as much as they are management or oversight tools. The ORS was designed as a clinical *and* outcome tool to provide real-time feedback to both clients and providers to improve the effectiveness of services, and as a way to measure outcome at individual, program, and agency levels.

Monitoring client feedback via the ORS is a natural fit with SFCST practice. In fact, my roots in solution-focused therapy were integral to the development of the ORS. When we discovered how infeasible longer measures of outcome were for everyday clinical practice, we sought to develop a way for clinicians to routinely talk with clients about outcome. Scaling questions are commonly used in SFBT to assess client perceptions of problems and goal attainment ("On a scale of 0 to 10, with 0 being the worst it's been with this concern and 10 being where you want it to be, where are things right now?"). Client-based scaling provides instant feedback and privileges the client's voice over all others when it comes to assessing the effectiveness of therapy (Franklin, Corcoran, Nowicki, & Streeter, 1997). With that in mind, I suggested that we take the four major domains from Lambert's measure, the OQ 45.2 (Individual, Interpersonal, Social, and Overall), and simply ask scaling questions to enable a total outcome score. That idea evolved into the use of a visual analog scale instead of scaling questions (although the oral script for use with the persons with visual or reading difficulties or telephonic use remains a scaling question format). The ORS is simply a more formal and systematic way to do scaling questions.

Monitoring the Alliance: The Session Rating Scale

> If a man will kick a fact out of the window, when he comes back he finds it again in the chimney corner.
>
> Ralph Waldo Emerson

Getting better results also requires monitoring the fit of your service with the client's expectations about the alliance. Routine assessment of the alliance

enables you to identify and correct potential problems before they exert a negative effect on outcome. Moreover, continuous monitoring helps you build a
strong alliance. Research repeatedly shows that clients' ratings of the alliance
are far more predictive of improvement than the type of intervention or the
therapist's ratings of the alliance. Paradoxically, virtually all alliance measures
were designed for research purposes,[4] not for everyday use for mental health and
substance-abuse professionals working in the trenches. Recognizing the much-
replicated findings regarding the alliance as well as the need for a clinical tool,
we developed the SRS (Duncan, Miller, Sparks, Claud, Reynolds, Brown, &
Johnson, 2003) as a brief alternative to longer research-based alliance measures
to encourage routine conversations with clients about the alliance.

Figure 0.4 shows that the SRS also contains four items, based in Bordin's
(1979) classic delineation of the components of the alliance: the relational bond
and the degree of agreement between the client and therapist about the goals
and tasks of therapy. First, a relationship scale rates the meeting on a continuum
from "I did not feel heard, understood, and respected" to "I felt heard, understood, and respected." Second is a goals and topics scale that rates the conversation on a continuum from "We did not work on or talk about what I wanted to
work on or talk about" to "We worked on or talked about what I wanted to work
on or talk about." Third is an approach or method scale requiring the client to
rate the meeting on a continuum from "The approach is not a good fit for me"
to "The approach is a good fit for me." Finally, the fourth scale looks at how the
client perceived the encounter in total along the continuum: "There was something missing in the session today" to "Overall, today's session was right for me."

The SRS simply translates what is known about the alliance into four visual
analog scales, with instructions to place a mark on a line with negative responses
depicted on the left and positive responses indicated on the right. The SRS
allows alliance feedback in real time so that problems may be addressed. Like
the ORS, the instrument takes only a couple of minutes to administer, score,
and discuss. The SRS is scored similarly to the ORS, by adding the total of the
client's marks on the four 10-cm lines.

The good news is that the SRS is also reliable and valid. Duncan, Miller,
Sparks, Claud, Reynolds, Brown, and Johnson (2003) found that the SRS had
a coefficient alpha of .88 and possessed a correlation coefficient of .48 with
the Helping Alliance Questionnaire–II (Luborsky et al., 1996; .63 with the
Working Alliance Inventory; Campbell & Hemsley, 2009); it was also validated
in Norwegian (Anker et al., 2009) and Dutch (Hafkenscheid et al., 2010).
Similar to other measures of the alliance, early SRS scores correlated significantly with outcome ($r = .27$; Duncan, Miller, Sparks, Claud, Reynolds,
Brown, & Johnson, 2003). Again we can get by with such a short measure
because all alliance measures tend to load on the same factors. Hatcher and
Barends (1996) revealed that in addition to the general factor measured
by all alliance scales (i.e., strength of the alliance), two other factors were
predictive: confident collaboration and the expression of negative feelings.
Confident collaboration speaks to the level of confidence that the client has
that therapy and the therapist will be helpful. Although overlapping with

Session Rating Scale (SRS V.3.0)

Name _____	Age (Yrs): _____
ID# _____	Sex: M / F
Session# _____ Date: _____	

Please rate today's session by placing a mark on the line nearest to the description that best fits your experience.

Relationship

I did not feel heard, understood, and respected. |--| I felt heard, understood, and respected.

Goals and Topics

We did *not* work on or talk about what I wanted to work on and talk about. |--| We worked on and talked about what I wanted to work on and talk about.

Approach or Method

The therapist's approach is not a good fit for me. |--| The therapist's approach is a good fit for me.

Overall

There was something missing in the session today. |--| Overall, today's session was right for me.

The Heart and Soul of Change Project

www.heartandsoulofchange.com

Figure 0.4 The Session Rating Scale. Download free working copies at www.heartandsoulofchange.com. Many translations are available.

Question 3 on the SRS (the fit of the therapist's approach), the fourth scale of the SRS directly addresses this factor and measures the client's view of the session, ranging from "There was something missing in the session today" to "Overall, today's session was right for me."

The other factor that is predictive beyond the general strength of the alliance is the client's freedom to voice negative feelings and reactions to the therapist. Clients who express even low levels of disagreement with their therapists report better progress (Hatcher & Barends, 1996). The entire SRS is based on encouraging clients to identify alliance problems, to elicit client disagreements about the therapeutic process so that the clinician may change to better fit client expectations. Remember that therapists who are better at forming strong alliances with more clients are the ones that are the most effective. The SRS is the only instrument on the planet designed to be a session-by-session real-time alliance measure. This is important because clients drop out of therapy for two primary reasons: one is that therapy is not helping (hence monitoring outcome), and the other is alliance problems (they are not engaged or turned on by the process). The most direct way to improve your effectiveness is simply to keep people engaged in therapy. In the EAP study mentioned earlier, we found that clients of therapists who opted out of completing the SRS were twice as likely to drop out and three times more likely to have a negative outcome (Miller et al., 2006).

We know the usual trajectory of change—early change predicts continued change—and we know that the good alliances predict ultimate treatment outcome. You can therefore predispose therapy to success by implementing an early warning system, tools that measure change and the alliance: the ORS and SRS.

Staying with What Works

> To follow knowledge like a sinking star,
> Beyond the upmost bound of human thought . . .
> To strive, to seek, to find, and not to yield.
>
> Alfred, Lord Tennyson

Psychotherapy is not an uninhabited landscape of technical procedures. It is not the sterile, stepwise, process of surgery, nor does it follow the predictable path of diagnosis, prescription, and cure. It cannot be described without the client and therapist, co-adventurers in a journey across what is largely uncharted territory. The common factors provide useful directions for this intensely interpersonal and idiosyncratic trip, and specific models and techniques provide well-traveled routes to consider—but feedback offers a necessary compass to provide bearings of the psychotherapy terrain and guidance to the desired destination.

Ericksonian, interactional, and solution-focused approaches can only be praised for their enormous contributions to all therapies. The significance of removing psychotherapy's pathology blinders can hardly be overstated. Today's competency-oriented therapists owe a debt of gratitude rarely expressed to these pioneers of positive perspectives of clients. SFCST's interest in client resources and client goals proved remarkably on track with the most robust finding in outcome research: that client contributions and attending to client preferences and goals accounts for the lion's share of outcome in therapy. Solution-focused pioneer Steve de Shazer introduced the radical notion that the solution need have no relationship to the problem, running directly counter to the medical model's insistence that a discrete, diagnosed disorder then dictates a specific, matched intervention. At the same time, an understanding of solutions as not problem-specific frees therapists and clients to travel multiple paths in a more client-directed and creative search for problem resolution. In addition, SFCST's attention to the future provides a natural enhancement of hope and expectancy factors, replacing the dismal past with a possibility filled future. Finally, solution-focused therapy's roots in Ericksonian ideas keeps the client's worldview center stage as well in an interest in learning and validating the client's theory of change as a critical component of strengthening the therapeutic alliance and enhancing positive outcome. Solution-focused models were almost prescient applications of what was later confirmed by the bulk of outcome research.

Similar to the other common factors, monitoring client feedback via the ORS and SRS is a natural fit with solution-focused clinical work, a mere extension of the practice of scaling. SFCST partnerships are founded on the belief that clients are better positioned than anyone else to know what is best for them as well as what works best for them. In addition, solution-focused approaches have a legacy of giving utmost attention to what works so both the client and therapist can do more of it. It also strongly adheres to the MRI idea: If it doesn't work, do something different. The ORS and SRS provide immediate feedback on what is working and what is not, cementing a relationship between the common factors and SFCST, a marriage made in heaven.

Barry L. Duncan

Notes

1. It is useful to compare each factor to model/technique to gain perspective regarding relative impact. The percentages, based in meta-analytic research, are best viewed as a defensible way to understand outcome variance but not as representing any ultimate truths. Because of the overlap among the common factors, the percentages for the separate factors will not add to 100%.
2. This term was coined by Bruce Wampold. The idea grew out of a discussion during the preparation of the introductory chapter in *The Heart and Soul of Change*, but was not included or developed in that chapter.
3. ES refers to the magnitude of change attributable to treatment, compared to an untreated group. The ES most associated with psychotherapy is .80 standard deviations above the mean of the untreated group. An ES of 1.0 indicates that the mean of the treated group falls at approximately the 84th percentile of the untreated one. Consequently, the average treated person is better off than approximately 80% of those without the benefit of treatment.
4. With the notable exception of Lynn Johnson's Session Rating Scale, which inspired the scale depicted here.

References

Anker, M.G., Duncan, B.L., & Sparks, J.A. (2009). Using client feedback to improve couple therapy outcomes: A randomized clinical trial in a naturalistic setting. *Journal of Consulting and Clinical Psychology*, 77, 693–704.

Anker, M.G., Owen, J., Duncan, B.L., & Sparks, J.A. (2010). The alliance in couple therapy. *Journal of Consulting and Clinical Psychology*, 78, 635–645.

Asay, T.P., and Lambert, M.J. (1999). The empirical case for the common factors in therapy: Quantitative findings. In M.A. Hubble, B.L. Duncan, & S.D. Miller (Eds.), *The heart and soul of change: What works in therapy*. Washington, D.C.: APA Press.

Baldwin, S., Berkeljon, A., Atkins, D., Olsen, J., & Nielsen, S. (2009). Rates of change in naturalistic psychotherapy: Contrasting dose-effect and good-enough level models of change. *Journal of Consulting and Clinical Psychology*, 77(2), 203–211.

Baldwin, S.A., Wampold, B.E., & Imel, Z.E. (2007). Untangling the alliance-outcome correlation: Exploring the relative importance of therapist and patient variability in the alliance. *Journal of Consulting and Clinical Psychology*, 75(6), 842–852.

Barkham, M., Margison, F., Leach, C., Lucock, M., Mellor-Clark, J., Milne, D., Evans, C., Benson, L., Connell, J., Audin, K., & McGrath, G. (2001). Service profiling and outcomes benchmarking using CORE-OM: Toward practice-based evidence in psychological therapies. *Journal of Consulting and Clinical Psychology*, 69, 184–196.

Baskin, T., Tierney, S., Minami, T., & Wampold, B. (2003). Establishing specificity in psychotherapy: A meta-analysis of structural equivalence of placebo controls. *Journal of Clinical Psychology*, 71(6), 973–979.

Bateson, G., Jackson, D., Haley, J., & Weakland, J. (1956). Toward a theory of schizophrenia. *Behavioral Science*, 1, 251–264.

Benish, S., Imel, Z.E., & Wampold, B. (2007). The relative efficacy of bona fide therapies for treating post-traumatic stress disorder: A meta-analysis of direct comparisons. *Clinical Psychology Review*, 28(5), 746–758.

Beutler, L.E., Malik, M., Alimohamed, S., Harwood, T.M., Talebi, H., Noble, S., et al. (2004). Therapist variables. In M.J. Lambert (Ed.), *Bergin and Garfield's handbook of psychotherapy and behavior change* (5th ed.). New York: Wiley.

Bohart, A., & Tallman, K. (2010). Clients: The neglected common factor in psychotherapy. In B. Duncan, S. Miller, B. Wampold, & M. Hubble (Eds.), *The heart and soul of change: Delivering what works* (2nd ed.). Washington DC: American Psychological Association Press.

Bordin, E.S. (1979). The generalizability of the psychoanalytic concept of the working alliance. *Psychotherapy*, 16, 252–260.

Bringhurst, D.L., Watson, C.W., Miller, S.D., & Duncan, B.L. (2006). The reliability and validity of the Outcome Rating Scale: A replication study of a brief clinical measure. *Journal of Brief Therapy*, 5(1), 23–30.

Brown, J., Dreis, S., & Nace, D. (1999). What really makes a difference in psychotherapy outcomes? Why does managed care want to know? In M. Hubble, B. Duncan, & S. Miller (Eds.), *The heart and soul of change*. Washington, DC: American Psychological Association.

Campbell, A. & Hemsley, S. (2009). Outcome Rating Scale and Session Rating Scale in psychological practice: Clinical utility of ultra-brief measures. *Clinical Psychologist*, 13(1), 1–9.

Carroll, L. (1962). *Alice's adventures in wonderland*. Harmondsworth, Middlesex: Penguin. (Original work published 1865)

Crits-Christoph, P., Barancackie, K., Kurcias, J.S., Beck, A.T., Carroll, K., Perry, K., Luborsky, L., McLellan, A.T., Woody, G.E., Tompson, L., Gallagher, D., & Zitrin, C. (1991). Meta-analyis of therapist effects in psychotherapy outcome studies. *Psychotherapy Research*, 1, 81–91.

de Shazer, S. (1982). *Patterns of brief family therapy.* New York: Guilford.

de Shazer, S. (1985). *Keys to solution in brief therapy.* New York: Norton.

de Shazer, S. (1994). *Words were originally magic.* New York: Norton.

Duncan, B. (2010a). *On becoming a better therapist.* Washington, DC: American Psychological Association.

Duncan, B. (2010b). Saul Rosenzweig: The founder of the common factors. In B. Duncan, S. Miller, B. Wampold, & M. Hubble (Eds.), *The heart and soul of change: Delivering what works* (2nd ed.). Washington DC: American Psychological Association.

Duncan, B., Hubble, M., & Miller, S. (1997). *Psychotherapy with "impossible" cases: Efficient therapy of therapy veterans.* New York: Norton.

Duncan, B., & Miller, S. (2000a). The client's theory of change. *Journal of Psychotherapy Integration*, 10, 169–187.

Duncan, B., & Miller, S. (2000b). *The heroic client. Doing client directed, outcome informed therapy.* San Francisco: Jossey Bass.

Duncan, B., Miller. S., & Sparks, J. (2004). *The heroic client: A revolutionary way to improve effectiveness through client directed outcome informed therapy* (revised ed.). San Francisco: Jossey-Bass.

Duncan, B., Miller, S., Sparks, J., Claud, D., Reynolds, L., Brown, J., & Johnson, L. (2003). The Session Rating Scale: Preliminary psychometric properties of a "working" alliance measure. *Journal of Brief Therapy*, 3(1), 3–12.

Duncan, B., Miller, S., Wampold, B. & Hubble, M. (Eds.) (2010). *The heart and soul of change: Delivering what works in therapy* (2nd ed.). Washington DC: American Psychological Association.

Duncan, B.L., & Moynihan, D. (1994). Applying outcome research: Intentional utilization of the client's frame of reference. *Psychotherapy*, 31, 294–301.

Duncan, B., Solovey, A., & Rusk, G. (1992). *Changing the rules: A client-directed approach.* New York: Guilford.

Duncan, B., Sparks, J., Miller, S., Bohanske, R., & Claud, D. (2006). Giving youth a voice: A preliminary study of the reliability and validity of a brief outcome measure for children. *Journal of Brief Therapy*, 5(1), 5–22.

Elkin, I., Shea, T., Watkins, J.T., Imber, S.D., Sotsky, S.M., Collins, J.F., Glass, D.R., Pilkonis, P.A., Leber, W.R., Docherty, J.P., Fiester, S.J., & Parloff, M.B. (1989). National Institute of Mental Health Treatment of Depression Collaborative Research Program: General effectiveness of treatments. *Archives of General Psychiatry*, 46, 971–982.

Elkin, I., Yamaguchi, J., Arnkoff, D., Glass, C., Sotsky, S., & Krupnick, J. (1999). "Patient-Treatment Fit" and early engagement in therapy. *Psychotherapy Research*, 9, 437–451.

Frank, J. (1973). *Persuasion and Healing: A comparative study of psychotherapy* (2nd ed.). Baltimore, MD: Johns Hopkins.

Frank, J., & Frank, J. (1991). *Persuasion and healing* (3rd ed.). Baltimore: Johns Hopkins University Press.

Franklin, C., Corcoran, J., Nowicki, J., & Streeter, C. (1997). Using client self-anchored scales to measure outcomes in solution-focused therapy. *Journal of Systemic Therapies*, 16, 246–265.

Gassman, D. & Grawe, K. (2006). General change mechanisms: The relation between problem activation and resource activation in successful and unsuccessful therapeutic interactions. *Clinical Psychology and Psychotherapy*, 13, 1–11.

Hafkenscheid, A., Duncan, B., & Miller, S. (2010). The Outcome and Session Rating Scales: A cross-cultural examination of the psychometric properties of the Dutch translation. *Journal of Brief Therapy*, 1&2, 1–12.

Haley, J. (1973). *Uncommon therapy: The psychiatric techniques of Milton H. Erickson, MD*. New York: Norton.

Hannan, C., Lambert, M.J., Harmon, C., Nielsen, S.L., Smart, D.W., Shimokawa, K., & Sutton, S.W. (2005). A lab test and algorithms for identifying clients at risk for treatment failure. *Journal of Clinical Psychology*, 61(2), 155–163.

Hansen, N., Lambert, M., Forman, E. (2002). The psychotherapy dose-effect and its implications for treatment delivery services. *Clinical Psychology: Science and Practice*, 9, 329–343.

Hatcher, R.L., & Barends, A.W. (1996). Patient's view of psychotherapy: Exploratory factor analysis of three alliance measures. *Journal of Consulting and Clinical Psychology*, 64, 1326–1336.

Hatcher, R.L., & Barends, W. (2006). How a return to theory could help alliance research. *Psychotherapy: Theory, Research, Practice, Training*, 43, 292–299.

Horvath, A.O., & Bedi, R.P. (2002). The alliance. In J.C. Norcross (Ed.), *Psychotherapy relationships that work*. New York: Oxford University Press, 37–69.

Horvath, A.O., & Symonds, B.D. (1991). Relation between working alliance and outcome in psychotherapy: A meta-analysis. *Journal of Counseling Psychology*, 38(2), 139–149.

Howard, K.I., Kopta, S.M., Krause, M.S., & Orlinsky, D.E. (1986). The dose-effect relationship in psychotherapy. *American Psychologist*, 41, 159–164.

Howard, K.I., Moras, K., Brill, P.L., Martinovich, Z., & Lutz, W. (1996). Evaluation of psychotherapy: Efficacy, effectiveness, and patient progress. *American Psychologist*, 51, 1059–1064.

Kim, D.M., Wampold, B.E., & Bolt, D.M. (2006). Therapist effects in psychotherapy: A random effects modeling of the NIMH TDCRP data. *Psychotherapy Research*, 16, 161–172.

Kirsch, I. (2005). Placebo psychotherapy: Synonym or oxymoron? *Journal of Clinical Psychology*, 61(7), 791–803.

Krupnick, J.L., Sotsky, S.M., Simmens, S., Moyher, J., Elkin, I., Watkins, J., & Pilkonis, P.A. (1996). The role of the therapeutic alliance in psychotherapy and pharmacotherapy outcome: Findings in the National Institute of Mental Health Treatment of Depression Collaborative Research Project. *Journal of Consulting and Clinical Psychology*, 64, 532–539.

Lambert, M.J. (1986). Implications of psychotherapy outcome research for eclectic psychotherapy. In J.C. Norcross (Ed.), *Handbook of eclectic psychotherapy*. New York: Brunner/Mazel.

Lambert, M.J. (2010). "Yes, it is time for clinicians to monitor treatment outcome." In B.L. Duncan, S.C., Miller, B.E. Wampold, & M.A. Hubble (Eds.), *Heart and soul of change: Delivering what works in therapy* (2nd ed.). Washington, DC: American Psychological Association.

Lambert, M.J., Garfield, S.L., & Bergin, A.E. (2004). Overview, trends, and future issues. In M.J. Lambert (Ed.), *Bergin and Garfield's handbook of psychotherapy and behavior change* (5th ed.). New York: Wiley.

Lambert, M.J., Hansen, N.B., Umphress, V., Lunnen, K., Okiishi, J., Burlingame, G., . . . Reisinger, C. (1996). *Administration and scoring manual for the OQ 45.2*. Stevenson, MD: American Professional Credentialing Services.

Luborsky, L., Barber, J., Siqueland, L., Johnson, S., Najavits, L., Frank, A., & Daley, D. (1996). The revised Helping Alliance Questionnaire (HAQ-II). *The Journal of Psychotherapy Practice and Research*, 5, 260–271.

Luborsky, L., Singer, B., & Luborsky, L. (1975). Comparative studies of psychotherapies: Is it true that "everyone has won and all must have prizes"? *Archives of General
Psychiatry*, 32, 995–1008.

Lutz, W., Stulz, N., & Köck, K. (2009). Patterns of early change and their relationship
to outcome and follow-up among patients with major depressive disorders. *Journal of
Affective Disorders*, 118, 60–68.

Martin, D.J., Garske, J.P., & Davis, M.K. (2000). Relation of the therapeutic alliance
with outcome and other variables: A meta-analytic review. *Journal of Consulting and
Clinical Psychology*, 68(3), 438–450.

McDonagh, A., Friedman, M., McHugo, G., Ford, J., Sengupta, A., & Mueser, K.
(2005). Randomized trial of cognitive-behavioral therapy for chronic posttraumatic
stress disorder in adult female survivors of childhood sexual abuse. *Journal of Consulting and Clinical Psychology*, 73, 515–524.

Miller, S.D., & Duncan, B.L. (2000). *The Outcome Rating Scale*. Jensen Beach, FL: Author.

Miller, S., Duncan, B., Brown, J., Sorrell, R., & Chalk, M.B. (2006). Using formal client
feedback to improve retention and outcome: Making real-time assessment feasible.
Journal of Brief Therapy, 5(1), 5–22.

Miller, S.D., Duncan, B.L., Brown, J., Sparks, J., & Claud, D. (2003). The outcome
rating scale: A preliminary study of the reliability, validity, and feasibility of a brief
visual analog measure. *Journal of Brief Therapy*, 2(2), 91–100.

Miller, S.D., & Duncan, B.L., & Johnson, L. (2002). *The Session Rating Scale*. Jensen
Beach, FL: Author.

Miller, S., Duncan, B., Sorrell, R., & Brown, G.S. (2005). The partners for change outcome management system. *Journal of Clinical Psychology*, 61(2), 199–208.

Murphy, J.J. (2008). *Solution-focused counseling in schools* (2nd ed.). Alexandria, VA: American Counseling Association.

Norcross, J. (2010). The therapeutic relationship. In B. Duncan, S. Miller, B. Wampold, &
M. Hubble (Eds.), *The heart and soul of change: Delivering what works* (2nd ed.). Washington, DC: American Psychological Association.

Norcross, J.C., & Lambert, M.J. (2005). The therapy relationship. In J.C. Norcross,
L.E. Beutler, & R.F. Levant (Eds.), *Evidence-based practices in mental health: Debate and
dialogue on the fundamental questions*. Washington, D.C.: American Psychological Association, 208–217.

Orlinsky, D.E., Rønnestad, M.H., & Willutzki, U. (2004). Fifty years of process-
outcome research: Continuity and change. In M.J. Lambert (Ed.), *Bergin and Garfield's
handbook of psychotherapy and behavior change* (5th ed.). New York: Wiley.

Project MATCH Research Group. (1998). Therapist effects in three treatments for alcohol problems. *Psychotherapy Research*, 8, 455–474.

Reese, R.J., Norsworthy, L.A., & Rowlands, S.R. (2009). Does a continuous feedback
system improve psychotherapy outcome? *Psychotherapy: Theory, Research, Practice, Training*, 46, 418–431.

Reese, R.J., Toland, M.D., Slone, N.C., & Norsworthy, L.A. (2010). Effect of client
feedback on couple psychotherapy outcomes. *Psychotherapy: Theory, Research, Practice,
Training*, 47, 616–630.

Rogers, C. (1957). The necessary and sufficient conditions of therapeutic personality
change. *Journal of Consulting Psychology*, 21, 95–103.

Rosenzweig, S. (1936). Some implicit common factors in diverse methods of psychotherapy. *American Journal of Orthopsychiatry*, 6, 412–415.

Sotsky, S.M., Glass, D.R., Shea, M.T., Pilkonis, P.A. Collins, J.F., Elkin, I., et al. (1991).
Patient predictors of response to psychotherapy and pharmacotherapy: Findings in

the NIMH Treatment of Depression Collaborative Research Program. *American Journal of Psychiatry*, 148, 997–1008.

Sparks, J.A., & Duncan, B.L. (2010). Couple and family therapy and the common factors: Have all won prizes? In B. Duncan, S. Miller, B. Wampold, & M. Hubble (Eds.), *The heart and soul of change: Delivering what works* (2nd ed.). Washington DC: American Psychological Association.

Stiles, W.B., Barkham, M., Twigg, E., Mellor-Clark, J., & Cooper, M. (2006). Effectiveness of cognitive-behavioural, person-centered and psychodynamic therapy as practiced in UK National Health Service Settings. *Psychological Medicine*, 36(4), 555–566.

Teyber, F., & McClure, E. (2000). *Interpersonal process in therapy: An integrative model.* Boston: Cengage Learning.

Wampold, B.E. (2001). *The great psychotherapy debate: Models, methods, and findings.* Mahwah, NJ: Erlbaum.

Wampold, B.E. (2005). The psychotherapist. In J.C. Norcross, L.E. Beutler, & R.F. Levant (Eds.), *Evidence-based practices in mental health: Debate and dialogue on the fundamental questions.* Washington, DC: American Psychological Association.

Wampold, B. (2007). *The great psychotherapy debate.* New York: Routledge.

Wampold, B., & Brown, G.S. (2005). Estimating variability in outcomes in managed care. *Journal of Consulting and Clinical Psychology*, 73(5), 914–923.

Wampold, B.E., Minami, T., Tierney, S.C., Baskin, T.W., & Bhati, K.S. (2005). The placebo is powerful: Estimating placebo effects in medicine and psychotherapy from clinical trials. *Journal of Clinical Psychology*, 61, 835–854.

Watzlawick, P., Weakland, J., & Fisch, R. (1974). *Change: Problem formation and problem resolution.* New York: Norton.

Wierzbicki, M., & Pekarik, G. (1993). A meta-analysis of psychotherapy dropout. *Professional Psychology: Research and Practice*, 24, 190–195.

Introduction

Solution-Focused Therapy can be seen and used as a meta-model that focuses on the therapeutic alliance, namely the common factors that account for 85–90% (Hubble, Duncan, & Miller, 1999; Lambert, 2013) of the efficacy of any therapeutic endeavor: that is, on the client factors (clients' objectives, resources, skills), on the placebo factors (hope and allegiance), and on the therapist factors (their qualities as a human being, their skills).

This handbook tries to tries to outline the present state of our knowledge on the effective practice of the psychotherapy, or more exactly (and more modestly) to summarize what we know about the factors that favor the success of a therapeutic endeavor.

It is composed of three volumes. The first (this one) lays the theoretical and practical bases of the Bruges model. The second describes some clinical and educational applications of the SF Model along with special topics. The third is dedicated to systemic and relational issues.

Inevitably, the description is extremely incomplete.

For example, the techniques and procedures that I describe are not better than many others that I also could have included. I chose them because they are simple to apply and effective.

Also, I absolutely do not consider as "true" the hypotheses that I propose on the functioning of the psyche and on the origin of psychological disorders. If I mention them, it is only as far as they can be useful to motivate customers and therapists, and by no means because I consider them as more than just narratives that can offer a handle to therapists and clients to make better use of their skills.

Regardless, all techniques that aim at getting rid of the clients' symptoms and the problems—or at eliminating their "causes"—fall under the Dodo Verdict that Barry Duncan describes in the Foreword. The reader is invited to continue to use his or her favorite interventions, as long as they do not divert the attention of what is essential: the therapeutic alliance, that is, the collaboration between therapist and clients with the aim to help these to live the life that they wish to live.

Origins and Evolution of the Model

The material covered here is not new. Four main influences contributed to shape the model—or rather the meta-model—that I present.

The Bruges Model Is an Ericksonian Model

First came the discovery, around 1980, of the work of Milton H. Erickson, as it was presented in Jay Haley's *Uncommon Therapy.*

One could see there a therapeutic genius at work who obtained results that left us stunned—but how did he do it? What was the logic behind his interventions, behind the tasks that he gave? My colleagues and I tried to do what others did, including Gregory Bateson, John Weakland, Jay Haley, Salvador Minuchin, John Bandler and Richard Grinder, Steve de Shazer, and many more.

I discerned several factors:

- The suggestions and the prescriptions that Erickson offered did not directly aim at solving his clients' problems. Rather, they created a context in which clients themselves would find the solutions that suited them.
- Rather than focusing on treating the symptoms, he urged his clients to use all their resources and their skills to reach their goals—goals that, blinded by their problems, they often did not see themselves and that he helped them to discover.
- Everything was done, everything was mobilized and utilized—the clients' resources, those of their family and acquaintances, their strengths as well as their weaknesses, often even their symptoms—to help clients to develop habits that satisfied them instead of habits that they wanted to get rid of.
- What finally struck me was his kindness, his caring, the way he loved his clients, that permeated the narratives that I read.

The Bruges Model Is a Systemic and Existentialist Model

The seventies were the time when the major systemic family approaches were formulated:

- Gregory Bateson (Bateson, 1972, 1975, 1979) and the MRI in Palo Alto (Bateson et al., 1956; Haley, 1985; Watzlawick, Beavin, & Jackson, 1967, 1974) for the analysis of communication in systems and for the paradoxical interventions that Knight Dunlap (Dunlap, 1928, 1930), Carl Whitaker (Neill & Kniskern, 1982) and the Milan group (Selvini-Palazzoli, Boscolo, Cecchin, & Prata, 1975) also contributed to develop;
- Salvador Minuchin (Minuchin, 1974; Minuchin & Fischman, 1981) and Jay Haley (Haley, 1976, 1984) for their analysis of structures and hierarchies in family systems;
- Guy Ausloos (Ausloos, 1995) who traveled a path parallel to mine, more interested in the skills of families than in their dysfunctional aspects.

Others also had a determining influence:

- Alfred Korzybski (Korzybski, 1921, 1933) who insisted on speaking a semantically exact language;

- Ludwig Binswanger's (Binswanger, 1962, 1965) and Viktor Frankl's Existential Analyses (Frankl, 1985, 1999) helped me to see that we have to leave to the clients the responsibility of the existential, semantic, and pragmatic choices by which they fit into the reality that they are part of.

Drawing on these diverse influences—constantly asking, "What would Milton Erickson have done with this client?"—my colleagues and I developed (dwarfs on the shoulders of these giants) the first elements of our model.

The Bruges Model Is Focused on Solutions and Skills

In 1989 we read *Keys to Solutions in Brief Therapy* (de Shazer, 1985), and in 1990 we invited Steve de Shazer (and a year later his wife, Insoo Kim Berg) for his first workshop at the Korzybski Institutes of Bruges, Paris, and Amsterdam. That was to be followed by more than fifty others.

We already were quite efficient, but it must be said that the interventions my therapist team at St. John's Hospital in Bruges and I had developed often were rather complicated. We loved to make a brilliant move. Steve de Shazer taught us to apply Occam's Razor.

Our principles and our methods were very similar to the ones developed by Steve de Shazer, Insoo Kim Berg, and their associates at the Brief Family Therapy Center in Milwaukee (Miller, 1997). Like them, we were disciples of Milton Erickson, but we lacked the rigor and the simplicity they taught us.

We discovered that we were solution-focused without knowing it. Years of friendship and collaboration followed.

The Bruges Model Is a Meta-Model Focused on the Common Factors and Directed by the Clients

The third revelation was the discovery of the work of Barry Duncan, Scott Miller, Bruce Wampold (Duncan et al., 2010; Hubble et al., 1999; Miller et al., 1996; Wampold, 2001), and their associates—and of Jerome Frank (Frank & Frank, 1961) as well as Michael Lambert (Lambert, 2013) who came before them—about the factors that make therapies efficient. These are essentially the non-specific factors, the factors that are common to all psychotherapeutic endeavors, whatever school or movement the therapist adheres to—and lo and behold, for us therapists who focused on solutions and skills, these were the factors that all our efforts were aimed at. It appeared that our methods were based on the most robust evidence available, that of thousands of research studies gathered into hundreds of meta-analyses.

What was left was to formalize client feedback through the ORS and the SRS, which we integrated into our procedures.

Therapy According to the Bruges Model

Therapy can be seen as a conversation between two or more people, who agree that one side is the therapeutic (helping, caring, etc.) side, the other the client (suffering, help-seeking, cared for, etc.) side. Non-verbal aspects of the conversation (mimic, prosody, etc.) are included in this.

However, this ignores non-verbal aspects of therapy such as body-centered interventions (bilateral stimulation such as EMDR, Alexander Techniques, etc.). It also ignores what goes on at a directly unconscious level, such as empathy through eye contact and the mirror neurons. So maybe we should say that therapy is a sequence of interactions between two or more people, through verbal and non-verbal, conscious and unconscious, cognitive, emotional, and behavioral channels.

However, what about computer-assisted therapy wherein a client interacts solely with a website, such as Paul Koeck's very effective program (www. 15Minutes4Me.com)? Or what about self-help books, some of which are quite helpful and therapeutic? So maybe we should stick to the idea that all therapy is self-therapy. People experience difficulties in their life. Some of these are problems that they solve, by themselves or with some help: help by family members, by educators, by therapists, by medication, and by self-help programs and books. Other difficulties they cannot change: They have to accept them, again by themselves or with some kind of help.

What is important is that, in therapy or otherwise, they make it clear for themselves what kind of life they want to live, or maybe just what kind of life they can accept, and that they set about implementing these existential choices in their daily life, that is, in their habits.

One term for this is *resilience,* or building strength to take on life's challenges. As Barry Duncan states in the Foreword to this book:

> It [the Bruges Model] takes seriously research that, over and over, places clients as the prime movers in therapy and the therapeutic alliance as the fuel for that movement—the client is the heart and the alliance is soul of therapeutic change.

Now if we take seriously this idea that it is the client who directs the therapy, the question arises: Who is the expert in the Bruges Model?

Who Is the Expert in Client-Directed Therapy?

In his seminars, Steve de Shazer often said that Milton H. Erickson defined psychotherapy as "What happens when two people get together and one tries to figure out what the other one wants."

Tom Andersen and Harry Goolishian (Anderson & Goolishian, 1992) introduced the concept of the "not-knowing" stance. The therapist works from the assumption that each client is different and does not assume that she, the therapist, being an expert, knows what is best for him, the client. So she may ask seemingly naïve questions that will help the client to reflect on what exactly he wants to change and what exactly he wants to achieve. The therapist puts the client in charge. This does not mean however that the client-directed therapist has to throw overboard everything that he or she knows.

The not-knowing stance applies to whatever the clients can bring into the therapeutic project:

- Goals, wishes (the optative), existential choices;
- Values, beliefs;
- The resources and skills that are present in the clients and in the clients' systems.

These are for the therapist to find out (and often to help the clients to find out).

The not-knowing stance does not apply to information the therapist has and that the clients do not have, such as

- Objective information about the clients' problems and possible solutions (e.g., physiological aspects of depression or addiction; stress mechanisms);
- Logical errors the clients make (e.g., the yellow polka-dot elephant paradox, whereby if you try not to think of something, you cannot help thinking of it).

Some Basic Assumptions in Client-Directed Cognitive and Systemic Therapy

The subject of this handbook is how to co-construct the alliance, how to work with client, therapist, and placebo factors.

It may be useful in this introduction to briefly state the basic assumptions of the Bruges Model of Client-directed Cognitive and Systemic therapy.

Assumptions about Client Factors

1. *All therapy is self-therapy.* Therapy is about change. We can change only ourselves; therefore, we are the agents of our own therapy.
2. *Therapy is about changing habits.* Problems and symptoms can be conceptualized as unwanted habits; therapy then consists in developing preferred habits that can take the place of unwanted ones.
3. *Therapy is about handling oneself differently in one's interactions with reality.* Problems and symptoms can also be conceptualized as problematic interactions with reality (mainly with oneself and one's environment); therapy focuses on more favorable interactions.
4. *All clients have the necessary resources to solve their problems and to accept their limitations.* It is the therapist's task to help clients to tap into these resources and to transform them into the skills they need to achieve their (existential and day-to-day) goals.

Assumptions about Change and Continuity

1. *Some aspects of reality can be changed, others cannot.* The therapist will help the clients to distinguish which aspects of their difficulties are problems that can be changed, and which are limitations that cannot be altered.

2. *Change is constant, as is continuity.* One of the main objectives of therapy is to strike a good balance between change and continuity.
3. *One step at a time.* Small and seemingly unimportant changes that build upon one another can lead to big and important changes.

Problems and Solutions, Limitations, and Opportunities

1. *Focusing on problems is less useful than focusing on goals, resources, and skills.* Some problems have to be solved, but many problems and symptoms thrive on the attention we give them. Looking instead at existential choices and the ways to implement them makes problems wither or even dissolve by themselves.
2. *Focusing on limitations is less useful than focusing on acceptance and on opportunities.* When clients stop searching for a door in the blind wall of their limitations and accept those limitations, they can turn around and discover a vast landscape of previously unnoticed opportunities.
3. *Techniques.* Tasks and experiments do not need to be directed towards solving problems or eliminating symptoms. They aim at putting the clients in charge again, that is, at creating a context in which the clients can build a better life by developing more satisfying habits.
4. *The solution-focused triad:*

   - If it ain't broke, don't fix it.
   - Once you find out what works, do more of it.
   - If it doesn't work, do something different.

Assumptions about the Therapeutic Alliance

1. *The therapist is the expert for the therapeutic method and for the therapeutic process. The client is the expert for goals, choices, resources, and skills.*
2. *Therapist and clients together construct the therapeutic alliance.*
3. *Clients are always motivated by something.* In the alliance between therapist and client, the client's motivation emerges and the goals for which he or she is motivated are implemented.

Part I

Client Factors

1 What Does the Client Want?
Setting Goals

Therapy is about restoring freedom of choice in setting one's goals. Therefore, helping the client to determine what he or she wants is the key.

Freedom of Choice

In SFCST, therapists don't set themselves the task of changing their clients, to solve their problems, to cure them. Instead, therapists try to help their clients create a context in which they will be able to choose to change what they want to change, and to keep what they do not want to change. As Eve Lipchik (2002) formulates this: "Therapists should not try to change clients; clients must decide when and if they are ready for change."

The goal of therapy is to help clients to recover their freedom of choice, which means:

- To clarify their existential choices;
- To express these choices in habits;
- To abandon the (pathological, problematical) habits they do not want;
- To find in themselves the resources and the skills to accomplish this;
- To recover the liberty to live the life they choose.

Considerations on the Nature of Symptoms

Often, our clients are stuck in a position where they have lost their freedom to choose. They seem to have lost the skill to construe their thoughts, their feelings, and their behavior in a way that satisfies them: depression, anxiety disorders, and obsessive-compulsive disorders are examples of this. Or, as in dependency, satisfaction on one level is nullified by suffering on another.

Symptoms can then be seen as thoughts, feelings, and behaviors that clients produce whether they want to or not. They cannot but suffer from them.

At first sight, it seems difficult to find a less normative definition of what symptoms are. There is no reference to pathology, to guilt, or even to responsibility.

The therapeutic goals would be to help the client to stop producing symptoms that are defined in this way. This, too, does not appear to be normative.

When we look more closely, however, some normative aspects appear that constitute a first difficulty inherent to the Bruges Model.

When therapists set themselves the goal to help clients to alleviate their suffering, they (implicitly) suggest that to suffer is not a good choice. Nonetheless, throughout history, scores of people have chosen to gladly accept the sufferings that came onto them, to endure them, or even to inflict them on themselves. They consider pain to be an important and necessary part of a good life. Its value is pedagogical (to build strength of character, to prepare oneself for an ordeal) or metaphysical (to imitate Christ in his sufferings). It shows moral strength to endure pain and sorrow with stoical acceptance.

How can we maintain that we should limit ourselves to helping our clients to recover their freedom of choice? How can we be convinced that they will then abandon their symptoms and their suffering? We have nothing but the experience that in the immense majority of cases, this is what they do—but this experience also shows that habits have a tendency to stick, and that showing alternatives to them may not be enough. Sometimes unwanted behavior tends to persist because clients seem insufficiently motivated to tackle it.

It is also possible that people for whom happiness is not a primary existential goal do not come in for therapy, or they quickly drop out of it. After all, many people live as if their primary concerns were to be very rich, exert power over others, hurt people around them, or simply keep up with the Joneses. People who come in for therapy rarely cite goals such as those when asked the Miracle Question: What would your life be like if you got rid of your problems? Maybe for some clients, what they formulate as their goals for therapy are just that, goals for therapy, their contribution to the therapeutic relationship, to be abandoned as soon as the crisis that brought them into therapy is over. For others, if the therapist helps them to reconsider what they want their life to be, what kind of persons (fathers, mothers, partners, etc.) they want to be—that is, if therapy helps them to reflect about their existential goals—it may be a defining moment in their lives. This is suggested by the fact that in long-term follow-up studies, like the ones we did in Bruges, clients answer that after therapy not only their symptoms are under control, but that their general well-being, their relationships, and so on, also are satisfying.

There is a second difficulty inherent to the SFCST model. If the absence of pathology means that we can freely choose our conduct at any time, then why do we so often act out of habit or to conform to a societal expectation? And what explains that up to a point, education means acquiring the habits that will allow us not to make choices all the time?

I will address these questions in the next chapter. For now, let me just indicate that the answer lies on a higher logical level than the simple act of choosing. We have adopted habits that we agree with so that we don't have to bother with making choices all the time. What distinguishes these "good" habits (i.e., the habits we agree with) from symptomatic ones is that not only do we practice the latter without choosing to, but we are even convinced that we cannot choose otherwise.

From this perspective, the goal of therapy is to help our clients to be able to choose to choose or not to choose: to feel free to determine the course of their actions, their thoughts and their emotions, or to let them happen as they come. This, I think, is the necessary and sufficient condition for them to let go of their symptoms. In this regard, therapists must know that clients can ascribe different meanings to situations, symptoms, facts, and to relationships. These meanings in turn will influence what each client chooses to do.

Semantic and Pragmatic Choices

Let us now turn our attention to the connections between perceiving reality, attributing meaning to it, and deciding which actions to take. This allows us to distinguish between semantic choice (choosing what meanings to bestow on facts and events) and pragmatic choice (choosing what to do and what decisions to make).

In the very act of perception, we attribute meaning to everything we perceive; we integrate it into a meaningful whole. Let's say I see a bird flying and alighting on the branch of a tree. Different categories of facts and objects enter into the meaning this event takes on for me: bird, branch, sky, to fly, and so on. My emotional reaction also colors the meaning, as does the linguistic symbolization (the words I use to describe the facts and objects), my rational understanding of the event, my operational apprehension (Can I do something with it?), and so on. For the same event, different meanings can come to the foreground, determined by external and internal circumstances. They can be (consciously or unconsciously) chosen. I call this process the *semantic choice.*

To take another example: The concept of "elevator" can evoke several associations, including a comfortable means of going from one floor to another, a long wait before it comes, or not a good idea if I want to lose weight.

From my semantic choice (What is the most important meaning for me now?) will follow my pragmatic choice (What shall I do, take the stairs or the elevator?).

Now let's suppose I am claustrophobic. Narrow spaces, like elevators, make me afraid. An elevator is no longer a means of transport that I can choose to use or not to use, according to the meaning I choose to attribute to it. One meaning stays in the foreground: Danger! Only one choice of action remains open: I have to take the stairs.

Pathologies, symptoms, and problems, are characterized by the loss of semantic and pragmatic choices, as shown in this example.

Jack and Alice have been married for twenty years. Every evening, while watching television, he drinks one can of beer after another. Alice is fed up with having him come to bed reeking of alcohol. She tells him that from now on he can sleep on the couch.

In Alice's perception, Jack has been reduced to a hopeless drunk.
Other aspects of him fade into the background. She doesn't want him
in her bedroom anymore, and soon she'll want him to leave the house.

Jack doesn't agree. For him, a man's got a right to a quiet evening
and a few beers. All his wife does is nag, nag, nag.

The way to pathology is paved with semantic restrictions. Therapy then will
aim at restoring freedom of choice, that is, at restoring the ability to choose
between different possible meanings and to opt for the most useful. This in
turn frees the way to choosing the most useful course of action from different
options.

What does this mean for Jack and Alice?

For Jack: A well-spent evening can mean something else than just
television and beer. Are there exceptions to this pattern? In what different ways did the couple spend their evenings before? If evenings
with Alice were just right, what would they look like?

For Alice: There are other aspects to her husband than his drinking.
His boss is satisfied with his work, and he can be funny when he is
in a good mood. Two weeks ago, on a sunny evening, they went for a
walk and had a good time. Finally, he never refuses to lend a hand in
the household chores.

Therapy should lead clients to broaden their semantics, help them out of
their one-sided, single-minded problematic views. Talking about solutions (i.e.,
positive goals, skills, and resources) and ways to implement them in daily life is
the simplest way of achieving this.

The Therapist's Responsibilities

- Work with clients to create a context in which they are willing to engage
  into therapeutic change;
- Help clients to know more clearly what they want (goals), by focusing away
  from what they don't want (problems).
- Present clients with a broader range of meanings that they can ascribe to
  perceived reality.
- Open up a range of options for possible actions and pragmatic choices;
- When a client has chosen a more satisfying way of handling reality, this
  can be repeated until more satisfying habits have become automatic.

Negotiating Attainable Goals

Many people don't ask themselves what they want out of their life in general, and out of their therapy when they come to us. When we ask them what they want to get out of therapy, they give answers like:

- "I'm not feeling well, and I don't know what to do."
- "It's like a dark cloud hanging over me. I want you to take it away."
- "Please help me to feel less . . ."
- "I'd like to get to know myself better."
- "I'd like to know why I feel so bad. Why do I do these things? Why can't I get myself to do . . ."
- "X sent me, but I don't know if it's worth it coming here."
- "I'd like to stop drinking, smoking, and so on."
- "My wife (husband, mother . . .) should . . ."

All of these responses are understandable and reasonable. One can try to find a therapeutic answer to them. What they don't say is what the client wants to feel, think and do when he or she stops feeling bad, stops drinking or smoking, knows her/himself better, and so on.

If we want to get therapeutic results, it is useful to help our clients to formulate their goals in a way that they are workable—meaning that clients can work on them themselves.

I can only change myself; I can change nobody else. No therapist can change a client; only the client can do that. Only the client can develop new and satisfactory habits instead of problematic and pathological ones.

It is much easier to replace an unwanted habit with one that is preferable than to just stop the unsatisfactory one. That isn't impossible, of course; it's just more difficult. Habits tend to come up automatically in the situations in which they belong. If clients knows what they want to do instead of what they don't want, they can start doing that rather than trying to do nothing.

Workable goals help clients know what they should (i.e., want to) do, not just what they shouldn't.

It is useful to distinguish between existential goals (or existential choices) and pragmatic goals (or choices). Existential goals are answers to the question, "What kind of person (father, mother, spouse, friend, etc.) do I want to be?" They are the personal morals that guides us and as such belong to the optative.

Pragmatic goals are the incarnation of our existential goals into daily life. They express themselves in the habits we practice and that we agree with, or that we want to develop. They belong to the present or future indicative.

The Client Sets the Goals

If the therapist wants to attain something other than the client, resistance comes up and motivation goes down. Clients are always motivated by something, though not always by the reasons that led someone (a spouse, a judge, their general practitioner) to refer them; or perhaps the institution to which they were admitted has decided that they need a therapy that they don't want to undergo.

The time that therapists spend to ascertain what their clients want is never spent in vain.

For therapy to be successful, clients have to change some habits. This is never easy. Unless violent means are used, it is almost impossible to get someone to change a habit that he or she doesn't want to change. One can only pity a therapist who wants to cure a client against his or her will. For rational as well as ethical reasons, it is better to let clients decide goals for themselves.

There are nevertheless a few exceptions to this general rule. Sometimes therapists—because of their clinical experience—see possible goals that a client does not, as in the following example.

> Maud, 25 years old, comes into therapy because of a bulimic eating pattern. She lives alone and she has few friends. She stays at home most of the time and she doesn't feel at ease with her colleagues at work. She thinks nobody is interested in her.
>
> The therapist asks her if she would like to have more confidence and more fun with her friends as well as tackling her eating binges. As an expert, he thinks these problems are related. Maud agrees immediately. She was so obsessed by her bulimia that she didn't think of working on these problems too.

It may happen that the therapist tries to convince a client to work on a goal that doesn't seem important to the client right away. In this case, it is better to start working on those points on which the client agrees, as shown in this example.

> Diana, 28 years old, complains that she feels depressed. She can't get anything done. She doesn't know why she has to go on living. Everything she undertakes leads to failure. She has made three suicide attempts. Two months ago she left her husband and went back to live with her parents. She wants to find an apartment nearby as quickly as possible where she can live with her daughter.
>
> At her parents' home she feels dependent, treated like a child; it is as if she doesn't have the right to be her daughter's mother anymore. She relives painful experiences from her past. She feels hate against her parents, who didn't protect her against her grandfather's sexual aggression.
>
> She says she married only to get away from home. Her parents didn't give their consent to her marriage; now she has failed, every day they remind her how right they were.

The therapist, who was trained in the systemic model, believes that her problems can be interpreted as a manifestation of loyalty towards her parents. He proposes that they work on her relationship with her parents and that they see how she can be loyal in another way. He would also like to work on the consequences of her sexual abuse.

Diana is not very enthusiastic about this proposition. She just wants to get along better with her parents, as she needs their help at the moment. The therapist follows her in this undertaking. After this goal is attained, and she has moved out and feels generally better, Diana herself asks to work on the consequences of the abuse.

Small Goals Are Beautiful

Clients don't come to see us for trifles. They (and their systems) have generally been suffering for some time because of their problems. They have tried without success to solve them. On one hand, it would be disrespectful to present their goals as easy to attain. On the other hand, the steps to take and the tasks we give should be as small as possible. The easier a task, the better the chances that clients will succeed and then go further on their own initiative.

Taking a small step in the right direction should not be too difficult, but for some clients, taking that first step may be daunting. Habits are not easy to change, and taking a step back is even easier than walking forward. It may be prudent to predict a relapse so as to excuse it in advance, rather to have to start the next session on a setback. The following example shows how this can be done.

Bruce is a man of 35 who shows psychotic traits. He thinks he is telepathically influenced: Somebody or something exerts power over his thoughts and his behavior. He lives alone. He has lost contact with his family and his former friends. His general practitioner has sent him.

In the first session, Bruce states as his goal that he just wants to keep doing what he does now: He works as an accountant and he goes to a computer photography course once a month.

One could think that, in relation to his psychotic symptoms, these are ridiculously small goals. But when the therapist discusses with him how much it costs him to do this—to get to work and to concentrate on it—the energy required appears to be enormous. The therapist says he must feel exhausted at night, and she wonders how he manages to practice his photo editing hobby. Bruce looks down and sighs that he can do this only on weekends.

> The fact that the therapist can acknowledge how hard Bruce has to fight every day just to survive as he does, and that she doesn't push for him to change anything, becomes the basis of a relationship in which Bruce feels respected and esteemed.
>
> In the next session, Bruce says he has contacted his sister, who seemed glad to hear from him. They have agreed to meet in two weeks. The therapist says how glad she is about that and asks him how he picked up the telephone and called. She adds that although she hopes that their meeting will be fine and that he will go on see- ing her from time to time, as often as he wants, still at some time a misunderstanding may occur. Some rain may fall on their relationship. She reminds Bruce that should that happen, he has shown that he can pick up the thread again whenever he wants.

If our clients do not sense that we are aware of what it costs them to attain their goals, they may have the impression that we minimize their sufferings, that their efforts are useless, even ridiculous, that their problems are unimportant, and that they have been too stupid to find a solution to them. Their self-esteem goes down and with it their capacity to solve their problems by themselves.

Splitting Up the Therapeutic Goal into Small Steps

To cure a client's psychosis is not an easy task. To help him to better cope with his auditory hallucinations is a little bit easier. Bad habits are easier to change than a personality disorder.

Big problems can be divided into small ones; with each small success, the client becomes more confident.

Clients are often impatient. They want to get rid of their symptoms as fast as possible, and they don't appreciate the small steps they take. Scaling their progress is generally helpful. The therapist can also propose small, intermedi- ary goals, and/or negotiate a treatment plan.

Negotiating Intermediate Goals

After the client has set a long-term goal (e.g., as an answer to the Miracle Ques- tion or another future-oriented technique), a first intermediate goal is negoti- ated, such as:

- "What would be the first small step that would show you (or your spouse, etc.) that you are going in the right direction?"
- "You say that, on a scale from 0 to 10, you are at 3. What would it take for you to go to 4?"

Small bits of progress can also be monitored between sessions:

- "Would you agree to take a moment at night when you look back on your day to see if at some moment you have been at 4, and how you managed that? It would be nice if you could do that at least three or four times a week."
- "You said you are at 3 now. Life isn't always easy, and at some times in the next days you may fall back to 2, or even to 1. If after that, you have managed to get back to 3, could you look at how you did that?"
- "Could you ask your husband (wife, etc.) to pay attention to any moments where you have moved to 4, and how you did that?"

Negotiating a Treatment Plan

In some cases, it may be useful to negotiate a detailed treatment that proposes specific steps to be taken in a predetermined order. This is particularly helpful in consulting relationships, for example with phobic clients who have to start by learning techniques for overcoming their anxiety. They will typically have to try out different techniques to see which one suits them best. Then they will have to practice first in a neutral environment, then in a context that elicits moderate anxiety, perhaps with a family member to reassure them, then on their own, and so on.

Whenever clients have to acquire new skills before tackling their problems, a treatment plan is useful. But the solution-focused approach tries to be as flexible as possible. If it is possible to build new habits by expanding exceptions and variations in problematic habits, it is preferable to proceed by asking the clients what the next step can be, and not to stick to a rigid procedure. This quickly gives clients the feeling that they can solve their problems by themselves and that they don't need therapy anymore.

Chronic Clients

With chronic clients who often have lost the ability to envision a wished-for future and for whom every change is a leap into the unknown, it pays to be even more prudent. In each session, the therapist discusses whatever changes have been made, makes positive comments on them, and abstains from urging the client to take further steps. This stimulates the client to make small changes on his or her own initiative.

Formulating Realistic Goals

Some clients have clear goals, but they have unrealistic expectations of themselves, the therapist, or their family. Many phobic or obsessive-compulsive clients would like to be instantly cured of their symptoms. We have to tell them they must heed John Weakland's recommendation to "go slow." Before they can attain their goal, they will have to practice self-control techniques and they will need time to do this.

Several criteria determine whether a goal is realistic:

- Does the client have the necessary qualities (e.g., self-confidence) and skills (e.g., meditation or auto-hypnotic techniques, relaxation, etc.)? If not, we will need to address these first.
- Does the therapist know the techniques the client will need to acquire?
- Is the context in which the client lives favorable?

In the following example, the client lacks the resources and the time to attain her goals.

Nancy is 16. She comes in with her mother because she has to take her first oral exam in four weeks. She appears to be very timid, looks at the floor, wrings her hands, and takes a long time before answering even simple questions. The therapist doesn't see how he can help her acquire the necessary skills in a such short time.

Useful questions may be:

- (After demonstrating a technique to control her thoughts and her emotions) "How often do you think you will need to practice this technique so you can use it in all circumstances?"
- "How do you think you can help yourself? How could you train yourself in that?"

A client who is a perfectionist may not agree with a realistic goal.

- Scaling his or her progress may be helpful: "Let's take a scale from 0 to 10 where 0 is the worst your problem has been in the last six months and 10 is when you have reached your goal. Where are you now? How will you know when you have gone up a notch?"
- 54321 with Acceptance, Joy, or Gratitude (see p. 188) can also be used here.
- The client may write a diary in which he or she notes every day what he or she has done, big or small, that goes in the right direction. This may help the client realize that moving forward is what counts, rather than reaching the goal.
- Prediction tasks (see p. 79) can have a similar effect: Clients tend to perform as they have foretold rather than to try to be perfect.

Formulating a realistic goal requires obtaining a concrete, observable, and measurable description of the milestones needed to reach that goal so that the client has clear criteria with which to measure his or her progress. If the client sticks to vague descriptions, a scale can be used to pseudo-quantify the progress, as shown in this example.

Frances suffers from severe feelings of guilt. They have become unbearable and she wants to get over them. When the therapist asks what would change for her if she did resolve her guilt, she answers: "I don't know," "I will do nothing different," and "I will feel lighter." She can say nothing more concrete.

The therapist proposes that she quantify her feelings of guilt on a scale, where -10 indicates that she feels totally guilty, and 0 means that she feels guilty only in cases where her best friend would agree that she has done wrong. This scale is used throughout therapy to measure her progress.

Describing the Goals as New Habits

If clients have described concretely how they will be thinking differently when they attain their goals, how their behavior and emotions will change, and what else will change in that context, then they will feel ready to tackle them.

Context and behavior are of particular importance in the following description because they can more easily be controlled and quantified.

A woman would like her husband to show more tenderness. The husband says he is ready to do so. Now it is necessary to describe this goal in such a way that both will be able to agree if the goal has been met and to what extent it has been attained—otherwise, she will stay unsatisfied and he will be discouraged.

They agree that when they meet in the evenings, he will kiss and hug her and she will respond to this, just like when they were courting.

She will try to show her satisfaction every time he does something that pleases her, and he will tell her if the way she shows this pleases him.

In this way the context is indicated and the behavior that corresponds to the emotions is rendered explicit. Each of them gets the feedback they need to adjust to what the other expects.

In the next example the four aspects of the wished-for habit are detailed. This makes it probable that the changes will be implemented.

CLIENT: "I want to get out of this damned depression!"
THERAPIST: "How will you recognize that you start to get out of it?"
CLIENT: "I will feel good again."
THERAPIST: "And what will you do when you feel good again? Let's say, tomorrow morning for example, how would your wife notice that you feel better?"
CLIENT: "I would sing in the shower!"
THERAPIST: "Oh! So you will take a shower and sing in it?"
CLIENT: "Yes, and I will smile to my wife and eat a good breakfast."
THERAPIST: "So how would that feel?"
CLIENT: "Good, of course!"
THERAPIST: "And how will your wife react if you smile at her?"

Both go on talking about what the client would do, and how he and his wife would react to that. The client cannot help but see that there are a lot of things he can do without waiting for his depression to go away, and that he would enjoy the reactions of his near and dear.

Interactional Description of the New Habit

If the goal, and the habits that go with it, are described interactionally, the client's family members and colleagues will take part in motivating the client. Shared habits develop and the client can let him- or herself be taken along by family members. For clients with an external locus of control this is a big advantage.

Here are a few examples of questions:

* "How would your husband, your mother, your son, your dog know that you are getting better?"
* "If your husband was sitting here, what would he say if I asked him how he would notice you're getting better?"
* (To the client's wife) "Your husband is like a lot of other people. He doesn't notice when he takes a step in the right direction. Would you agree to tell him when you notice something like that, and in general, to tell him whenever he does something you're happy with?"

On the stage of our life, we see not only with our own eyes, but also, perhaps even mainly, through the eyes of the others.

In couples therapy or in therapy with an adolescent the client often comes up with a goal that is dependent on the goodwill of someone else (the spouse, the parents). In this case, we can start with the wished-for action of the other and construct an interactional sequence that starts from there, as shown in the following example.

> The wife wishes that her husband would be more affectionate and that he would tell her more about his work. He would like for her to be less jealous, to show more trust in him, and to nag less, in particular when he has to go out for professional reasons.
>
> THERAPIST: "What would you do if your husband were more affectionate?"
> WIFE: "I would feel more secure in our relationship."
> THERAPIST: "And what would you do differently if you felt more secure?"
> WIFE: "I wouldn't bother him with all my questions when he has to go out."
> THERAPIST (to husband): "And you, what would you do differently if your wife wasn't nagging so much?"
> HUSBAND: "I think I would feel closer to her."
> THERAPIST: "How would you show that you feel closer to her? What exactly would you do? And how do you think she would react? Would that be all right with you? And how would you react to that?"

The clients notice that they can start changes at any point in the interactional sequence (i.e., the sequence of interactions) and so start a new interactional habit (i.e., a habit that involves other persons).

A conversation like this is often easier to make if we see the spouses (or the adolescent and his or her parents) separately. We can confront them more easily and talk about the qualities of the other without them "losing points."

Positive Formulations

When somebody says: "I don't want to smoke anymore," he or she thinks of a cigarette. When someone says: "I will not drink any alcohol today," he or she thinks of alcohol. This is why successful dieting programs stress the idea of eating differently, not of eating less.

Unfortunately, many clients know what they don't want, but they have not thought about what they want instead. Here follow a few examples of useful questions:

- "What would you do instead?"
- "Could you tell me what you will be doing when your fears have gone?"
- "What did you do on those days where you have been drinking less than usual or not at all?"

> A negative statement . . . feeds discouragement, low energy, and a sense of being stuck or trapped. In addition, it focuses what little energy the client may have left on trying to keep this negative something away. It is usually much easier for people to do something they perceive as positive. For example, it is easier for clients to lose weight by getting up and taking a walk than by continually reminding themselves not to go to the kitchen for a bag of potato chips and a soda. Consequently, well-formed goals are described as the presence of something positive rather than the absence of some perceived problem.
>
> (De Jong & Berg, 1998)

A well-formulated therapeutic goal is the start of new habits, the end of old ones. This implies that (with the exception of chronic clients who lack perspective) once new habits have been established and become automatic, therapy is no longer necessary. It may even be enough for clients to have their attention turned to their goals and what they are doing already to achieve them. They can find their own way after that.

Scales of progress are useful in this respect. If in the first session we ask: "If 10 stands for the point where you will need no more therapy and 0 for the opposite, where are you now on that scale?" and the client says he or she now stands at 3, we can monitor the client's progress on this scale. In most instances, the client will decide when he or she no longer needs our help. At the outset, clients (and therapists) often overestimate the amount of help they will need.

Some clients can tell right at the start what they want. Others have only a vague idea. A future-oriented question doesn't always lead to a clear and concrete description of a wished-for life, for the excellent reason that clients can be too blinded by their problems to think of anything else. In this case, observation tasks like the Three Questions for a Good Life (see p. 129) or the First Session Formula Task (see p. 105) can help clients to have a better view of what they want to keep and what they want to change.

Hidden Problems, Hidden Goals

Some clients come and talk about their symptoms without mentioning other problems they have. They may feel ashamed or guilty, or they don't see any connection. Psychosomatic symptoms like muscular aches, headaches, abdominal pain in children or gynecological and urinary complaints in women are often caused by stress mechanisms that are themselves the expression of other problems. Anorexia, self-mutilation, and suicide attempts may point to a history of trauma and abuse.

The therapist needs to tread with caution here:

- Suggestive or direct questioning may reactivate a trauma that the client had more or less successfully dealt with, causing unnecessary suffering;
- False memories may be induced, causing even more harm;
- Questions may be couched so obliquely that the client doesn't understand what they mean.

If there are hidden problems, it is a (frequently made) error to think that they must be solved before the actual complaints can be addressed. On the contrary, helping the client to lead a better life now will lead to a trusting and empowering relationship in which trauma, guilt, and shame can be successfully addressed.

Goals May Change

At the outset, many clients have no map for what they will be doing once their problems have been solved. Goals are discussed in the first sessions, but sometimes they can change in the course of even brief therapy. For example, an alcoholic who first wanted to control her drinking may change to a desire for abstinence. The client of course has the right to do this. It can even be seen as a good sign: She takes her therapy in her own hands, she assumes responsibility and acts as an expert, and an internal locus of control is established. Or, as Lipchik (2002) puts it: "Solutions are the end product of a process of discovery. They may be far removed from what the clients thought their goal was when they entered therapy. Based on this reasoning, 'goal clarification' is better thought of as an ongoing monitoring of, and reevaluation with, clients during therapy of what they want the outcome to be."

Goals are an evolving co-construction. Throughout the course of therapy, new perspectives open after each bend in the road. Clients discover new territories that they want to explore and to chart.

This has implications for therapists who work according to a preestablished protocol:

- The protocol shows the way that therapists and clients have to travel along to reach the goal.
- If, along the way, the client wishes to take a shortcut or if he or she wants to change his or her destination, the therapist must be ready to follow that lead. Goals are like the Pole Star: They are useful not to lose the North. If the client decides to go East instead, that is his or her decision. One can still use the Pole Star as a guide.

- Goals are constructs, and in this sense they are hypotheses that we will use as long as they are helpful.
- We have to let go of the client as soon as he or she decides we are not needed anymore, even if the protocol says there is more to do.

What to Do with Dangerous Goals

Client may set their goals in such a way that they endanger themselves, their family, or their friends. In this case, the therapist may have to step out of the therapeutic relationship and assume a protective one, as in this example.

> Sarah, 15, has been prostituting herself since she was 12. She is hospitalized now but will be leaving the clinic shortly. She tells her therapist that after discharge she will take up prostitution again. The therapist must alert the child protection service.

Another example would be a psychotic with dangerous delusions or an alcoholic in a delirium tremens. In such situations, protective measures take the lead over therapeutic considerations. Even so, trying to share responsibilities and offering choices will often prove more helpful than directly imposing a protective measure. In the psychiatric emergency ward in St. John's Hospital Bruges, aggressive and agitated psychotics who are brought in by the police are told that they cannot go home right away, they need to rest first. They will need a sedative to be able to rest, but they can choose between a tablet and an injection. Nine out of ten choose the tablet and take it, obviating the need for five male nurses to overpower them while they are administered an injection against their will.

Some useful questions for clarifying goals include:

- The Miracle Question (see pp. 124–125);
- Three Questions for a Good Life (see p. 99);
- The spiritual testament (see pp. 135–136);
- How will you know your problems are solved?
- What needs to be different for you to be able to say: "If my life goes on as it is now, that's OK with me?"
- How will that feel different?
- What will you do differently?
- What will (significant others) say is different with you?
- What will be different about (significant others)? What will be different about your relationship with them?
- What needs to change so you don't need to come and see me anymore?

2   Tackling the Semantics

Useful Views

A client will need to develop new habits if he or she wants to get rid of (or, at least, to suffer less from) his or her problems and symptoms. Problematic habits will have to make way for acceptable ones. When constructing these new habits, other emotions and feelings, other patterns of behavior will emerge, as will other meanings and views.

I will not discuss here the question of the reality of reality. Does reality as we know it exist only inside our conscious mind, as the sensualist, solipsistic, and constructivist thinkers maintain (Watzlawick et al., 1967, 1974)? Is reality a social construction, a consensus among the groups of individuals who compose our social and cultural context, as the constructionists assert (Gergen, 2001)? Or should we adopt a materialistic view, as many neuro-physiologists do, in which reality is what our senses (and the instruments that extend them) perceive?

With Alfred Korzybski (1933) and Gregory Bateson (1972, 1975, 1979) we would like to adopt a pragmatic viewpoint. We cannot know reality itself, as anyone who has tried to understand modern physics will admit, but we can draw maps that help us to orient ourselves in the landscape of reality. These maps should be sufficiently congruent, that is, analogous to the reality whose structure they represent. According to the aspects of reality we want to highlight, various features can be added to a map, or different maps can be drawn. Michelin maps of Europe in the years following 1945 adapted to the reality of the times by showing which bridges had been destroyed. As Korzybski famously said, "The map is not the territory," and as the Chinese Emperor in the J.L. Borges story discovered, no map can show all the features of the territory—but we can at least try to make the map (the description of our client's reality) as helpful as possible for our purposes, by discarding unhelpful and distracting features and by including useful ones.

Here is a description of a case, with various viewpoints, some of which can be helpful and others that cannot.

Maud is 31 years old. She lives alone in a small flat. She visits her parents twice a week, to get a warm meal and to give them her laundry to wash. She has no work and gets no social benefits; her parents support her. They are just wealthy enough to do so, but they feel unsure about how to provide for Maud after their death.

When Maud goes shopping, her mother is always with her. Outside of her family, she has almost no social contacts. Still, for a few hours every week, she goes to a seniors' residence and pushes elderly people in their wheelchairs through the city park.

She goes to bed around 9 P.M. and rises at 11 A.M. She hears voices that offend and insult her. In the morning, Prince Charles comes into her room and makes expert comments on her appearance: Her hair is done all right; her lipstick is a mess; and so on. She appreciates these appearances and feels a little flattered by them. When he is otherwise engaged and cannot come, she feels insecure. She doesn't read anything, not even a fashion magazine, because she cannot concentrate.

This condition has been present for eight years, after she was hospitalized in a psychotic and agitated state.

What hypotheses can we make? What maps can we draw? And how can we use them?

Maud has been diagnosed as a schizophrenic. From a biological perspective, neuroleptics will be prescribed as a matter of course. If she doesn't show enough compliance and if she doesn't take her medication punctually enough (e.g., because Prince Charles stops appearing when she takes her pills), she will get a monthly shot.

A psychoanalyst could hypothesize a pre-Oedipal disorder and treat her according to this view.

A family therapist might detect a symbiotic relationship between mother and daughter and try to work towards more autonomy. The therapist might also look at the father-mother-daughter triad, and as a first move, restore parental authority (Haley, 1973). Or the therapist might think that Maud is "triangulated" between father and mother, and might want to re-establish clear frontiers between the generations and a "normal" hierarchy. He or she may observe paradoxes in their communication patterns, such as an escalation of symmetry (Selvini-Palazzoli et al., 1975), and deploy a counter-paradox.

Questions of loyalty might also inspire the family therapist, or transgenerational theories for the origin of a schizophrenic psychosis.

A behavior therapist might perhaps view Maud's voices as a learned behavior that should be unlearned through an operant conditioning. This therapist might also try to break through her social isolation by using social skills training.

There are many other approaches, each founded on their own hypotheses and leading to different strategies.

There are also some unprofessional opinions about Maud's condition. She has her views, and her relatives have theirs.

Her elder brother says she is lazy and she profits from her parents. They should stop being so soft and instead kick her laziness out of her.

Her mother sees Maud as being seriously ill. She considers it her duty to do all she can for her. Her father shares this opinion. They hope against hope that some day a doctor will find a cure for her.

Maud says that she suffers from a great weakness, induced by those same people who abuse her with their voices. She feels helpless; she has no idea what she could do about it.

In addition to these more global views, certain specific aspects of Maud's behavior are subject to different interpretations. To take just one example:

She stays in bed for more than 12 hours every night. This can be seen as:

- A bad habit;
- A flight from her responsibilities;
- A side effect of the neuroleptics she takes;
- A negative symptom of her psychotic disorder;
- A maneuver to induce care-giving behavior in her mother.

Perhaps) she stays in bed so she can listen to her voices without being disturbed—or she might have other reasons of her own (one could ask her).

Each of the manifold hypotheses I mentioned connects different facts and aspects of Maud's reality. All have their merits insofar as (but, in my view, only insofar as) they can lead to a successful strategy.

I will now try to show a few features of what are, in my opinion, helpful viewpoints.

Ten Tips for Useful Semantics

Useful interpretations help to:

1. Take a positive view.
2. Put the symptomatic habit in a larger context.

3. Highlight the positive aspects of the symptomatic habit.
4. Lessen feelings of guilt.
5. Build hope.
6. Stimulate clients to make their own decisions and take their own responsibilities.
7. Postulate a circular rather than a linear causality.
8. Adopt an allocentric rather than an egocentric viewpoint.
9. Supplement old views with new ones (not replace them).
10. If possible, develop several alternative and mutually non-exclusive views.

Well-Formed Hypotheses

A Hypothesis Can Never Be True, It Can Only Be Useful

Facts exist, and in that sense they can be said to be true. Hypotheses do not happen; they do not belong to the realm of reality. Facts and events belong in that realm, not hypotheses. These are abstractions that permit us to interpret and structure the facts we perceive. We do this by connecting them with each other by, for example, causal connections, analogies, and so on. Since Karl Popper, the illusion has been abandoned that we can verify hypotheses (and so declare them to be true). Instead of this, we can try to falsify them and prove that they are not true. If we don't succeed in this, a hypothesis can provisionally be accepted.

Well-formed hypotheses stay very close to the observed, concrete facts. They tend to connect facts with facts, not hypotheses with hypotheses or abstractions with abstractions. Here follows an, admittedly exaggerated, example of how interpretations can spin out of control.

Charlotte is 13 years old. She has taken up the habit of retiring to the bathroom whenever her mother calls her to help in washing up. One could keep it simple and suppose she doesn't like to help with the household chores. One could also go a little further in constructing hypotheses.

It may be that she's afraid the skin of her hands might become dry from the soapy water. If she wants beautiful hands, it follows that she wants to look good. This may mean that she has a boyfriend. If, at her age, she has a steady boyfriend, perhaps she doesn't feel understood by her parents. If she doesn't feel understood, they probably pay her too little attention. When parents pay too little attention to their children, the reason is often that they have too many conflicts between them. So it's obvious that Charlotte doesn't help with the cleaning because her parents are quarrelling. Relationship therapy is indicated.

The only concrete fact we have is that Charlotte, not unlike many other girls of her age, locks herself inside the bathroom when her help is requested in a household chore. If her parents wanted to change this habit, they might go into couples therapy. One may have doubts about the usefulness of such a procedure.

Her parents may also use a strategy based on hypotheses that are nearer to the concrete facts. Mother could wait with the washing up until Charlotte comes out of the bathroom; they could lock the door before calling her; they could give her pocket money depend on her readiness to help out in the household; or they could use any other strategy that starts from the observed facts.

Hypotheses being abstractions, it is not relevant to ask how true they are. Much more interesting is the question of how helpful they are in attaining the goal that client and therapist are negotiating.

Let's suppose that Charlotte's parents have requested our advice on how to address their daughter's disobedience, with the washing up as an example. To advise them to enter couple's therapy would speak very little to their expectations and to the mandate they wanted to give to the therapist. They would probably break off therapy.

It should prove more productive to look out for other observable facts that can be linked to Charlotte's flight into the bathroom. Does she do her school tasks without prompting? What other activities does she have? How does mother ask her to help with the chores? Are there other children in the family, and do they help? Does Charlotte refuse all chores, or does she do some without demurring? Perhaps even without being asked? Which ones? (Compliments are due to Charlotte for doing them and to her parents for educating her, with these results!)

When we stick to the facts, and when we investigate the habits of Charlotte and her family with their nuances and alternatives, chances are that, together with our clients, we discover ways out of the problems and that we can share with them a mandate to solve them.

Hypotheses may be useful or not. Useful hypotheses are those that inspire both clients and therapists towards effective strategies. If such a strategy succeeds, this does not mean that the underlying hypothesis is true. It means only that it is useful.

Some hypotheses are simply useless, while some are positively harmful: They take away hope, they discourage or ridicule useful explorations, and they close up possible solutions. Whenever a harmful, discouraging hypothesis raises its ugly head, however "true" it may look, just lock it away in the back of your head and use it to go easy on pressing the client for change. Orient the therapy to the concrete details of the problem sequences: Chances are you will soon find something useful there.

Our clients themselves show us how dangerous it is to stick to a hypothesis under the pretext that it explains the problems and go on repeating the same unhelpful solutions. Here is an example of a vicious circle that turns round and round when people stand by their unhelpful views.

Harriet drinks too much because (she says) her husband shows her too little affection and consequently she feels lonely. So she goes on drinking and reproaching him bitterly. He disengages himself even more from this (in his eyes) vicious drunk.

Hypotheses Are Flexible and Disposable Working Tools

Well-formed hypotheses are based on facts, not on interpretations. They connect facts, and these connections are useful or not. When they cannot be used to implement a successful strategy, they should be replaced by other constructions: Hypotheses are disposable goods. Beautiful as a hypothesis may be and as proud as we may be of having designed it, one should never fall in love with a hypothesis.

Hypotheses are constructed, checked, and retained or rejected in a dialogue with clients about their concrete difficulties. The aim and worth of hypotheses lie only in helping to solve problems and to promote new habits.

A hypothesis that seemed useful in one session may prove useless in the next. In that case, it should be abandoned.

The following example shows how one should drop even the most plausible and captivating hypotheses when one doesn't need them any more.

Hester, 35 years old, is separated from her son Sandy's father. She now lives with a new partner. Sandy shows behavior problems; he is in group therapy in a child psychiatry facility. Parallel to this, he is in family therapy with his mother.

During one session, Hester talks about her fears when Sandy spends the weekend with his father. She wants Sandy to go on seeing him and to maintain a good relationship with him, but she suspects physical abuse without being sure of it. She also expresses fears for her own security if she should oppose the visits. Sandy's father has made threats already and he is capable of anything when he has been drinking. She thinks it might be even worse if her boyfriend intervened, as he has proposed. In this session, she appears very anxious and agitated.

The therapists know that Hester was a victim of childhood abuse and that her parents' separation was very painful for her. They resolve to take up these matters in the next session. They think Hester may need a trauma therapy of her own.

Two weeks later, Hester is very relieved to say that her fears were groundless. She, her uncle, and her boyfriend have talked to Sandy's

father; the mood was relaxed, they came to an agreement, and everything went all right. Her worries are over; she wants to address other
problems.

The therapists still may have questions for themselves and watch out for signs
that Hester's childhood problems are interfering with her relationship with
Sandy. But it would be misplaced at this point to insist on individual therapy for
Hester. This would put into question the solutions she has put into place by herself. Advising individual therapy would imply that Hester's skills are inadequate
and her self-efficacy would be undermined. In addition, this would impose upon
her a goal that she hasn't formulated herself: She came into therapy for her son's
sake, not for her own.

Use Dynamic Language

Korzybski (1933) and later O'Hanlon & Wilk (1987) have shown that habits,
being dynamic features, are better described in dynamic rather than in static
language. In other words: It is better to describe processes than personality
traits or diagnoses. Or in yet other words: It is better to make descriptions that
do not link the verbs "to be" or "to have" with an adjective or a substantive that
stand for a lasting characteristic. Here are two examples.

Example 1: A static way to describe Charlotte's flight to the toilet
would be: "She's lazy." A more dynamic description might be: "When
it's time to do the dishes, Charlotte goes to the toilet." It will be easier
to change this habit than to cure her of her laziness.

Example 2: Gertrude, 30 years old, married with two daughters,
was sexually abused during her childhood. She suffered from a number of sequels to this abuse, including nightmares, flashbacks, difficulties in washing herself, and automutilations.

Every day, while going home after her work as a secretary, she was
pursued by male voices insulting her, calling her a whore, and so on.
In order to escape her persecutors, she ran as fast as she could—but
the voices kept up with her. When at last she reached home, she was
so confused, distraught, and exhausted that she had to lock herself
into her bedroom for half an hour to recuperate.

She had been diagnosed with PTSD, with differential diagnoses of
Borderline Personality Disorder and, after an agitated depressive episode and a serious suicide attempt, Psychotic Depressive Disorder.

She underwent a neuroleptic treatment that reduced her general anxiety level.

The therapist proposed that she answer to the voices as if they were real people. He did a role play with her in which he played her role and she played her voices. He asked her to explain what precisely they meant when they called her a whore and on what concrete facts their accusations were founded. They had no answer. So he told them they were neither truthful nor polite, as they should be towards a lady. The voices, through the client's mouth, didn't know what to say.

In his approach, the therapist used the dynamic procedure of taking the client's experience at face value. If voices talked to her, why not do like the client and take them as actual people's voices? Confront these persons, hold them responsible for their statements, and bid them to explain themselves and to mind their manners.

The client was somewhat confused but she felt that no one before had taken her as seriously. She promised to apply the method right away. In the next session, she reported that the voices were still there, but they were much less intrusive. On a scale of 1 to 10 measuring how well she felt while going home, she had risen from 2 to 7.

Hypotheses Should Build Hope and Offer a Perspective of Change

According to Rabkin (1977), clients come into therapy when they have lost confidence and believe they cannot solve their problems by themselves. Nonetheless, they hope that the therapist will show them the way to a solution, though they have no idea of what this way might look like. Negative expectations dominate their field of vision. They are focused on their problems as on a mountain: They stand before it with no idea how they might climb it. It seems impossible to them to get out of this predicament. They use words like *powerless, impossible, victim,* and *destiny.* These words are part of the logos aspect of their habits; they keep them locked inside the witches' circle of their negative feelings and behavior patterns.

Frankl (1999) points out that discouragement is the main motive for clients to seek therapeutic help. In Frankl's view, it is therefore just as important for therapy to open up perspectives and to foster client self-efficacy as it is to alleviate their symptoms.

Accordingly, a well-formed hypothesis should not only offer a new explanation for the symptoms and stay close to the concrete reality of the client, but it should also build the space in which new habits can be tried out. Gertrude provides an example of this.

The hypothesis that it is possible not to just suffer from the voices, but that one can stand up to them and challenge them to explain themselves and behave civilly, opened up a wholly new perspective for Gertrude. The therapist did not seek to eliminate the dissociative disorder, but to open a new perspective from which Gertrude could become able to use her own resources: She became more self-efficacious.

Her past stays the same, but she found new ways to cope with its effects.

Well-Formed Hypotheses Are Useful and Respectful for the Client and Important Family Members

From a systemic perspective, habits are rules of the system. Our relatives (or our colleagues, our team mates, our class mates, according to which system we consider) interact with our habits; we have seen that all habits have an interactional aspect and that almost no habit is so private that nobody interacts with it.

Habits are repetitive interactional behavior patterns; this is a definition for rules of a system. The more a hypothesis appears as useful and respectful for all members of the client's system, the better the strategies that follow from it will be accepted. This will become more clear in the following section.

Hypotheses Can Be More Productive When Including Positive Functions of the Symptom

Habits are rules of the system. These are not there for nothing; they have a function. Even when a habit generates suffering, some aspects of it may be advantageous. I call these the *positive functions* of the symptom. Most of the time, the clients and their relatives are blind to this. When the therapist points their attention to it, they are surprised by the discovery that their problematic behavior might be based on a choice, and that under the circumstances this choice might even not be the worst one.

Following is an example of how even grave symptoms can have positive effects and how the therapist should take these into account:

Jackie, who is 35 years old and has three children, is a medical doctor. She works half time in a youth care service. Her husband is a surgeon in the local clinic. She drinks heavily two or three times a week, sometimes ending up in an alcoholic coma. Several times she has driven her children to school while heavily drunk. She drinks mostly beer; she says she doesn't like the stuff and has no idea why she drinks it. She has nothing to complain about except perhaps her job that bores her, but then it's only half-time. Her husband is very concerned about her and their children. He has tried all he could to curb her drinking binges. He locks the cellar, where the beer is kept; he calls several times a day from the clinic; and he has enlisted Jackie's mother, who has been widowed for a couple of years. She came to live with them a month ago and keeps a constant watch on her daughter. In spite of all these precautions, Jackie succeeds again and again in outwitting her family's vigilance.

We see immediately that Jackie's drunken episodes have two concrete and positive consequences. Her husband, whose job is very demanding and time-consuming, stays present through his repeated telephone calls. Her mother suddenly doesn't find herself alone and useless anymore—to the contrary, her presence with her daughter has become indispensable.

One could hypothesize that these two consequences are positive functions of the symptom. To corroborate this, we can look a little closer into the family interactions. It appears that Jackie's husband not only is more engaged with her, but that he also is more active in educating the children. Grandma consults him as well as Jackie; together, they make the little decisions of everyday life.

Together with Jackie, the therapist can now look how the positive consequences of her symptomatic habits can be attained by other means. How can her husband go on being a concerned and active father and husband? How can mother go on feeling useful and involved?

Allocentric and Circular Hypotheses Work Better Than Egocentric and Linear Ones

By *egocentric hypotheses*, I here mean hypotheses that depict the client as producing the symptoms for his or her own benefit. Allocentric explanations look at the advantages for persons who are near to the client, such as the partner, parents, or children.

Linear causal hypotheses try to find a cause that precedes the effect, so they generally look for explanations in the client's past. Circular hypotheses postulate that the positions of "cause" and "effect" are often mutually interchangeable. At the end of a problem sequence, the conditions for a new one are established. What "caused" the problem comes back as its consequence.

Let's illustrate this with Jackie's example.

One can see Jackie as an unworthy mother and an unthankful wife who thinks only of her own pleasure—an egoistic monster. This hypothesis, which certainly fits a lot of the facts, doesn't help the therapist to develop the empathy he will need or to respect her as a fellow human being who has big problems. It would not be easy to design a strategy based on this hypothesis: Should one try to make her less egoistic? How should one go about that? An allocentric view (based on the positive consequences for her husband and her mother) looks at the hidden possibilities and resources that are present in the symptomatic interactions and thereby show possible alternatives.

I would like to point out that in my approach, these allocentric and positive hypotheses are not formulated in order to stimulate the client to a paradoxical reaction, such as has been described by Mara Selvini-Palazzoli and colleagues in "Paradox and Contraparadox" (1975). My aim is to help the therapist to adopt a positive and respectful attitude, to help the client to lessen her feelings of guilt and to show the way to positive interactions.

The circular view is complementary to the linear. From a linear causal perspective, one could say that Jackie started drinking because she felt neglected by her husband. The ever-stricter control to which he subjected her does not fulfill her expectations and her needs. To the contrary, she feels humiliated; this has pushed her to drink even more. Of course, one could say that her husband had no choice but to exert such strict control in order to maintain a minimum of security in their home.

In these opposing linear views, either Jackie or her husband are guilty. A circular hypothesis looks to the symptom sequences and their consequences rather than to the causes, to the "how," the "when" and the "to what effect" rather than to the "why."

We can only *observe* that Jackie's husband has been more involved since she has started to drink. She has gone on drinking and her husband has stepped up his efforts to be present by trying to exercise control over whatever he could. She has continued drinking and her mother has become involved, being present and controlling when her husband is at the clinic. Nobody is guilty, but all take part in what is happening (even the children, whom I have left out for simplicity's sake).

When we ask who is guilty, our attention and our thoughts are focused on the past. However interesting this may seem, it does not lead us to a solution.

The therapist makes no judgments but instead helps everyone to find the way to make the right choices and to accept his or her responsibilities: How can each one contribute in his or her own way to solve the problem?

To conclude, I would like to remind the reader that new hypotheses do not annul old ones. A therapist's hypotheses are not more true than those of the clients; they only open up new perspectives. That is their only function and their only justification.

3 How to Promote Freedom of Choice

The Pragmatics

In my view, it is not a therapist's task to rid clients of their symptoms. That is something that clients have to do. Nobody can change someone else; we can change only ourselves. Therefore, all therapy is self-therapy. The therapist's task is to help clients to (be able to) choose to do what they want to do, as opposed to feeling compelled to do something they don't want to do. A therapist should help clients to develop (or to revert to) alternative habits (i.e., habits other than the problematic ones) in the situation in which the problematic habits occur. Then, when clients can choose between a problematic and a non-problematic, between a healthy and a pathological habit, they recover the freedom to choose how they want to live.

This is a radically permissive position. It is not always easy for therapists to keep it up. Many clients profess themselves to be powerless and incompetent. They ask us to cure them, by which they (explicitly or implicitly) mean that we should remove their problems and their symptoms, like a surgeon who cuts out a tumor. A therapist who accepts this mandate and who sees it as his or her task to change a client's behavior of steps into a minefield.

A therapist who attempts this shows too little respect for clients:

- However much clients suffer from their symptoms, they often have developed them as an answer to a given situation, a specific context of meaningful stimuli, and until now they haven't found a better answer. Symptoms often have good consequences as well as bad ones. If one doesn't take this into account, resistance is the result. The clients, and they alone, must decide how they want to live.
- Out of the best of intentions, a therapist may pursue a goal that his or her client doesn't share. The therapist is in danger of treating his or her own troubles through the client.
- Clients often don't collaborate as eagerly as we would like them to. We may safely assume that they have good reasons for that. They know their present problems and they have more or less learned to live with them. They ask us to help them; but, not knowing what awaits them when their problems are gone, they may fear the outcome.

- Sometimes the symptoms bring some gain for someone else in the family: Caring for an anorexic, a phobic, or a depressive sibling may be as rewarding as it is sometimes frustrating.
- Struggling with one's problems can be difficult, but also stimulating; living without them may then be more easy, but also more boring.

Clients like these "don't know what they want." An authoritarian therapist who thinks he or she knows what's good for clients will then be tempted to impose his or her own goals. The therapist means well enough and sometimes clients will accept his or her help and feel the better for it. Still, the therapist will not have helped the client to determine his or her own existential goals, to adjust his or her behavior to these and so to bolster self-efficacy.

So how can we help our clients to make the right decisions and to internalize these as healthy habits?

Building the Context for Good Decisions

To build a context for good decisions we have several options (and of course all their combinations).

We can *look for alternative habits*: What is the client already doing differently in the context in which the symptoms habitually arise? Many clients occasionally do something else in the situation in which their symptoms come up. A post-traumatic client cuts himself whenever a flashback comes—but now and then he takes a cold shower instead. A lonely woman drinks to soothe her sorrows—but when the weather is fair, she sometimes drives into town and drinks a coke in a sidewalk café. Such alternative habits are proof that some freedom of choice still exists. Sometimes clients are so blinded by their problems that they don't think of these exceptions while we are talking with them. If this is the case, we will give an observation task.

A second consideration is that *all symptom sequences end sooner or later*. A depressed client might rise at 11:00 A.M., but she eventually gets out of bed, washes, and eats something. A heavy drinker leaves the bar at some point in the evening, mostly when he is drunk—but sometimes earlier, when he hasn't had as much as he's used to. A compulsive client washes her hands seven times, then stops. Although few clients see it this way, the end of the symptom sequence signals a move away from the symptoms and towards a more healthy functioning. Here too, an observation task will give interesting information on how much the client is still able to choose.

Although the therapist never dictates a solution, sometimes the therapist may want to *suggest an alternative to the unwanted habits:* "What do you think would happen if you . . . ?" It is always better not to directly propose a solution, but rather a context in which the client has more chances of finding his or her own solution. If for some reason the therapist feels he or she has to offer a solution, it is better to offer more than one possible solution. This way, the client still has some freedom of choice and his or her self-efficacy will be stimulated.

An elegant technique is for the therapist to *suggest small changes in the symptom sequence* (such as the Last Five Minutes, the Worrying Chair, 54321, etc.) (see pp. 138, 183, 549). As these interventions induce only minor changes, they don't elicit much resistance. Instead, they help clients to reflect on their position: They take the time to see themselves as the actors of their symptoms and perhaps to ask themselves if, this time too, they want to let the symptom habit unfold itself in exactly the same way as they are used to, or if they want to change something. As soon as this freer stance is acquired, these methods have achieved their goal. The clients then generally stop using them.

Building upon *pre-session change is yet another possibility:* As Steve de Shazer (1985) and colleagues have shown, in ambulatory therapy clients often start moving in the right direction as soon as they have made their first appointment, before they have seen the therapist. They rarely tell about this without being asked. This "pre-session change," though, can give important indications on what direction the therapy has to take: They came about on the clients' own initiative and show how well their self-efficacy work.

Milton Erickson was a master at putting his clients in a meta-position, helping them to take a good look at what they were doing and deciding if they wanted to change something about it. His *therapeutic double binds* (p. 140) put the client into a position where only good choices are possible. This makes for more freedom of choice than when he or she can choose only between good or bad, sick or healthy.

Some clients seem unable to fully accept the consequences of the choices they are considering: A client who, like Hercules at the crossroads, wants to take the left road but keep the advantages of the right, ends up having little freedom of choice. A husband wants to stay with his children and therefore with his wife, but he doesn't want to break up with his mistress. An adolescent wants more pocket money and the use of his father's car on weekends, but he also wants to sniff as much cocaine or drink as much beer as he likes.

Often, these clients don't realize that the different things they want are incompatible with each other. Two strategies may help them to see more clearly:

- the homework task "A Day, a Year Later . . ." (p. 133);
- a Socratic dialogue, in which through logical questioning (without moralizing!) the client gets to see the consequences of his or her views, decisions, and behavior and so to make a well-reflected choice.

Still another, and very effective, way of creating a context of choice is to *propose a projection into the future* such as de Shazer's Miracle Question (p. 124) or the spiritual testament (p. 000) in order to help the client to visualize a wished-for future and to envision not only what they don't want, but also what they could do instead.

Yet another, and often funny, way to proceed is to *suggest possible choices that would have consequences that the client would want to avoid.* In this way, those clients who are convinced that they are the hapless victims of their symptoms some-times come to see that they are able at least to do something about them. They then can move from a searching to a consulting relationship. For example, con-sider the following scenario.

A woman drinks secretly whenever she feels depressed. When she has these dark thoughts, she sees only one solution: to drink and so to forget. The following dialogue could occur between this woman and her therapist.

THERAPIST: "So then you think only of the wine and of forgetting, and then you see no other choice than to drink."

CLIENT: "That's right, I'd like not to do it. I've tried I don't know how many times, but I never succeed."

THERAPIST: "What would happen if at such a moment you called your sister or a good friend?"

CLIENT: "Oh, I have tried everything. Well, yes, sometimes that helps. But I can't bother my sister all the time, can I?"

THERAPIST: "No, of course, I can see that. But has this been useful already—that you got busy with something else, and that the bad moment passed?"

CLIENT: "Well, yes, but I can't do that all the time, can I?"

THERAPIST: "Your sister wouldn't agree?"

CLIENT: "I don't know, perhaps she would. She wants to help me. But I can't do that."

THERAPIST: "And something else that would sufficiently keep your attention?"

CLIENT: "I wouldn't know what."

THERAPIST: "Mmmmh . . . What would happen if at that moment you would drop a ten-pound weight on your big toe? Would that capture your attention?"

CLIENT: (Laughs) "Yeah, that would do the trick, I think."

THERAPIST: "But I suppose you wouldn't like to have your toe crushed."

CLIENT: "Well, actually no, I'd rather not."

THERAPIST: "You know what we often do with people who don't know what they could do when the craving is as strong as it is with you? We try, together with them we try to look what possibilities there are, what you still could do that stops short of crushing your big toe. You know, a kind of first aid kit for when you're about to stumble. Sometimes we call it a treasure chest, or, well, a first aid kit. Let me show you how it works."

The client has been "softened up," she is less convinced that she can't do anything, and she cooperates more readily.

Finally, *creating a context of choice* during the therapeutic session is also quite helpful.

Creating a Context of Choice

How can we create a context of choice? By, whenever possible, inviting clients to make their own choices.

- One can *let the client decide if he or she wants to come to see us alone or with a family member.* Generally speaking, therapy moves faster when the family is involved. Information comes from different sources. We can hear directly from the client's husband, wife, and so on, what their views are on the problems and on possible solutions. We can discuss alternative hypotheses with them. We can compliment them on how they have been coping with the problems, on their good intentions, on their resources, on their love for the client, on the help they have been giving already. We can discuss with them how they can help the client to help himself or herself. When the therapy succeeds and the client gets better, we can compliment them on their contribution to the client's progress. This can help prevent resistance that might arise if they haven't been involved in the direction the therapy takes and if (for whatever reason) they don't agree with it.
- Insofar as our appointment calendar permits, we can ask clients when they want to come back. In this way, clients take responsibility for structuring the timing of their own change. It is sometimes astounding to see clients who have merely complained and made themselves dependent upon us during consultation choose long intervals between sessions, thereby committing themselves to their own therapy. There seems to be no relationship between the frequency of therapeutic consultations and the duration of therapy. In solution-oriented cognitive therapy, success depends not so much on what has happened during the interview as on the work that clients to between sessions, in their own context. For this, and because clients need to develop new habits, they need time. To this rule that clients preferably choose the date for the next session there are at least two important exceptions: (1) psychotic clients who think they are not ill and who don't see why they should come back and (2) depressive clients who have low self-esteem and who might feel rejected if the therapist doesn't show that he or she wants to see them back soon.
- *With hospitalized clients, one can let them have their say in the duration of hospitalization*—taking into account of course therapeutic and economic considerations.
- We can *let them co-decide which therapeutic strategy will be implemented* by briefly describing the different possibilities and asking for their opinion.

- *After agreeing on well-formulated goals, we can ask clients which goal they want to start with*. Of course, we may suggest that they start with a goal that's not too hard to achieve, so success is more probable. Or we can suggest that clients choose a goal that their families can help them with. But even so, compliance will be better if clients have their own say in the matter.
- *When we give homework tasks, we can offer the choice between more than one task*. One can also tell clients that they can choose not to do any of the proposed tasks. In that case, they will certainly do something else, which will be more interesting still than the outcome of the tasks themselves, as it will have come out of their own initiative. Here is an example of this in couples therapy.

Therapist: "I would like to propose two possible exercises. The first would be that in the evenings, for the first quarter of an hour after you have met again, you try to observe only what your partner does that you're happy with, everything that you find all right. And while you do that, observe how you react to that, and how your partner reacts to your reaction. You don't have to talk about it, just to observe. But of course you can say something about it if you want to; it's up to you. The second possible exercise would be for you to toss a coin every morning, and when it's heads, each of you would do a small kindness to the other without telling. Then the other one could try and guess what it was—but you don't talk about that either, you write it down and we'll talk about it next time. So why don't you try out each of these exercises, which one you like most. You don't even have to tell each other which one you continue. Perhaps you don't like either one of them, in which case I'm sure you'll find something better. I'm already curious what that might be."

- *Permissive formulations* give clients the choice—and the responsibility—to follow the therapist's suggestions more or less exactly.
- *Observation and prediction tasks* generally presuppose that the symptoms will continue to be produced to a greater or lesser extent. It is then up to clients to know how much effort they want to expend to control their symptoms, and how much suffering they are prepared to endure from them.
- When clients are in a consulting relationship with a therapist (p. 180) and they have to learn new methods to use their own resources, it's useful to *teach two or three new techniques in each session*, so clients can try them out and choose those that work best.
- *Scales (p. 108) help clients to free themselves from the dictatorship of black/white, sick/healthy, abstinent/relapsing mode of thinking*, in which the only choice is between good and bad—in other words, no choice at all.
- While *looking for exceptions, and at the end of the symptom sequence*, clients realize that their unwanted habits are more flexible than expected.
- *Therapeutic double binds* (p. 140) allow clients to choose how much they want to limit their symptoms.
- One can also *create situations in which clients will realize that they have options they hadn't thought of before*, as illustrated in the following example:

A young nurse with a traumatic past was living alone. She kept having episodes (mostly after a telephone call with her parents) in which she felt very bad and drank a whole bottle of wine. As she normally didn't drink any alcohol, the effect was disastrous. She would awake in the morning in an unknown room with an unknown man, or in a friend's flat where she had arrived in the middle of the night, half naked and crying and unable to explain what had happened. Being a well-mannered and religious young woman, she was horribly ashamed about this. She didn't dare to have alcoholic drinks in her apartment, and this made her feel a bad hostess when she couldn't offer any beer or wine to visitors. The therapist asked her to fill a chest with things that gave her joy. She also suggested that she was to buy a bottle of wine, open it and pour one glass per day into the sink without tasting it so as to realize that even after opening a bottle, she could do something else with it than drink it. This combination gave the client the feeling that she could choose her own behavior.

- Another possibility: We can *talk about possible choices that clients rightly have not made, as they would have unwanted consequences for themselves or for others.* Clients often have the feeling that they have no choice and don't realize that they have already excluded on very good grounds a number of possibilities. When we remind them of these alternatives, they realize that they did not make such a bad choice, even if it has unwanted consequences. The following case is an illustration of this.

An airline pilot came complaining about various psychosomatic complaints. He attributed these to the stress occasioned by his irregular working hours, repeated jet lag, and the boredom in the cockpit during the long hours on automatic pilot. The conversation came to bear on alternatives and their consequences. He could quit his job, but it would be hard to find another one that paid as well, and his wife and two children depended on his income. He felt he had no choice but to go on working, even if his health suffered from it. He felt a powerless victim of circumstances, living an unbearable existence. The therapist conceded this, while saying that he also had made a difficult, indeed a heroic choice. His duties as a husband, a father, and a pilot were more important to him than his well-being. However hard the consequences were to bear, he had chosen them. The goal now could be to see how he could go on upholding these values while making life more bearable.

- In general it pays to *offer more than one choice for each intervention*. Clients need to be assured that they co-determine the direction that the therapy takes.

Ten Ways to Ensure Good Pragmatic Choices

1. Learn about alternative habits.
2. Analyze the end of the symptom sequence.
3. Find out about variations in the problem habit.
4. Suggest small changes.
5. Ask about pre-session changes.
6. Propose therapeutic double binds.
7. Discuss the consequences of the client's choices.
8. Make projections into the future.
9. Talk about possible choices that entail unwanted consequences.
10. Establish a context of freedom of choice.

4 The Link between Choice and Habits in the Bruges Model

The following factors work together in making choices possible and in governing the clients' interaction with reality:

- Education
- Genetic factors
- Context
- Experience
- Creativity

Freedom of choice is the basis of psychological health: When one loses the freedom to choose, one acts and reacts in a pathological way.

This does not mean that one has to make conscious choices all the time. Our life is structured by habits that allow us to make unconscious choices. A successful therapeutic outcome means that our clients will be able to choose between different habits. They will again be able to make conscious choices, but only when needed. They can just as well let a wished-for habit unfold.

Therapy has to widen the scope of semantic and pragmatic choices. In the first phase of treatment, these will almost always have to be conscious. Before a habit automatically comes up in its context, it has to be practiced and repeated again and again.

Perhaps the reader will object that such a therapy can only be superficial.

Utilizing the metaphors of psychological "depth" and "surface" is, in my opinion, a grave logical error. There is no depth or surface in the mind. The whole human being is in constant interaction with reality. There is no such thing as "penetrating the surface" to the "depths of the human psyche." To reason like this is to reify a metaphor.

In my view, it is useful to consider the "structures of personality" not as fixed, so to speak mechanical, structures in our minds, but as clusters of habits that regulate our semantic and pragmatic activity in the reality around (and inside) us. "Surface" and "depth" are then topological metaphors that are inseparable from one and the same dynamic insertion of the individual in his or her world.

Exterior changes can happen in the client's reality or can be induced by a therapeutic system. They can be useful for creating a situation that makes therapeutic change easier, but they are not therapeutic in themselves. For instance, one can change one's workplace or one's home. Or, in the case of father-daughter incest, it will generally be necessary that they do not go on living in the same house in order to protect the victim. Changes like these make it possible to reestablish freedom of choice. They may be necessary, but they are not sufficient.

The mandate of the therapist in the Bruges Model is to co-create (with the clients) a context in which the clients will feel able to make a therapeutic change and to help the clients to see more clearly what they want (their goals) and to focus away from what they do not want (their problems). To accomplish this, on the perception side of the client's interface with reality, one-track semantics are broadened into a larger semantic choice. From this broader semantic choice, a number of pragmatic choices will emerge. Finally, when the clients have chosen a more satisfying way to cope with reality and with themselves, this has to be repeated until the more satisfying habits have been internalized.

The Structure of Habits

One possible definition of a human being—or at least of the human personality—would be to say that the individual is the sum of his or her habits. If we could take the time to describe all of someone's habits, we would have a pretty complete description of who he or she is.

Pathology could then be defined (along with other possible and complementary definitions) as a cluster of unsatisfactory habits: habits that we practice although we don't want to, habits that do not correspond to our existential choices. Existential choices could be defined as projections of ourselves as the persons we want to be, for example, what kind of father, husband, therapist, and citizen I want to be.

What kind of persons we want to be (our existential choices) determines what we do (our daily choices, our behavior). Any behavior that is not linked to an existential choice can be considered as unsatisfactory and/or pathological. The habits of an alcoholic, for example, are not related to an existential choice. One can hardly choose to be a good alcoholic in the same sense that one can choose to be a good mother, a good doctor, and so on.

Smoking habits are another example. Most ads for cigarettes appeal to an existential choice: the rugged cowboy with his cigarette and his horse stands for a free and masculine life, the attractive woman in her elegant suit suggests a successful career woman who has just concluded an important business deal. In this way, Madison Avenue tries to construe the smoking habit as being part of the consumer's existential choices. Of course, by the environment—if not by the smoker—smoking will "objectively" be perceived as malodorous, unpleasant, unhealthy, and addictive. Two existential choices clash. The smoker—like the drinker—may respond by declaring himself powerless: "I'd like to quit, but try as I may, I'm not able to." Or an addict may go into denial: "I don't want to stop. I don't drink too much. If I smoke, that's my choice," and so on. In fact, when one talks to them after they have given up smoking or drinking, most addicts who said they didn't want to stop agree that they would have liked to, but after several failed attempts to stop or at least to limit their consumption, they were convinced that it would be too difficult. If they had seen the possibility of quitting without any effort and without withdrawal symptoms, they would have given up their unhealthy habit. So the task of the therapist will be to help them recover their trust in their own resources.

Everybody has some habits that they don't like and that can be pathological if they get out of hand. Many people have small irrational aversions or fears (of mice or spiders, of crowded elevators) or small compulsions (checking to see if the door is really closed, turning back to make sure that the percolator has been switched off). As long as these habits do not hinder normal life activities, they are simply annoying quirks that people have and without which life would perhaps be too monotonous. However, as these habits get in the way of translating important existential choices into satisfactory habitual behavior (satisfactory, that is, for the client and his or her environment), one can say that these habits are pathological.

The goal of therapy can then be defined as to help clients to develop new habits (or to revert to old habits) that are more satisfactory and that are congruent with their existential choices. The task of the therapist is to help clients to create a context in which they will again be able to choose and not be stuck in an unsatisfactory habit.

It is often sufficient to help clients make a small change in some aspect of their unsatisfactory habits, such as helping them to focus on exceptions to a pathological habit. Exceptions are helpful variations on the unsatisfactory habit, which have the advantage of already being there. Doing more of what is already there represents a change without the challenge of the unknown, and elicits less resistance. By enlarging these variations, a variety of possible choices appear. The client may then develop a satisfactory new habit or revert to an old one without further help. New and related habits will emerge to sustain and complete the new or recovered satisfactory habit. Therapy with these clients can, and indeed should, be brief.

Chronic clients mostly have no satisfactory old habits to revert to. Too much time has passed, and the clients' life circumstances have changed too much. The process of installing a set of wholly new habits can then be a long and tiring one. The therapist may need to foster the new habits over a longer period of time, until they have permanently superseded the unsatisfactory habits.

Freedom of choice according to the Bruges Model means the freedom to choose between habits. Clients often have no clear view of what their habits are and even less of what habits they want (they often do not know what they want, only what they don't want). In order to help them to find out how their habits function, it is useful for the therapist to know (i.e., to have a model of) the structure of habits.

What are habits composed of? What is their structure? What are their dynamics? How do they arise and how are they maintained?

In cognitive behavioral therapy (e.g., Bandura, 1969), cognitions, emotions, and behavior are described as influencing each other. I think that it is a useful hypothesis to assume that these are not three separate elements that influence each other, but rather that they constitute a triadic gestalt, that is, a whole that can be looked at from three viewpoints. Cognitions, emotions, and behavior are to be regarded as three ways of describing one gestalt, the habit. This then is the basic structure of habits.

This triad harks back to Aristotle. In his writings on rhetoric (Aristotle, 1952), he describes three elements that are well suited to serve as a basis for a reflection about the nature of habits. The triad of logos, Pathos, and Ethos can be completed with a fourth element: oikos.

Habits can also be described on three levels: the conscious, the unconscious, and the systemic or interactional level. As stated earlier, it must be stressed that the distinction between these various elements and levels is an artificial one. This distinction is useful for a structured description in the language of traditional models, but it is important to consider a habit as a whole, a gestalt. It can be looked at and described from different perspectives but it keeps its indivisible wholeness. In this sense, it is incorrect to speak of emotions "influencing" behavior, of changed cognitions "leading to" changing emotions. If the emotional aspect of a habit changes, the whole habit changes, and the same goes for the cognitive and the behavioral aspects. This makes for a host of therapeutic opportunities: Habits can be changed by means of their emotional, cognitive, or behavioral aspects.

I will now try to illustrate this theory of habits with two examples.

Example 1: Iris is a 45-year-old housewife. She has been in treatment for an obsessive-compulsive disorder for the past 20 years. Her husband is 50 years old and a school principal. Her three children are married. She used to work as a kindergarten teacher, but 15 years ago her compulsions and a grave depression led her to leave her profession.

In the course of the treatment, she has been able to drop her various repetition compulsions. Now, she still broods compulsively over feelings of guilt. For example, she is always musing about whether she could inadvertently have said something wrong to her sister or to her mother-in-law. Every morning, she drinks a mug of a thick brew she makes by filling it to the brim with instant coffee and adding water. She gets up early so she can do this while nobody is around. The taste is revolting, but she has read somewhere that drinking too much coffee is bad for her health and will shorten her life. On one hand, her husband has a pacemaker and she doesn't want to live longer than him. On the other hand, she doesn't want to die before he does, because she thinks that he couldn't get along without her. So she feels she is walking a tightrope. Every now and then, she gets heartburn or palpitations. She then drinks only half a cup for a few days, or she stops altogether, then, when the symptoms have gone, she starts again.

Example 2: Hank is a 40-year-old construction worker. He drinks about 20 units (7 fl. oz.) of alcohol every day. At work he drinks only beer; at the bar with his friends he drinks beer and liquor. He is a hard worker and a good friend, always ready to lend a hand. At home he can be aggressive. He has been married for 20 years and has two daughters, 16 and 14.

On the Conscious Level

Logos. One meaning of the Greek word *logos* is *word*.

A habit can be described with words. We occasionally do this in an internal monologue, when we want to be conscious of something we are doing or experiencing, for example, when we are trying out a new habit and we are still paying close attention to it.

The words we use to describe a habit can determine what it means to us. If a man drinks a bottle of wine in the evening, it makes a difference if he says: "I enjoy a good meal and I usually drink a bottle of wine with my dinner" or if he says "I'm an alcoholic and I can't stop myself from drinking a bottle of wine at dinnertime." The liver may not notice the difference, but to the mind the meaning is not the same.

Logos, in this sense, stands for the words with which, and the way in which, we describe reality. We use words as symbols for the reality they describe.

Logos can also stand for *rationale, understanding,* and *cognition.* From this meaning the names of most scientific disciplines are derived, such as zoology, entomology, anthropology, and so on. We understand our habits more or less clearly, and we can discuss them rationally. In the act of reflecting upon them, we give them a meaning. What are the logos aspects ot Iris's and Hank's habits?

Example 1: Iris drinks her coffee because sometime, somewhere she read that people who drink too much coffee have a shorter life expectancy. Although she is now much happier than she used to be, she wouldn't like to live too long. "Coffee will shorten my life," is how she describes it.

Other logos aspects of her habit are that she knows how she buys the coffee, how she hides it from her husband, and how she makes her bitter brew.

Example 2: For Hank, drinking beer means just that: drinking beer. He doesn't consider himself an alcoholic. He likes beer and that's it.

Pathos means *emotion* and *affect.*

Habits have an affective component. With some habits, the affective component is what strikes us most, as for instance when we express our feelings in the way we are used to: how we laugh, how we burst into tears, how we express our anger, and so on. In other cases, the affective component will contribute less to the structure of the habit, as in a technical behavior (writing, walking, turning on a faucet). The pathos aspects of Iris's and Hank's habits can be analyzed as follows.

> **Example 1:** Feelings of guilt are part of the Pathos. Iris is always feeling guilty about something. For example, she may have said something wrong on the telephone with her sister, and she feels both guilty and relieved when she has finished her coffee.
>
> **Example 2:** Hank drinks his beer with pleasure. The craving gets strong when he has to wait.

Ethos. With *ethos,* things get a little more complicated.

In Greek, *ethos* can be written in two ways. When it is written with *epsilon* (here shown in lowercase, as ethos), it means one's usual behavior—the movements, the mimicry, all the non-verbal elements that are part of our habits. The term *ethology* (the science that describes the habitual behavior of animals) derives from this.

Pathos and ethos are linked in proprioceptive perception: the perception of our body, our muscle tension, our heart rate, and so on. We sense our emotions through their expression in our body.

Ethos written with *etha* (here shown in capital letters, as ETHOS) means *morals* or *ethics.* (See Figure 4.1.)

Both these concepts are more narrowly linked than one might think at first sight. Our personal morals are composed of our existential choices (which themselves of course were influenced by the values and the ethics of our family, our society, etc.), for example, what kind of father or mother I want to be; how, as a therapist, I want to help my clients; what relationship with my parents, my neighbors, and so on, seems right to me. All these are my moral principles.

My ETHOS also determines how I project myself into the future. Let us take the example of the spiritual testament technique, in which the client answers the following question: "How do you want your children, your grandchildren, and so on to remember you after your death?" With this technique, the therapist proposes to look back, from the perspective of the hour of our death (i.e., the end of our personal future), on the existence the clients would have liked to live. The answers correspond to their existential choices: What is the image of a parent, a grandparent, and so on, that I want to leave?

In so far as I live according to what my conscience tells me, my habits will agree with these principles. Ethos follows ETHOS. Habits are formed according

```
Logos  - - - - - - - - - - - - - - - - - - - - -  Pathos

    \                                       /

      \                                   /

        \                               /

          \                           /

            \                       /

              \                   /

                \               /

                  \           /


              ethos   - - - - - - -   ETHOS
```

Figure 4.1 The Structure of Habits

to moral principles. This relationship is a circular one: Aristotle rightly says: *E ethike ek ethous periginetai*, morals arise out of habit.

Simple daily behavioral choices are integral to all habits, and through the connection between ethos and ETHOS, our morals are expressed in our habits. When there is a discrepancy between our behaviors and our morals, we live in disharmony with ourselves.

When we change our habits, we often adapt our morals. Morals are the offspring of habits (Tavris & Aronson, 2007).

When we develop a habit that doesn't tally with our personal morals, one solution is to construe a justification. A young cyclist who enters a team with a firm decision never to take drugs nonetheless gives in, telling himself that everyone does it. A wife who cheats on her husband tells herself it's his own fault: If he were home more often, it wouldn't happen, and so on.

Another solution is to consider this unwanted habit as pathological: We cannot help it; it's stronger than ourselves. The binge eating of a bulimic woman, the self-harming of a post-traumatic client, or the inaction of a depressed person are experienced by the clients as a non-choice, or as an inevitable and imposed choice, not as a satisfying, wished-for choice.

One can want to be a good mother or a successful lawyer or a loving and loved grandparent. But one does not say: I want to be a super alcoholic. The habit of an alcoholic who gets drunk every day does not correspond to his or her existential choices. We can apply this to Iris and Hank.

> **Example 1:** How Iris habitually prepares her coffee, how she feels disgusted but still drinks it, how she has been hiding this from her husband and children for 15 years now: this is the ethos. How she stops from time to time because she doesn't want to abandon her husband by dying too young: this is part of her ETHOS.
>
> **Example 2:** How Hank drinks his beer, how he works hard, what he does consciously when he becomes aggressive, these are some of the conscious ethos and ETHOS aspects of his drinking habits.

On the Unconscious Level

Most of our habits happen on the unconscious level. We just do them without paying attention.

Logos means here the logical structure, the logical matrix that dynamically structures the habit. It makes the habit unfold in the usual way; it can often be expressed in mathematical-logical formulas. In this sense, the series of nervous impulses, of neuromuscular innervations and of muscular contractions that constitute a movement have a logical structure and are part of the logos. Most of the time, we are not aware of them: They remain unconscious, as in these examples.

> **Examples 1 and 2:** the somatic (muscular, proprioceptive, etc.) behavioral patterns that constitute the habit, such as opening a bottle, pouring beer in a glass or drinking it from the can; opening the coffee jar, pouring water on the coffee powder, mixing it.

Pathos on an unconscious level includes all the emotions that are part of the habit, but that we are not conscious of at the moment. A chain smoker will have lighted a cigarette without being aware of the craving that stays in the background. A mother will do a host of things for children without being consciously aware of the love that makes her do them (peeling potatoes for lunch, washing clothes, etc.). These are the unconscious aspects of Iris's and Hank's habits:

> **Example 1:** Even when Iris is not thinking of her guilt, much of what she does, thinks, and feels is determined by her guilty feelings.
>
> **Example 2:** Like most addicts, Hank doesn't have to consciously feel his craving in order to drink.

Here, ethos comprises the innumerable movements and elements of behavior that happen outside of our conscious attention. For most of our habits, one can even say that we do them much better if we don't pay attention to them. This the case for most well-internalized habits.

ETHOS is the latent moral sense, comprising the existential choices that we are not aware of and that constitute the moral frame on which our habits are formed. In the following examples, ethos includes all automatized behavioral sequences, such as the movements needed to drink beer or coffee, while ETHOS includes the underlying ethical principles that we never think about.

Example 1: ETHOS. When Iris fills her cup with coffee powder, she doesn't think consciously about her desire not to abandon her husband by dying before him. Still, in the background, this ethical principle contributes toward her not drinking three or four cups and not choosing a stronger poison than hyper-concentrated coffee.

Example 2: The idea to behave like his mates makes Hank adapt his drinking pattern to theirs.

On the Interactional Level

Finally, there is an interactional level to our habits. No man is an island unto himself; we live in an uninterrupted exchange with the reality that surrounds us, and so with our fellow human beings.

The logos stands here for the stories we tell ourselves and the others about ourselves. One could also say the interactional logos is the scenario of the play we enact with the others and that we co-author with them as it unfolds. We build our identity in mimesis, in the mirror of the other's eyes. On the stage of our life we play again and again, in dialogue with the others, the same scenes we are used to: these are our habits. For Iris and for Hank, this could be an interactional description of the logos aspect:

Example 1: When Iris's husband comes home, she welcomes him by saying, "Hi, honey." He kisses her and asks her about her day. She talks about the children and grandchildren. They live in the neighborhood and she is afraid that she doesn't make herself available enough to them. Or, she has had her sister on the phone and she doesn't remember exactly what she has said, but it certainly wasn't what she should have.

Iris stands on her inner stage as if driven by the goddesses of Fate to say and do the wrong things again and again, though she doesn't want to. She talks and afterwards she fears that her tongue has betrayed her into saying things that could have awful consequences.

Example 2: Hank is the archetypal construction worker who works like a horse, drinks like a fish, and is always ready to lend a hand, but who can be violent at home—though only, as he sees it, when he is provoked.

In the pathos, we show others our feelings by mimicry, by gestures, by the tone of our voice (tender, angry, etc.), and by the words we choose. We feel with the others—or we think we feel with them—what they feel. Sympathy and antipathy are part of the interactional pathos. Here is a description of the pathos aspect:

Example 1: Iris has been angry with her cat for depositing a dead pigeon under her bed. She can vent her feelings to her husband when he comes home. Her husband has scored a professional success; he shows his joy and Iris shares it.

Iris is forever making mistakes in her empathy in that she thinks that her mother, her sister, and so on are angry with her and don't want to talk with her. She tries to show a friendly face, but makes an inauthentic impression.

Example 2: For Hank, it is easier to share his feelings with his friends than with his wife.

To the ethos pertain our habitual gestures on the stage of our life, the moves we make together, enlaced in the dance of our common existence. Ethos also means the image of ourselves we show to the others—and through them, to ourselves.

The ETHOS stands for the morals we share with our family, our company, our culture, and that seem self-evidently right to us. Family myths are part of this, our views on the qualities and the failings of our ancestors and our relatives: we have them "in our genes." For Iris and for Hank this translates into the following.

Example 1: Iris's husband kisses her when he comes home, because he feels this is what he must do as her husband. For the same reason, she interrupts her cooking to sit down with him and discuss the day.

These are interactional habits that are sustained by common moral principles.

Example 2: Hank shows himself a good worker and a good friend. At home, he alternates between friendliness and aggression, when he thinks this is justified.

Oikos. A fourth element completes the description of the structure of habits: the *oikos*. In Greek, *oikos* means "house" (hence: economy, the science of the laws or *nomoi* that govern housekeeping) and "surroundings, context" (hence: ecology). Habits are produced in a context. If we change the context, the habit changes. Most often it will not be produced at all. But in the habitual context the habit manifests itself, in a self-evident or a compelling way.

Here is an example.

A chain smoker sits in a team meeting. After one hour, there is a pause. He goes outside and smokes a cigarette. During the meeting, he didn't think about smoking. If it had gone on for one and a half hour, he probably wouldn't have felt any craving. However, it would be torture for him to go outside after an hour and not have a smoke.

The context may be seen as the stimulus for the habitual reaction. This can be initiated through a cognition, an emotion, or an action.

Perception is our way of assessing external reality, the oikos, and fitting it into the meaningful whole of our mind-in-the-world. Logos, pathos, ETHOS, and ethos participate in varying ways in each perception, as they participate in each habit.

Although dogs, cats, and other animals dream in their sleep and may twitch a muscle or salivate in reaction to their dreams, they normally react to external stimuli only. A mouse, as far as we know, is not afraid of a cat that isn't there (although it will peep out warily when entering a room where it has seen a cat before: That room has become a "catty" environment, and so a threatening one).

We humans are blessed with the wonderful (but sometimes baleful) capacity of creating internal contexts. This creative function allows us, among other things, to plan strategically what we will do in the future. It also allows us to conjure, out of our imagination or our memory, situations and contexts that aren't there, and produce habits of fear, loathing, anger, sadness, and so on, in reaction to these inner contexts. Many techniques that are described in this book aim at enabling clients to disconnect the automatic link between cognition and emotion or emotion and action, and so change the structure of the unwanted habit.

Seeing a Habit as a Whole

Let me stress again how useful it is to view a habit as a whole, as a gestalt, even when we distinguish between the aspects of logos, pathos, ETHOS, and ethos. In a panic attack, for example, we can describe the fear as an emotion; the anxious thoughts as cognitions; and the muscular tension, the trembling, the body movements as behavior. But these are merely different aspects of a unit. There is no such thing as a purely psychological fear that we do not perceive in our body (as muscle tension, transpiration, a dry mouth, etc.) and that is not accompanied by anxious thoughts.

In the problem context (i.e., in the context in which the problem habitually arises), one can have the impression that the emotions are the primary response. For example, a client feels fear as soon as he sees the elevator.

At other times, the symptomatic thoughts seem to be the first to arise. For example, a compulsive client closes a door and starts immediately to doubt if it is really closed.

In still another context, the behavior is what first seems to happen. For example, a smoker comes out of a meeting. She is talking to a friend; she lights a cigarette without thinking about it and without (at least consciously) feeling any craving.

Although one element stands in the foreground in each of these examples, all three are present on the conscious, the unconscious, and the interactional levels.

How Can One Change Habits?

Only very few habits follow a strict course without any variation. We will see that this opens a host of opportunities for therapy. Variations, however tiny they are, can be seen as exceptions that we can develop and enlarge until a new habit is formed out of them. In order to offer actual and possible variations in the habit as alternatives that can be chosen, it is useful to address the elements of logos, pathos, ETHOS, and ethos, and oikos in the therapeutic conversation. Change can be initiated through any of them.

For example, consider a client with agoraphobia who is dependent upon her husband. He has to accompany her everywhere and has to spend a lot of time with her.

On the conscious level:

- The client is aware of her reduced mobility, and of her dependence on her husband. She knows that she obeys him even when she doesn't want to out of fear that he might leave her. She knowingly pays this price. (logos)
- She has feelings of fear, panic, and dejectedness. (pathos)

- The client does not leave her house when she is alone. (ethos)
- She feels guilty about this. (ETHOS)

On the unconscious level:

- In the background, the phobic cognitions are always there. (logos)
- Fear and anger at herself are always hovering on the background. (pathos)
- She is often not conscious of how much she clings to her husband, or of how tense her muscles are. (ethos)
- Even when she is not consciously concerned with her feelings of guilt, on the unconscious level these feelings influence what she does. (ETHOS)

On the interactional level:

- The client speaks of her fear and her husband understands. Both talk about her fears and about how to avoid them. (logos)
- The client shows her fears; her husband empathically feels with her. Sometimes he also feels and shows irritation. (pathos)
- She clings to her husband. He has to accompany her everywhere. (ethos)
- She submits to her husband in that she does anything for him she thinks he might want. (ETHOS)

Distinguishing between the different elements and levels is useful to find out how a habit can be changed. Another application concerns projections into the future, such as the Miracle Question. Asking about the different elements of the new and wished-for condition helps the client to draw a more complete picture of it. This applies to observation tasks as well as to projections in the future, such as the Miracle Question:

- How would you notice that the miracle has occurred?
- What would you be doing differently?
- How would that feel?
- Who else would be there? What would they notice?
- Any idea how they might feel about that, or what they might be thinking? What they would say?
- And what would you do then (in response to the other's reactions and observations)?
- How would that feel?

The client draws such a complete "map" of the new "territory" he or she wishes to live in, so that it almost feels as if he or she had been there already.

Neuroanatomy of Habits

Habits are incarnated memory: Patterns of habits, that is logos-pathos-ETHOS-ethos that we have memorized through repetition and that, when we have practiced them often enough, have become automatic in their context. This automatization can be experienced as a choice, as a necessity, as a self-evident fact or as a compulsion; in all cases, it has a neuroanatomical foundation.

For each new habit we develop, new connections form in the brain. A new neuronal circuit is created in which the limbic system takes part (pathos), as do the prefrontal cortex (logos and ETHOS), the temporo-parietal cortex (ethos with the movements and the proprioceptive sensations), the cerebellum, and of course all the nuclei that participate in this particular habit (visual, auditory, motor nuclei, etc.).

In this way, every habit has its own neuroanatomical substrate. To lay down this circuit, it is enough simply to repeat the habit.

Some clients are so happy that they have solved their problem (with the help of the therapist), that they spontaneously repeat the habit, making it automatic without any further help. Therapy with these clients is brief.

Others, mainly chronic clients, need more time: They need a warm and trusting, caring relationship to effect any change that arouses their suspicion. The new routine has to be supported again and again before it becomes automatic.

Still other clients relapse. They have found solutions to their problems; they have implemented them: They have repeated them and the habits have become automatic. The problems seemed to be solved—but then they fall back upon their former habits, they drink or they smoke again, they become anxious or depressed again, and so on.

When clients have a biological excuse, such as Bipolar Disorder, we can understand. We can also empathize if there is a death in the family, a separation, or a trauma. But what about all those who, without apparent reason, as if by chance, start drinking or smoking again, or producing any other symptom?

From an anatomical perspective, once a habit has been strongly internalized, we cannot simply unlearn it. If a habit is no longer practiced, its circuit is put out of service, but it is not dismantled. It stays inscribed in the anatomy of the brain. It stays available for when the context comes up again.

For example, suppose that when you were young you learned to ride a bicycle. Then you lived for 15 years in a big city and you didn't ride one. You move back to the country and you try again: You will not need more than ten minutes to ride without falling over. After a week you will not even need to pay attention anymore. The automatism has kicked in.

So how to manage relapses?

A client explains how she has started smoking again after having stopped for two years: She was with friends who were smoking and she tried just one cigarette. It tasted bad. However, the next day—without really wanting to—she smoked another cigarette, and then another two days later. In two weeks she was back to one pack a day.

What happened? She repeated a few times in a rather quick succession a behavior that was very similar to an old habit. The brain decoded this as a call for a return to this former habit; without the woman having to choose, her brain, so to speak, choose for her and set the old automatism in motion: the whole habit with its logos (lighting up without thinking), its pathos (the craving), its ethos (the same gestures as before, the same deep inhalation of the smoke), and its ETHOS ("There we go, I relapsed. I will never be able to stop. I have no willpower").

What conclusions can we draw from this?

- One cannot unlearn a habit. Even we don't use it, it is not lost. It is the therapist's task to help the client to develop a "good" habit in the context where the "bad" habit comes up. After that, it is the client's task to choose between them. If he or she practices the new habit only, this will set up itself automatically. But if the client repeatedly does things that resemble the "bad" habit, he or she is in danger of relapsing.
- It is important that the new habit is as different as possible from the old one. Otherwise the risk is great that the old circuit will kick in again. This is particularly important with clients suffering from eating disorders or with alcoholics who opt for controlled drinking: here, the old and the new habits have much in common.
- During a relapse, the "good" habit stays just as available as the "bad" one was during remission. If the client takes it up again and repeats it assiduously, it will gain the upper hand by itself.
- A relapse can be seen as a failed attempt to the control the problem. Seen from this angle, it is also a test for the old and new habits and for their applicability. When one examines the relapse in this light, one often sees that the client, while stumbling into the relapse, tried to hang onto the branches of the new habit. A careful interrogation reveals that the client has tried a lot of small solutions that have enabled him or her to limit the damage. These will be helpful when next time the client starts skidding off the road.

5 Positive Comments and Compliments

Building Confidence

Success builds confidence; failures sap it. Clients come to us because they have failed to solve their problems and to control their symptoms. Their confidence is at a low ebb.

They may be so convinced that no change is possible that they don't even ask for our help. Or their problem-focused attitude blinds them to the partial control, the partial solutions they are already applying, and they expect the therapist to take over and help them out, removing their symptoms like a surgeon who excises a tumor.

Therapists have to turn clients' attention to their own skills and their resources. Positive comments (compliments, in Solution-Focused language) are major tools for doing this.

What Are Compliments For?

Compliments build and reinforce the therapeutic alliance in a variety of ways:

- They express the respect the therapist feels for his or her clients.
- They express agreement with the clients' self-image and with their existential choices.
- They convey the therapist's confidence in the clients' abilities, skills, and resources.
- They help clients to emerge from their problem trance, their fascination with their problems.
- They point out what clients are doing well already, and what positive changes they have already made.
- They are generally received as suggestions to go on doing similar things.
- They may point out positive aspects of the problem behavior, helping clients realize that they aren't doing so badly after all.
- They help the therapist to stay in a confident, "together we can solve this" attitude.
- They are a gift, an act of kindness, and as such make clients and therapists feel better.

- If the therapist has negative feelings towards a client, they help him or her overcome them.

Let me illustrate these different aspects with a case study.

A divorced mother who suffers from depression feels particularly bad in the morning. Nevertheless, she gets up at 7:00 A.M. to give her two children their breakfast and get them ready for school. Immediately after this, she gets back into bed and stays there until noon.

The therapist knows how hard it is for a depressed client to get up so early in the morning. She also knows this has an anti-depressant effect. She focuses on the client's merits: "I can sense how sad and tired you feel. I don't know where you find the strength to get up and see to your children in the morning. It's not easy, when one is so depressed as you are, to see to it that your children suffer from it as little as possible. Not every mother manages that. How do you do it?"

Compliments Stimulate Creativity

Compliments are useful for achieving an agreement on existential choices. They throw light on values, qualities, skills, and resources that clients have and of which they can give examples, but that they didn't conceive of consciously as qualities. Creativity and motivation are stimulated: "If I have these qualities, perhaps I could also. . . ." As O'Connell (1998) says: "Genuine compliments, as distinguished from manipulative flattery, help to motivate people, especially those with long experience of failure and isolation. We have all experienced the encouragement which an unexpected compliment gives."

Here are two examples of compliments that a client didn't expect:

- A single mother with two children has been complaining of how exhausting it is to combine her work with the care for her children, and of how inadequate she feels as a mother. The therapist could say, "It touches me to see how fond you are of your children, and how much you are willing to do for them."
- The same client has mentioned that she often has to ask for help from her friends because she cannot cope on her own. A compliment could be: "Your friends really are doing a lot for you. You must be a good friend to them, or they wouldn't do so much for you."

Using Compliments as a Bridge from Problems to Solutions

Compliments can be used to lead the client from describing problems and symptoms towards exploring healthier and more satisfying behavior that is still there, or that was there in the past.

The therapist can show compassion and empathy with a client's suffering by complimenting him or her on coping with a difficult situation: "You are feeling very sad. I think it's admirable that you still do as much as you do in the household. There must be times when you really aren't up to it. When you do succeed in doing what you do, how do you manage to do it? What helps you in those moments?"

Compliments about what the client has done already to get better are more effective when they are formulated in the client's words (if possible, by repeating literally something he or she has said). It also helps to get them accepted if we use non-verbal means of showing approval, such as slightly bending forward, looking in the client's eyes, nodding, or adopting the client's posture.

Using Compliments to Construct a Yes-Set

de Shazer (1985) says that "Compliments may or may not have anything to do with the complaint. The purpose of the compliments is to build a "Yes-Set" that helps to get the client into a frame of mind to accept something new— the therapeutic task or directive." This Yes-Set is a circular one: the therapist approves what the client does, and the client approves what the therapist says.

Compliments Build a Respectful Relationship

Compliments show that the therapist has listened carefully, and with both ears: one has heard the concrete description of the problems and their nuances; the other has listened for the resources and the tentative solutions. In one movement, the therapist is able to acknowledge the client's suffering, to show attention for his or her strengths and skills, and to offer new (and often unexpected) insight on the client's and his or her systems' functioning.

In this way, sincere compliments are an important element in building a respectful relationship.

Using Compliments for Positive Reframing

As Gale Miller (1997) states,

> eco-systemic brief therapists and team members might interpret virtually any aspect of client's statements and behavior during interviews as positive signs. They tell married couples who don't get along, for example, that their strong feelings really demonstrate how much they care about one another, and contrast the clients' situation with other couples who care so little that they cannot muster enough emotion to fight with one another over their differences.

This use of compliments is akin to the Milan Group's (Selvini-Palazzoli et al., 1975) use of positive connotation as a paradoxical strategy: Clients are apparently encouraged to go on with their problematic behavior. The therapist's hidden hope is that, in Milan terms, they look at their problems from a "meta-position," deflate the strong emotions that are inherent in them, and ask themselves if they could find a way to keep the positive aspects (how much they care about one another) while abandoning the negative ones (the fighting).

Systemic Use of Compliments

Our clients' relatives often have suffered with them, they had to adapt to their symptoms, and they have tried again and again to help them. It is important to acknowledge their suffering and to utilize their resources. If we forget to include them in our compliments, we deny them the respect they have earned and we exclude them from the therapeutic alliance. They might then fail to cooperate and even sabotage a therapy that doesn't take them into account.

Characteristics of a Useful Compliment

Direct vs. Indirect

A compliment may be direct: "Wow!," "I am amazed that you . . .," "That's fantastic," "It takes a lot of commitment and I'm just really impressed by you" (Berg, 1992).

Direct compliments put the therapist in the position of the expert who knows what is good and what isn't. They are most useful with insecure clients and with dependent clients who operate with an external locus of decision.

A compliment may also be indirect: "How did you do that?," "Where did you learn to do that?," "How did you learn to cope with such a terrible situation all by yourself, with no help?" (Berg, 1992)

This type of question sets clients thinking about their skills and resources. Their answer is a compliment that clients give to themselves. In the words of I.K. Berg (1992), "This question (i.e. 'How did you do it,' or 'how do you do it'), when asked with the appropriate intonation and facial expression has been found to be the most 'empowering' question anyone can ask a client who has been repeatedly given a message that he is inadequate. In order to answer this question of 'how,' the client is forced to think about the resources and ingenuity with which he has confronted a difficult situation."

Indirect compliments can be used in couples therapy to give a compliment to both sides: For example, "What did you do to help your wife have such a positive reaction?"

Authentic

Praise and compliments must be authentic and nuanced, otherwise the client may find them dubious or too general and "too good to be true." With some clients, any direct compliment, however authentically meant by the therapist, gives rise to suspicion. If this is the case, it is better to give only indirect compliments.

Empathic

Authenticity is a consequence of the therapist's empathy. One may compliment a feat that in itself is not spectacular, but that for this client means he or she had to work hard to overcome his problems. For example, with a depressed woman: "I must observe that, although you feel so tired in the morning and you would prefer not to get up at all, you still have managed to wash and dress, to put on some make up, and to make yourself some tea. How did you do that?"

Nuanced

As Dolan and Pichot (2003) observe, some clients understand compliments as (positive) criticism. This may bring them to think that the therapist is hiding negative observations. In this case, talking also about the negative aspects makes the positive comments more credible: "I see in your drinking diary that in the past two weeks you have managed not to drink on six days out of fourteen, and that you have been drinking less than three glasses on four more days. On Saturday and Sunday, and also on Wednesday, you lost control quite heavily. How did you manage to pull yourself together again on Monday and on Thursday?"

Commenting on Actions Rather Than Traits

Research in school and work settings has shown that compliments on traits ("You are a good student, a hard-working employee") sometimes have the paradoxical effect of leading to a less-good performance after the compliment was given, whereas a compliment on actions accomplished ("You learned your vocabulary very well this time," "You made a very convincing presentation") stimulates to do at least as well next time. When giving a trait compliment, as is often done at the end of a session, it is useful to cite one or two concrete examples that have come up in the session.

Using Humor in the Compliment

When the therapeutic relationship is good, a little humor, some gentle irony, or even a benevolent provocation may prove stimulating.

Well-formed compliments have the following characteristics:

- based on concrete facts;
- commenting on actions rather than traits;
- often formulated in an indirect way;

- authentic;
- based on empathy;
- nuanced;
- sometimes humorous or even provocative.

Possible Difficulties with Compliments

Compliments are intended to support clients and to motivate them by making them realize the skills and resources they have. They must sound true and credible. So how can one compliment a client when he or she (at least seemingly) did nothing to make the solution or the exception to his or her problems happen—when it happened by accident, or when someone else did it?

If a solution came up by accident, one may enquire if the client didn't do something that contributed to create a context in which the coincidence was more likely to happen. If this isn't the case, the client still has made use of the chance he or she was offered: "You used this quite skillfully! How did you do that?"

If the solution came from someone else, the compliments may concern the client's reaction and whatever he or she did to make good use of what the other person did. For example:

- "Now that was a good reaction to (what X did)! Do you think your reaction might help X to do something like that again? Or could you do something else to make X do that again?"
- "As you see it, the initiative came wholly from X. But I think you may have contributed to X doing this, you may have so to speak helped to make the climate in which this idea came to X. Do you have any idea how you could have done this?"
- "If X has done this, in my opinion you must have helped to create the conditions in which this could happen." (For example, when a child makes a lot of trouble at home, but behaves himself very politely in other people's company, this means that his parents have been successful in teaching him good manners. Or when a spouse, a child, or a friend has been kind to the client, this means of course that they are kind people, but also that the client has earned their kindness.)

What can the therapist do if his or her compliments fall flat, if the client doesn't accept them, or if even gets angry about them?

Perhaps the therapist's style was too direct or too enthusiastic for that specific client. More tentative formulations may be appropriate, such as:

- "In fact, I would think that . . ."
- "You know, one might say that . . ."
- "I'm asking myself if one couldn't say that . . ."

Perhaps the client thinks that what he or she has done isn't important enough to merit a compliment. This means that one has to pay attention to better adapt the compliments to the client's scale of values.

Clients who refuse all compliments may accept gentle provocation and lightly paradoxical formulations:

- "I know you will be mad at me, but I can't help it, I must say that . . . (the compliment)"
- "Can I tell you something really cheeky?"
- "You will no doubt be very offended, but nevertheless I want to say that . . ."
- (If with a couple one wants to make a compliment to the husband, one could turn to the wife:) "Your husband will not want to hear this, so I'd like to tell to you that . . ."

Part II

Therapist and Relationship Factors

6 Therapist Qualities and Attitudes

To forge a therapeutic alliance and reinforce the client factors, a successful therapist makes a targeted use of her or his qualities as a human being. He or she also adopts an attitude that will help the clients to invest their resources in attaining their goals.

Interest, Curiosity, Understanding

In research about what clients felt most helpful in a session, interest generally comes in first:

- "I finally found someone who was really interested in me."
- "I've been to some doctors and I got the impression that they just wanted to tick boxes on their form. This one, she really listened. That felt so good."
- "I felt understood."
- "Sometimes I don't understand myself, and sometimes I feel that my therapist understands me better than I do myself."

It is not necessary to perfectly understand our clients. That would be impossible anyway. What is important is to show one makes an effort to understand them as they understand themselves, as their relatives understand them, and—if possible—to add, from our expertise, some further elements of understanding that help them to better accept themselves and to change.

For Nelson and Thomas (2007), "Therapists' optimism plays a part in maintaining curiosity within the SFBT frame. Curiosity is not so much directed toward causes, explanations and categorizations as it is toward positive outcome, partial success, and clinical/contextual resourcefulness."

Solutions are in the details: A conversation in which the therapist asks the clients to describe in detail a symptom sequence (e.g., "Could you tell me exactly how this happened the last time it did?") always reveals how the clients used their resources to limit their problems, to solve them partially, and to end the symptom sequence.

Acceptance and Respect

The therapist respects and accepts clients as they are, with their good and their bad habits, with their qualities and their failings, with their inconsistencies, their contradictions, and their mood swings. Acceptance does not mean neutrality: It is an attitude of active respect for the whole person of the client. Saint Augustine said: "I love the sinner, but I loathe the sin." I think one must go further and include all aspects of the clients' personality, even those that they do not accept themselves and that they would like to get rid of.

There are several reasons for this:

- In general, the problems and the symptoms that clients produce have some positive aspects. They are good for something. They entail, for the clients and their relatives, so-called secondary benefits that can be quite important. They are part of the system's rules and they have their function there. The therapist is well advised to take this into account and to help clients to preserve, as much as possible, these benefits: The therapist is a guarantor of continuity as much as an agent of change.
- Our attitude of acceptance serves as a model for our clients who do not admit their symptoms, who sometimes detest them, and therefore do not admit and detest a part of themselves. They want to fight this part. In this war on themselves, they end up losing even if they appear to win.
- Our clients' energy and their attention are focused on these symptoms they want to eliminate. But a lot of symptoms (e.g., anxious, depressive, obsessive thoughts) are kept alive precisely by the attention that clients pay them and disappear when their interest turns elsewhere.
- "Perhaps the most prominent aspect of a respectful posture is the recruitment and endorsement of clients' expectations for therapy" (Nelson & Thomas, 2007). What counts is what the clients see as problems and how they describe what they want.

Of course, there are limits to what a therapist can accept. Physical or moral violence and sexual abuse are examples of this. To accept does not necessarily mean to assent. But even in these cases, experience shows that the more understanding the therapist can show towards these clients (of course, without condoning their behavior), the greater the chances will be that he or she can get them to cooperate in a program where they learn to control their impulses in order to achieve their existential goals by other means.

Empathy and Sympathy

The term *empathy* refers to a certain number of phenomena that can be distinguished in several ways:

1. Direct emotional or affective empathy, which works through the mirror neurons and that allows one to feel "from the inside" what the other feels

and to communicate that one feels it is one aspect of this. (The original German term of which empathy is the Greek translation is *sich hineinfühlen*, literally "to feel into the inside of the other.") This empathy by the mirror neurons is a kind of nonverbal communication that needs no conscious reflection (Bauer, 2006). Communication by eye contact (seeing in the eyes of the other what they feel, "the eyes are the mirror of the soul") is an important part of this. The client's emotion is reproduced in the brain of the therapist, who therefore feels an analogous emotion to the client's and shows this in words as well as in body language. The therapist is directly affected by the client's emotional state by a process of emotional transference of which he is not necessarily conscious.

2. Indirect emotional or affective empathy, where the therapist, without the aid of mirror neurons, tries to reconstruct in herself, based on her experience and her creativity, what she understands (by listening and by observing) of the client's emotions, and to communicate this in her words and her body language. The therapist succeeds in understanding and taking the perspective of the client.

3. Cognitive empathy, to understand (and to show one understands) others' thinking, their view on the world and on themselves, and their existential choices, and to show that one shares them when one can, or that one respects them when one cannot share them.

4. Relational empathy, which comprises the preceding three and which constructs itself in systems that last long enough, such as families. This form of empathy is part of the habits the system shares; it contributes to mimesis and therefore is a factor of cohesion as well as of dissension. (Oughourlian, 2013).

The term *empathy*, as it is used in psychotherapy, is often restricted to resonance with the client's suffering; it is then close to compassion. Used in this sense, empathy is problem-oriented; sympathy would then be its solution-oriented equivalent. Other meanings of the term are of less concern to us as therapists—those of Dilthey or Husserl (Husserl, 1969) for instance, who made use of this notion in phenomenology to discuss a "knowledge from the inside" of different aspects of reality.

In empathy, I observe myself in order to better observe the other. It goes without saying that many errors can occur in this process, and that the therapist must not trust his or her empathic reactions too far.

In solution-focused therapy, the therapist's empathic attitude is closely linked to care for the clients' well-being, to unconditional acceptance of the clients as they are: It is not therapeutic to feel what the clients feel and not bother with it or even to condemn it.

Some authors (e.g., Lammers, 2007) consider that as a rule clients "refuse, fight or avoid" negative emotions. The therapist must then use his or her empathy to feel the emotions the client hides and "adopt a corrective, accepting and respectful attitude" in order to help the client more efficiently.

Sympathy with clients' qualities, their resources and skills, their existential choices and the way they express them in their daily life, probably is even more important than empathy with their sufferings. It is nourished by the four clusters of positive feelings that follow:

1. friendship/attraction/love/tenderness;
2. compassion/care/comforting/charity;
3. respect/esteem/admiration; and
4. recognition/gratitude.

A few comments on some of these notions:

- In long-term therapeutic support, a kind of complicity often develops that is close to friendship. This motivates the client to make efforts to please the therapist—efforts that, without this relationship, they may never make. The therapist of course must see to it that this benefits the client. The friendship that the therapist feels can help him or her to tolerate client attitudes that otherwise would be irritating.
- It is not unusual for clients to feel attracted to their therapist. The erotic component of this is of course prohibited. The client has to be referred if it cannot be controlled. But the friendship component can foster cooperation.
- One of Erickson's daughters wrote of him: "My father loved all his patients" (Erickson & Keeney, 2006). Some therapists have this faculty of being able to love their clients with a paternal or maternal affection. This warm relationship is very beneficial to the great majority of clients. They feel secure and they are more willing to take the risks that are inherent to change. I heard Carl Whitaker, one of the founding fathers of family therapy, say in one of his seminars that "A patient who isn't worth caring for isn't worth treating"—by which he meant that if one cannot feel some measure of affection for a client, one should refer him or her to a colleague.
- Tenderness, Jean Vannier said in an interview in the Vatican newspaper *Osservatore Romano* (on 03.31.2014) "offers security, it reveals the importance and the sacred value of the other, it becomes exhortation to grow . . . it is a welcome, without any judgment." In child therapy, but also with adults, it helps the anxious, the timorous, and those who have been deeply wounded and who do not dare anymore to give their trust, to abandon of their reserve.
- Compassion is the foremost virtue for the Buddhists, and they are right. Charity can be defined as compassion put in action. It is not very well considered these days. It smells of the naphthalene of Victorian charitable ladies with their condescending and reproving attitude; it makes one think of the baskets they brought to the deserving poor. It is, however, the expression of a nobility of the soul that is beneficial to those who are in need of

material and spiritual resources. A respectful sense of charity can inspire acts of generosity that are helpful to the most destitute of our clients.

- When therapy is successful, clients tend to express their gratitude to the therapist, who answers that it is they who have done all the therapeutic work; he or she did no more than support them. But as therapists we also often have reason to be grateful to our clients: To feel that we have helped someone is a source of joy, and it is our clients who give us this feeling.

Empathy can help us to bear, to accept, and to respect clients that irritate or annoy us. If it is not enough to inspire a positive attitude, a little exercise just before I receive them can be useful: I tell myself that every human being has something that inspires sympathy in someone. One has only to look for it. I then take three minutes to find out who among the client's acquaintances may feel some sympathy towards the client, and I try empathically to evoke in myself this movement of sympathy.

Intelligence

Because I think they are the most directly useful to clients, those aspects of intelligence that I see as the most important for therapists are emotional intelligence, the sense of logic, and what the Greeks called *metis* (ruse).

Emotional Intelligence

Mayer and Salovey (Salovey, Brackett, & Mayer, 2004), who first defined the concept of emotional intelligence, distinguish between these two aspects:

- an experiential dimension, or our emotional reaction to reality and how we (often unconsciously) integrate this emotion as one aspect of the meaning we give to our experience;
- a strategic dimension, or the ability to manage our emotions and to integrate them (again often unconsciously) into our interactions with reality.

Obviously, it is this strategic aspect that is most important in therapy: Therapists should not let themselves be carried away by emotions; they must choose among different emotional reactions those that will be most helpful to clients.

For Goleman (2004), our emotional intelligence allows us to inspire others, to stimulate their resources and to join them so as to help them to convert their existential choices into habits.

Sense of Logic

I am mainly concerned with practical logic here: the kind of logic that helps the therapist to detect logical errors that clients make and by which they poison their lives.

Consider, as a first example of a logical error the paradox of the pink elephant on roller skates, also called the "paradox of Kant's manservant": Kant's manservant of many years, Martin Lampe, had taken to drinking to excess. Kant dismissed him, but afterward was seized with doubts: "Lampe is out of employment," he said to himself. "Everyone here in Königsberg knows that he has become a drunk and no one will give him work. His wife and children are in need. Shouldn't I have given him another chance? But I warned him often enough! How could I have kept in my service someone who is drunk half of the time? I would have never had any peace."

This dilemma obsessed him so much that he could no longer concentrate on the Critique of Reason, pure or other, which he was writing at the time. To make matters even worse, he had got into the habit of calling his new valet by the name of Lampe, so he was constantly reminded of the offending servant.

To get out of this conundrum, he put a note on his desk: "The name of Lampe must be totally forgotten from now on." Obviously, every time he saw this note, the memory of his valet came back to him.

If I do not want to think of something, I think of it each time I tell myself to forget it. The Alcoholics Anonymous member tells himself every morning: "I'm an alcoholic, though it has been two years since I have touched alcohol. I decide today, as I do every morning, not to drink any alcohol." This reveals excellent resolve, but it brings up the idea of alcohol and the memories that are associated with it. Coupled with the concepts of "Once an alcoholic, always an alcoholic" and "The first glass is a relapse," this approach, though well-intentioned, has led to many relapses. After one or two drinks (which in themselves are nothing more than a banana peel: You can slip on it and fall down, but there is no reason why you should not get up again) the former drinker who is now sober thinks: "This is the proof. I am an alcoholic and I will always be one." So he goes on drinking and the prophecy fulfills itself: He is in relapse.

It is more useful, instead of perpetuating one's interest in alcohol, to focus on all the other nice things one wishes to do.

- A second example of a logical error is the paradox of forced spontaneity: A couple's wedding anniversary approaches. The wife hopes her husband will remember that this time and bring her a nice bouquet of flowers. But she does not want to remind him: If he loves her, he should think of it by himself. If she needs to tell him, then it is not spontaneous and it doesn't count. The anniversary arrives, and the husband, however much he loves his wife, of course has forgotten as he does almost every year. A domestic scene ensues: profound disappointment, bitter reproaches, tears flowing freely. The aggrieved wife is convinced that she counts for nothing in her husband's life.

  A small reminder—two words slipped into a conversation—would have avoided much misery.

- The illusion of all or nothing is the logical error of perfectionists. "If I do not perform to perfection, I have failed. I am a perfect (mother, wife, collaborator . . .) or I'm a bad (. . .)." Let us remember that the only infallible way never to fail is never to try, that 50% or 60% are adequate, and that "optimal" is rarely synonymous with "maximum." 54321 with Acceptance, Joy, or Gratitude is often useful for these clients, as are scales.

There are many other logical errors that people slip into their interactions, by means of which they torture each other. These errors put a pinch of salt in their relationships—and in their wounds. The therapist who detects them can make his or her clients aware of them with a short Socratic dialogue, or by asking questions that confront them with their contradictions and paradoxes, and that leave them free to choose what they want to do about them. For example, one dialogue could proceed like this:

"How long have you been married?"

"Twenty years."

"And after twenty years, you still hope that you will be able to change your husband? Well, of course hope springs eternal, but I must say you don't lack courage. In your place I would have given up a long time ago and I would have said: 'Either I leave him, or I'll take him as he is.' In fact, it is not such a bad thing that he has his flaws. If he were perfect, you would have to be perfect too. At least his flaws excuse yours, so you don't have to worry too much about them."

Metis

For the ancient Greeks, metis was perhaps the most important form of intelligence. The Odyssey is the epic of metis: It is through his metis that Ulysses succeeds time and again to wriggle out of the seemingly intractable problems in which he finds himself.

To quote Detienne and Vernant, who devoted a major study to metis:

> To reach one's goal in the most direct way, to follow unswervingly one's path in a world that is fluctuating, constantly swerving from one side to the other, one has to proceed at a slant, make one's intelligence twisted and flexible enough to bend in every direction, use an approach that is "curvy" enough to be open to all directions at once.
>
> (Detienne & Vernant, 1978)

It is this flexible intelligence, this slanting approach that allows the therapist to never tell clients what to do, but to turn them—by skillful questions and indirect suggestions—into explorers of themselves, of their desires and their goals, of their abilities and strengths:

> The metis is fast, she is swift as the opportunity she snatches as it flies by, without letting it go. But she is nothing less than light, leptè: a dense

thought, bushy, tight—pukinè; instead of floating here and there according to circumstances, she anchors the mind deeply in the project she engineered in advance, thanks to her ability to predict, beyond the immediate present, a more or less thick slice of the future.

(Detienne & Vernant, 1978)

"The project engineered in advance": none other than to bring forth the clients' self-efficacy in the helping relationship, to bring clients to the point where help is no longer needed, where clients themselves can struggle free from the grip of their conflicts, their problems, and their symptoms.

There is a close relationship between metis and opportunity or chance (*kairos* in Greek):

Anticipating the kairos, as fast as this may be, it is the metis that takes the opportunity by surprise: it can "grab the opportunity precisely because, not being "light," it was able to predict the course of events and prepare for them from early on.

(Detienne & Vernant, 1978)

Authenticity

Carl Rogers (Rogers, 1951) considered congruence, which he also called *genuineness* or *authenticity*, to be an important quality of good therapists.

Following are some remarks about well-tempered authenticity.

- Authenticity in the motivations of the therapist: The therapist truly wants to help his clients. Of course, he also has to earn a living, but he will never let this stand in the way of helpfulness.
- Authenticity in expressing emotions: The therapist truly feels the emotions she expresses in her words and in her non-verbal attitude. This does not mean that she shows all her emotions: She selects those that she deems useful to the therapeutic process. She is neutral not in the sense that she shows no emotion, but in the sense that she selects what emotions she shows to fit to what she perceives as the clients' needs.
- Authenticity in positive comments, in compliments: On one hand, the therapist compliments whatever goes in the direction of the clients' goals. On the other hand, he may sometimes make a negative comment in order to increase the credibility of his positive comments (Pichot & Dolan, 2003); some clients accept compliments only if they are seasoned with some criticism.
- Authenticity modulated through empathy: The client is the reference with his habits, his choices, and his possibilities. The therapist can show herself authentically enthusiastic when a depressed client got up at 8:00 A.M., put his clothes on, and went out to buy a newspaper. For herself, it is nothing; for the client, it is an achievement.

- Authenticity when making suggestions by telling therapeutic tales: Like Milton Erickson (Gordon & Anderson, 1981), one can make a suggestion by telling the story of a client who suffered from similar problems to the client's. One needs of course to modify and leave out details in order to protect the privacy of the client in the story.

Humor

Humor can be a wonderful tool in the therapeutic relationship. It helps clients put problems into perspective; it allows the therapist to gently criticize a negative attitude that the client shows (for example, self-loathing, self-condemning, or self-criticism), or an attitude of irresponsibility and dependency: In these cases, humor helps to show that therapists hold the client in greater esteem than they do themselves.

Humor often helps clients to question their monosemic vision, to take off the blinders that keep them from seeing the vast array of possibilities that were there all the time, but that they couldn't see.

Humor helps clients to accept and correctly understand the kind of paradoxical prescriptions and suggestions that are given in the MRI model (e.g., Fisch et al., 1982) or in strategic therapy (e.g., Haley, 1976, 1984; Madanès, 1991, 2014).

The element of aggression that is always present in humor must of course be kept under control. Rudeness, cynicism, and sarcasm have no place in therapy. One has also to make sure that humorous remarks will be well understood and accepted. Clients (for example, those who have a very concrete way of thinking) may not always catch the meaning of a paradoxical formulation and may feel hurt or confused by a witticism that they understand too literally.

This being said, a little humor does wonders to soothe and to lighten a problem-focused conversation; it strengthens the bond between clients and therapists; and it often lets a ray of hope shine where no openings were visible.

I personally think that a therapy session where clients and therapists have not been able to share at least one little laugh is a wasted session.

7   Four Levels of Intervention

The interventions that the therapist and the client make can be classified on four levels of abstraction:

1. epistemological and ethical;
2. mandated;
3. strategic;
4. tactical or technical.

The Epistemological and Ethical Level

Explanatory Models

Before they come to see us, clients and their relatives have given much thought to the reasons and the causes of their problems and symptoms.

What is the client's explanatory model? Let us take the example of a client suffering from an anxiety disorder with somatic complaints.

- She may be convinced that her symptoms come from a somatic illness (heart pounding + chest pains = impending coronary thrombosis).
- She may have looked up the relationship between anxiety and neurotransmitters on the Internet, and she wants to get a specific drug treatment.
- She may see herself as a traumatized person whose mother gave her too little love and attention.
- Maybe she thinks she suffers from an Oedipal complex.
- She may be convinced that the upstairs neighbor has installed an electrical machine that sends her magnetizing beams.
- She might believe that spirito, djinns, or the devil have entered her body.

Whatever their nature, the client's hypotheses clearly are not sufficient to solve their problems, or they wouldn't be seeking our help. Sometimes we can get the client to agree that we shouldn't look for explanations at all and instead just get on with the business of building a better life. Still, our best plan is to try to see if we can start from their explanation, maybe add or subtly change something that will help to construct a rationale on which we can peg our strategy. If not, alternative hypotheses will be necessary if we want to establish a constructive collaboration. This doesn't mean that we need to convince the client that her or his opinions are wrong. They just have to admit the therapist's ideas sufficiently to agree to change, even if just as an experiment, some of their habits.

In some cases it will be useful to go along with the client's views even if we cannot share them. With psychotic clients it works better to start from their vision of reality: They will develop less resistance against strategies that appear consistent with their convictions. With orthodox Muslims it may be worthwhile to collaborate with an imam, and with Catholics who suffer from obsessive guilt feelings, with a priest to whom they go for confession.

The Epistemological and Ethical Principles of Solution-Focused Cognitive Therapy

Like any other therapeutic model, solution-focused cognitive therapy is founded on a certain number of epistemological and ethical principles. Here are the most important:

- Every person has within themselves the resources to solve their problems and accept their limitations. In the therapeutic process, these resources are activated. To achieve this, the focus is directed towards the healthy strengths rather than towards the problematic weaknesses.
- We live in the here and now. The past is no longer real; the future isn't here yet. We can use knowledge, insights, and habits acquired in the past. We can project goals and desires into the future. Both past and future contribute to create reality, but are not part of it.
- Habits, once acquired, stay wired in the brain and cannot be lost (unless the brain itself is damaged). But new habits can be developed. The goal of therapy is to facilitate the creation of wished-for habits that one can choose instead of the unwanted ones.
- We can only be changed by ourselves. Only clients can "therapize" themselves: All therapy is self-therapy. Together with the clients and their relatives, the therapist makes the context in which this self-therapy is made easier.
- Only clients can decide on their therapeutic goals. However benevolent and useful the therapist's intentions are, as long as clients don't share them, they must not be pursued. If the therapist has good reasons to take matters into his or her own hands and to impose a change, he or she should be aware that he or she leaves the therapeutic mandate and that takes on a protective or a charitable one.

- Our role is to help clients to change what they want to change, to accept what they cannot change, and to be satisfied when they live the life they want and are able to live. This means mainly that clients practice the habits that they want to practice.
- If one accepts that the goal of therapy is to help clients to live the life they want to live—that is, to use the habits they want to use—then it is obvious that the question of what the clients' existential choices are cannot be avoided. These may often remain implicit. Sometimes they must be addressed explicitly, as when a client wants to make a choice but doesn't accept its consequences and so drives himself or herself into an existential impasse.

Most Commonly Used Epistemologies

Most people's epistemologies can be classified into three categories: common sense, scientific, and metaphysical.

Everyday or Common Sense Epistemology

Examples: The sun goes up in the morning and goes down at night. Matter and energy are different things. An apple falls down onto Sir Isaac Newton's head.

Scientific Epistemology

Examples: The earth turns on its own axis. $e = mc^2$. Earth and apple attract one another through the force of gravitation.

Different paradigms can be distinguished in scientific epistemology.

- **Biological:** In its pure, materialistic form, the biological paradigm states that the mind can be reduced to a function of the brain. The idea that the mind is not limited by the body appears absurd. Psychological disorders are disorders of the brain.
- **Analytical:** For the reductionist, analytical paradigm that underlies psychodynamic and behavioral models, individuals are seen as separate entities. They have an intra-psychic structure and can communicate and establish relationships with each other. Here, the question of whether the mind is located in the body is not relevant. Psychological disorders are seen as disorders of the individual's psychic apparatus.
- **Holistic or systemic:** Here, the central concept is that human beings are part of greater units, called systems, such as the family or a professional team. What is inside the individual's consciousness is less important than the patterns of relationships between the elements of the system (i.e., its members). Psychological disorders are the expression of a malfunctioning system, while individual clients are called "Identified clients": they are designed as clients, as individuals who do not function well, whereas it is the whole system that should be considered as the client.

Metaphysical Epistemology

Religion, atheism, and superstition belong in this category. Examples: There will be another life after death, in heaven or hell or in a reincarnation, or there will be no life after death. The stars influence us. God (and maybe his saints) will favor us if we pray often and if we live in fear of God. It makes sense to play our lucky number in the lotto or a casino. Psychological disorders are God's punishment for the sins that our forefathers or we have committed, or they are the expression of demonic possession, or we were born under an unlucky star.

A Few Epistemological and Ethical Traps

From an ethical as well as a practical perspective, it is important that the therapist joins in the client's epistemology as closely as possible—at least at the outset. Minuchin's phrase "start where the patient is" applies here (Minuchin & Fischman, 1981).

This can give rise to conflict of conscience. For example, a young Islamic woman is hospitalized with depression. She doesn't love the man whom her parents want her to marry. However, she is very devout: She loves her parents and doesn't want to disobey them. The therapeutic team believes in the individual's freedom of choice and thinks that the woman should marry the man she loves. Is it certain that this view will be helpful for the client? There is no easy answer to this question.

Different Experiences of Space

Sometimes our opinions seem so evidently true that we are not aware of the gap between our views and the clients'. Here are a few examples that concern the way we experience space and time.

- **The individual experience of space:** In Cartesian Western thought it is evident that human beings are separate individuals who can communicate between themselves. This communication may be adequate or full of errors, but one thing is certain: We cannot read each other's thoughts; we cannot feel their feelings.
- **The collective experience of space:** As Ludwig Binswanger (1962) showed, the identity we experience may also be a supra-individual one. This collective space of identity still plays an important role in non-Western societies, where the family or the tribe is the unity of reference. Until the Renaissance, when the individual became "the measure of all things," this was also the case in the Western world (Gourevitsch, 1973). Emotions and thoughts are experienced as collective processes. There is no need to exercise empathy in order to sympathize: One's relatives' feelings are not felt as being separate from one's own feelings. It is self-evident that

the other thinks as I do: Thoughts are shared. Hours of palaver under the baobab constitute the emergence of a collective thinking rather than an exchange of different opinions. The Self has not so much developed as an individual and discrete Self as seems evident in Western society. Rather, a collective consciousness of Self has emerged which, to our Western eyes, appears as a symbiotic or fusional relationship.

It is useful to think of these different ways of experiencing space and identity when we therapists label a relationship as "symbiotic." Perhaps some of these relationships are not as abnormal as we think.

Some of these so-called symbiotic clients are in the autism spectrum. Lacking well-functioning mirror neurons, they didn't develop empathic understanding. They perceive the world of others by observing their gestures and mimicry; time and again, they make disturbing mistakes that render them insecure in their relationship with others. They need a symbiotic partner (normally one of their parents, or their partner once they enter into a relationship) who supplements their observations with his or her emotional intelligence. Only then can they form reliable and useful opinions.

They need this reliable partner for other reasons too. If we look closely and without assumptions at the interactions between both partners of the symbiotic relationship, we can observe that at first the individual on the autism spectrum feels his or her own emotions in a vague and ill-defined way. Only after the symbiotic partner has co-experienced them empathically and commented on them do they become differentiated and reliable. So a symbiotic relationship may present considerable advantages. We should think twice before we decide that separating partners in the symbiotic relationship is a good thing to do. Do the clients wish it? Will it really be helpful for them?

If we decide that some loosening of the symbiotic bond is in order, it will seldom be useful to do this by too direct means (e.g., by telling the symbiotic partner not to speak in place of the client). The usual response to this is resistance. Two indirect strategic moves may prove more useful:

- Asking the client to, out of his or her own initiative and without telling beforehand, do small acts of kindness towards the symbiotic partner;
- Asking the symbiotic partner to observe what the client does that makes him or her (the partner) happy and/or grateful.

This lessens the dependence and favors a more equal relationship. In a second phase, the "dominant" partner will be more willing to delegate responsibilities to the "dominated" one.

Different Experiences of Time

Linear: Our main experience of time is linear. The seconds tick; time moves on inexorably; we cannot return into our past. A hundred years, even twenty years ago, the world was very different from what it is now. Change is constant. New opportunities and possibilities arise; we have to continually adapt to new circumstances, new demands.

Circular: For thousands of years, the way humankind experienced time was mainly circular. For a herdsman or a farmer a thousand years ago, what was important was to know if it was summer or autumn, and that after each winter, spring comes back. Night and day, rain and sunshine, sowing and harvesting: What keeps returning is what is important. A good hunter, a good farmer tried to emulate his father. Today a farmer who would try to do exactly as his or her father did would soon be ruined.

Some clients have a difficult time with the compulsory changes we have to live with. Many autistic and obsessive-compulsive, as well as chronic clients in general, have a loathing for change. They ask for our help, but progress implies change, which they resist. This is not to the liking of most therapists. For these clients, their present state—as uncomfortable as it may be—is the best solution they have found to their difficulties.

We will get better results if we accept their attitude and appreciate their resistance as useful information. We can focus on changes that have already happened instead of negotiating what they want to change in the future. We can ask them what they did that went well since we last saw them and make positive comments about that. A therapeutic relationship in which they are appreciated for what they are doing well already will encourage them more to experiment than a relationship in which they are expected to change.

The Level of Mandates

In psychotherapy, the term *mandate* means the power and the responsibility that clients hand over to the therapist, and vice versa. The therapeutic mandate consists of the expectations that the different actors of the therapeutic process bring with them, and of the constraints to which they are subjected.

I will first discuss mandates in general, and then review different types of mandates.

Circularity of the Mandates

The Bruges Model focuses on the therapeutic alliance, and the circularity of the mandates is essential.

Communication science postulates that all communication implies a power relationship. This comes in two types: symmetrical and complementary (Bateson, 1972; Watzlawick et al., 1974).

In a symmetrical relationship, neither of the partners dominates the other. The relationship is egalitarian: territories are managed by common consent; conflicts arise frequently.

Resolving conflicts often means that one partners yields power to the other. The relationship then becomes complementary.

If this is not the case, if none of the parties involved yields, the power struggle leads to a symmetrical escalation. The instability that is inherent to symmetrical relationships leads to repetitive conflicts.

All living systems tend to evolve a hierarchy, to install complementary relations.

In complementary relations, one partner exercises power over the other. One is in the upper complementary position (the alpha dog), one in the lower position (the underdog).

The most stable relationships are generally those where the different territories—the different aspects of living together—are managed in a complementary way. Those who are in the subordinate position accept the authority of the one who manages the territory, but when they formulate requests or remarks, these are accepted.

In therapy, the clients expect to be listened to, to be given advice, to be supported and helped. They put themselves in the subordinate position. To start with, the therapist accepts the dominant role. In the Bruges Model, the therapist then uses the dominant position to allow him- or herself to take a subordinate role.

On one hand, the therapist has to be accepted as the expert, the person who knows, who can help, and whose help the client will accept. On the other hand, the therapist uses this position to constantly put the clients in the expert position, to search for their skills and strengths, and to ratify their solutions. In this to-and-fro movement, in this circulatory mandate, a virtuous spiral is created that fosters the clients' resources and skills, that stimulates their creativity to solve their own difficulties.

Following the Clients

Following and joining the clients are two movements that are essential for establishing a circular mandate.

The therapist listens in an active way. By his or her questions and rewordings, the therapist patiently helps clients to clarify their difficulties, their goals, and their solutions, while respecting their rhythms. Clients come to see us because of difficulties they have had for some time. They have explored them and they know them well. So let us accept their definition of their problems and their goals.

To impose your views means telling them that they are in the wrong and that you have the knowledge. The clients will not necessarily agree; they will lose confidence in themselves and become more dependent, which is the reverse of what we want to achieve. If clients do not know their problems, if we claim to know them better than they do, how will they be able to solve them? How will they know when they are solved? And if we know better that they do what their goals must be, how will we motivate them to work towards them?

If your definition of the clients' problems and goals prevails, you become your own client, you even become the client of your client! You ask them to work towards a goal that you have defined, not they. Chances are that you will have to work much harder than them to attain a very uncertain result.

To accept the clients' definition, to follow them in their progress, asks for a great alertness and tenacity. When the problem's description remains unclear, when clients ask for your help and then immediately resist the help you offer them, do not let yourself be tempted to "take matters into your hands" by imposing your definition of the problems and of the way to solve them. Clients in a searching relationship need us to reassure them about themselves, about their views of themselves, about the reliability of the therapeutic relationship.

"Take matters in our own hands" means underscoring our clients' incompetence, ratifying their loss of self-esteem and their loss of confidence in their ability to help themselves. Perhaps at first they will get better—but then their self-doubting, their fears, their loss of self-confidence will rise again and so will their dependency on the therapist. A relapse is then the safest way to ensure the therapist's support. In the extreme, maintaining the therapeutic relationship becomes the goal of the therapy.

When the Client Gives No Mandate

When the request for help comes from a referent and not from the client, do not automatically adopt the goals of the referent. You will probably walk into the same dead end they did.

These clients come to you in a non-engaged relationship. Their goal in consulting you is to solve a difficulty they have in their relationship with the referent. However, the clients do not necessarily want to solve the problem they were sent for. That is not their problem; it's the referent's problem.

Let us take the example of an alcoholic who is sent by his general practitioner and whose wife threatens to leave him. He denies his dependency and minimizes his consumption. What he wants is for his wife to stay with him and maybe for his doctor to stop preaching abstinence. What his wife and his doctor want is to convince him to stop drinking. Of course, from a medical viewpoint, they are right! But their strategy of preaching and threatening has failed. The more they try, the more he resists. It makes no sense to try to do the same.

Still, someone has succeeded in motivating him to come to your consulting room. What is his motivation? What problem has he come to solve, and with whom?

Following our clients does not prevent us from giving information that will help them make their own choices. Precise and personalized information makes them better experts. For an obese person to control his or her diet, he or she needs objective information about diet and exercise. A depressive client needs to know about sleep hygiene. An alcoholic can benefit from personalized information about the medical, psychological, and relational aspects of his or her drinking habits. This medical and psycho-educational information answers to the motivation they had to come. It has more chance of being accepted when it is given in a question-and-answer mode where we discuss what the clients objectively do wrong and what they do right, where we try to hitch our suggestions to things they already do—and above all, to what they want.

Let us now discuss some different types of mandates.

Mandates Coming from Clients

First and foremost comes the mandate that clients give to the therapist. Clients ask us for some kind of help. By doing so they enter the subordinate position in a complementary relationship.

Typically, clients have three ways to solicit our help:

- The "surgical" demand: Clients expect us to cure them without having to do anything themselves. It is as if such a client might say: "Take my problem away the way a surgeon excises a tumor. When you are ready, I want to be rid of my problem, and nothing else must have changed." Clients who are strongly convinced of an external locus of control have this attitude. So do clients who come asking for hypnotherapy and who think that the hypnotherapist can impose change. A therapist who accepts this surgical mandate may be able to help clients with their current difficulties but will scarcely stimulate their self-efficacy.
- The "medical" demand: Clients expect us to make a diagnosis and to prescribe a treatment that must be taken in order for them to be cured. Problem-solving strategies follow this pattern. They have the same drawback of being helpful in the current situation without boosting the clients' self-efficacy.
- The psychotherapeutic demand: These clients want to learn how to help themselves. We can train them in methods and techniques to make an optimal use of their resources (consultancy relationship), discuss what variations already exist in their unwanted habits (exceptions, partial control) that can be extended into satisfying habits (expert relationship). The resulting psychotherapeutic mandate is a shared one: The therapist accepts the dominant position that clients yield: He or she is an expert in questions of pathology and health, of problems and solutions. At the same time, the therapist gives clients the mandate to do their own therapy: He or she gives the client the dominant position in this. Thus, the therapist accepts responsibility and gives it back in the same movement.

Mandates Coming from the Client System

In most cases, the family gives us the same mandate as the client: Help us to make things better. As the new habits that the client has to develop will affect the other family members, it is better to take these people into account. They have tried to help: How did they do that? What was useful, even if only for a short time? What are they prepared to do in order to help? How can the client help them to help him or her?

If different family members have different goals for the therapy (parents/ adolescents, couples, and so on), and consequently give us different mandates, it becomes necessary to help them to negotiate a compromise. An elegant way to do this is have them separately respond to a goal-oriented question (such as the Miracle Question), and then have them situate themselves on their own and each other's scale. For instance, the husband describes his miracle; then the wife describes hers; the therapist abstains from commenting on the discrepancies; the husband situates himself on his own scale (10 = situation after the miracle, 0 = the opposite) and says how he came there; the wife situates herself on her own scale; the husband says where he thinks they stand on his wife's scale; the wife says where she thinks they stand on her husband's scale. Of course, at each point the therapist asks: What makes that you can say you are at that number on the scale? The result is that they first make positive comments about themselves, and then about each other and about their relationship.

Another strategy is to give them as an experiment the second question for a happy life: "Every day, when you come together (in the evening), you could do the following: For 15 minutes, and while you do whatever else you have to do, you pay attention to what the other does that you are satisfied with or grateful for. And you also pay attention to the way you react in a positive way." The result is that they come to agree more easily on common goals.

Mandates from the Referent

What the persons who sent us the client expect from us often is a delicate question. They often have goals that are different from the client's, and views on how the therapy should be conducted that are not ours. A problem drinker must stay abstinent for six months before he or she can get a driving license; we are expected to make that happen. A judge has given a client the choice between therapy and a jail sentence. A cardiologist has sent a hypochondriac so we cure his cardiophobia.

If we are completely independent from the referents, we may take no heed of their expectations. But if we have to take them into account, it is better to put the responsibility squarely on the client's shoulders. This empowers the client, increases self-efficacy, and helps us to keep our peace of mind. In the referent-client-therapist triangle, the therapist's task is to help the client do what it takes to satisfy the referent. Useful questions are:

- "What do you have to do so X (the referent) is satisfied?"
- "What would need to happen so that X says you don't have to come to see me any more?"
- "How could you convince X that you don't need any more therapy?"
- "What would need to change for X to give you back the custody of your child?"
- "What will you need to show to your parents if you want them to give you permission for . . .?"

Official Mandates

We all have official mandates given us by society (as a medical doctor, a psychologist, social worker, teacher, and so on) and by the institution that we work for. This latter mandate is partly official: What a nurse is permitted and required to do is different from a social worker's task. Another part is unofficial, dependent on the institutional culture, the alliances and friendships or enmities. It is wise to limit us to the explicit or implicit mandates that the team has agreed upon.

Personal Mandates

There are also the expectations we have of ourselves as therapists. My personal professional ethics determine what kind of therapist I want to be, what I consider to be my duty. I will in any case exert some influence over my clients, even if I try not to, because they expect that coming to see me will bring about a change for the better. In the Bruges Model, the therapist strives to make a therapeutic alliance that will help his or her clients to do their own therapy more easily.

Other Possible Mandates

Most of us are charged with other mandates than the therapeutic one. We may sometimes have to protect clients from themselves, or to protect others from the clients. We must then assume responsibility for the client, at least temporarily. A client may not agree with this and may not want our help anymore.

For this reason, whenever it can be arranged (e.g., in a clinical or educational context), the therapeutic and the protective roles may be assumed by different persons. For instance, the consultant psychiatrist may take on the protective function, while the psychotherapist goes on in the therapeutic role—or an educator may see to it that the rules of the institutions are respected, while the therapist may compliment the adolescent on his creativity in exploring the limits of what is allowed (Ausloos, 1995).

The Strategic Level

Topics on the strategic level of intervention include:

- Should one focus on the problems (illness, symptoms) or on the therapeutic alliance and the solutions (healthy aspects, resources, skills, strengths)? A focus on the illness and the symptoms is useful for the medical and pharmaceutical aspects of the treatment and for filling out forms. A focus on solutions is helpful to empower the client and stimulate his or her self-healing capacities.
- In the Bruges Model, empowerment of the client is essential. This calls for a permissive and inviting, rather than an authoritarian, attitude. With

small children, intellectually disabled, or mentally ill clients the therapist may have to take over, but even there it pays to try to offer choices rather than just imposing one's decisions.

- The therapist tries to take the "not-knowing stance"—that is, to let the client be the expert on his or her own life. Sometimes however it may be useful to point out logical errors the client makes (e.g., when a husband expects his wife to spontaneously behave in the way he wants). Sometimes the therapist may also let a client profit from his or her experience, as when Erickson told clients stories about other clients who had been going through similar problems to their own.

- Therapy is about change, but also about continuity. How much, at each stage in the therapy, should the therapist be the agent of change, and how much should he or she be the reassuring guardian of stability? And how fast should the desired change go forward? Sometimes a client's family members cannot follow the pace at which he or she changes. In chronic cases, the affective economy of the system has become organized around the symptoms. As interactional habits, these have become important rules of the system. A phobic woman needs her husband to come with her when she leaves the house. An obsessive-compulsive husband has taken on the chore of checking all of the windows, the doors, and the knobs on the stove before the couple goes to bed. These roles have become essential in the exchange of proofs of affection and of interdependence in the exercise of power. This is why it is almost always preferable to involve the family members in the treatment: As co-therapists, they cooperate to define common goals and to shape new habits.

- Indirect strategies and formulations are preferable to direct interventions, because they leave more freedom to the client to choose how to implement his or her auto-therapy.

- The therapist leads the client from behind, by carefully choosing questions and by making positive comments and compliments. But if the client strays from what is seen as the right way (by both, though sometimes more clearly by the therapist because he or she has his expertise and has no stake in the matter), the therapist will have to make corrective suggestions.

- When the clients know what they want and there are enough exceptions, partial solutions, and useful variations in the habits, one can directly proceed to an expert relationship and simply follow the clients' lead. If not, it is better to work with techniques oriented towards the optative. Techniques that help to find out what the clients want.

- Sometimes the problems can be tackled right away, in a direct, concrete, and congruent manner. In other cases, indirect, metaphoric, and even paradoxical techniques will yield better results, mainly because they elicit less resistance.

- Observation tasks are indicated as long as the client shows that he or she expects the therapist to "operate," to take away his or her troubles. Action tasks can be given when the client asks for advice and is ready to follow it.

In SFCST, action tasks are not meant to provide a solution, but rather to make a context in which the client will find his or her own solutions.

The Tactical or Technical Level

On the tactical level, we ask ourselves: What do I say now? What shall I do now?

We may be clear about the higher levels of the therapeutic relationship. The client's and the therapist's epistemology and ethics are the same, or they respect each other's vision. The therapeutic mandate is shared. The goals are clear and the therapist knows what strategy will lead to them. In other words, there is a shared allegiance to the therapeutic model and an agreement to cooperate.

Now comes the practical question of how to say clearly what has to be said. How should the therapist formulate questions, remarks, and comments? What facial expression, what posture and gestures should he or she assume?

Multipurpose Techniques

However experienced you are as a therapist, there are moments when you don't quite know what to say or to do. Fortunately, there are a few multipurpose techniques that you can use in such a situation.

- The echo (or parrot) technique: Repeat word for word what the client just said.
- Repeat what the client said in a questioning tone, as if to ask for more details.
- Repeat with a little nuance. (Client: "He never says a friendly word to me." Therapist: "He rarely says something friendly to you.")
- Ask for a concrete example of what the client is complaining about, and go on asking for more precise detailed to make a detailed analysis of the problem (and therefore also of the exceptions and the partial solutions).
- Ask if what is being discussed is helpful for the client.
- Propose a general or a specific scale.
- Make an indirect compliment. ("How did you succeed in . . .," How did you cope with . . .," "Would your husband also say that . . .")

When you are totally confused, useful interventions include:

- Ask a scaling question. If they answer "I'm at 3," for example, and you ask what allows them to say they are at 3, they necessarily will talk about skills, resources, and successes. (Clients rarely put themselves at 0.)
- Ask for a concrete example: "Can you describe to me the last time you had this problem?" There will be instances of partial control of the problem, that is, of skills.

End-of-Session Interventions

If you have difficulties in bringing a session to a close, here are a few possibilities:

- Use the First Session Formula Task.
- Ask the Three Questions for a Good Life.
- Assign observation tasks concerning the start (context, emotions, perceptions, and events that precipitate the symptom sequence), the sequence itself (logos, pathos, ethos), and how it comes to an end.
- Action tasks (prescribing an activity that the client does not do yet) should be given in a consulting relationship only. If the relationship is still in the searching stage, only observation tasks are indicated. If one absolutely wants to give an action task, one should wrap it up as an observation task: "I wonder what would happen if you did . . .? Would you be willing to try it out and to carefully observe what happens to you and to X?"
- Don't forget that between sessions, the client often slides back a little higher up in the flowchart: Basking in the soft glow of a good therapeutic relationship, a client agrees to do an active task. But after the session, buffeted by the cold wind of reality, he or she loses courage and does nothing.

8 Levels of Engagement in the Therapeutic Relationship

The Bruges Flowchart

We who use the Bruges Model strive to build a relationship in which clients can become the expert of their own therapy. It is often a difficult task to create this bond, to develop it and to support it. The way is full of pitfalls and hidden traps.

The therapist's desire to help his or her clients as much and as fast as possible can easily lead into such a blind alley. Each time we think that it is our responsibility to find a solution to our clients' problems, we start working in their stead; and while the therapist works, clients politely rest. In this situation, self-efficacy will not grow—and the danger is great that we will propose our own goals to our clients, that we push them in a direction they didn't choose for themselves. This leads either to dependence or to resistance.

Four questions can help us to analyze the level of engagement (of both the client and the therapist) into the therapeutic alliance. Keep in mind that this is not a static classification but a dynamic and constantly changing reciprocal process, a dance of engaging and letting go of each other.

1. Can we reasonably expect the client to be able to solve his or her difficulties?

    YES: PROBLEM   NO: LIMITATION

2. Does the client request our help?

    YES: Proceed to Question 3.
    NO: UNCOMMITTED RELATIONSHIP

3. *Does the client show that he or she is ready to work in therapy?*

    YES: Proceed to Question 4.
    NO: SEARCHING RELATIONSHIP

    Three types:

    *   Too little or too much information;
    *   "It's stronger than myself";
    *   "Someone else has to change."

4. Does the client know how to use his or her resources?

    NO: CONSULTING RELATIONSHIP
    YES: EXPERT RELATIONSHIP

The flowchart that we (I and my colleagues at the Korzybski Institute in Paris) have developed aims to help the therapist not to go too fast: This would only elicit resistance. At each level of the relationship, I will propose a certain number of possible interventions. Please keep in mind that these are only suggestions; there are many more useful techniques and each therapist will add those that he or she likes best.

There are different reasons why I and my colleagues have not adopted the three categories of visitors, complainants, and customers that de Shazer and Berg proposed.

- These categories designate states, or positions, of the client, whereas it is the relationship that should be described;[1]
- The BFTC made only an implicit distinction between problems and limitations, whereas we think it useful to make it explicit.
- The "consultancy" level, where the therapist helps clients to make skills out of their resources, is absent from the de Shazer and Berg categories.
- In addition, while the term *visitor* is neutral, *complainant* sounds rather negative, and *customers* seems inappropriate because clients are not there to buy anything, but to share their expertise with that of the therapist.

For therapists who use these categories, visitors roughly correspond to the uncommitted relationship, complainants to the searching level, and customers to the level of shared expertise, or experts' relationship.

Problems and Limitations

Clients come and talk to us about their complaints, their symptoms, and their sufferings. The first question we can ask ourselves is: What can we reasonably expect the client to be able to solve among these difficulties? And what part of them cannot be solved? "We" meaning therapist and clients together.

A difficulty for which a solution can be found is a problem. If there is no feasible solution, then the difficulty is not a problem: It's a limitation. It's as simple as that. Unfortunately, most difficulties are of a complex nature. Part of them are problems; part are limitations.

Limitations Come in Different Kinds

Biological limitations include gender, age, genetic predispositions, chronic illnesses, physical disability, and so on.

Social and cultural limitations include the era in which we live, the region we inhabit, the country where we were born, our family and cultural background, our education, and so on.

Other limitations include any decision we have made with effects that are still noticeable, such as the choice of a partner (or of successive partners), our children, the studies we did or didn't finish, the profession(s) we chose, and so on.

In addition, past events that had a strong emotional charge put their mark on us, influencing our personality and our habits. Limitations may therefore also include emotional traumas we suffered in the past:

- We may have witnessed a death by accident or escaped from a fire or have been saved from drowning.
- We may have been a victim of sexual abuse.
- We may have been tortured physically or mentally.

Acceptance

The past is over and the difficulties it brought often cannot be undone. Loss and grief are examples of this, as shown in the following scenario.

Example 1: A woman has lost her husband through cancer. This is a limitation: Her husband has passed away and nothing can be done about that. She will have to live with it. A therapist can help her overcome her grief (this is the problem part), so she will be able to accept the loss (the limitation part). Rituals may be helpful.

Example 2: After a motorbike accident, a young man's leg has been amputated. This is a limitation: However sophisticated an artificial leg may be and however good the rehabilitation, the fact is there: He has lost a leg.

Example 3: A man's wife has left and has taken their three children with her. She has to care for them, so she stays at home and has no income. She struggles to make ends meet. The man pays alimony to her and child support for the children; this leaves him with little money to spend, much less in any case than when they lived together. This makes him angry. He feels his wife, and life in general, have cheated him. These sentiments are typical of someone who wants to solve a limitation and adopts a victim stance. The therapist will have to try to help him to accept what he cannot change, and see what options and opportunities are still open.

The past cannot be reversed. In spite of the title of Ben Furman's book, *It's Never Too Late to Have a Happy Childhood* (Furman, 1998), an unhappy childhood remains unhappy forever. Nonetheless, clients often come to see us with a magical and unexpressed wish that we may change their past:

- "If only my mother had loved me a little bit more, then . . ."
- "If I hadn't been abused . . ."

- "If my father had paid a little more attention to my accomplishments, and not just to where I failed . . ."
- "If my child hadn't died . . ."

Whenever we refuse to accept a situation from our past, we waste our energy in a futile and hopeless fight. We see ourselves as victims and lock ourselves in a paralyzing past.

The therapist's task is to gently help his or her clients to accept their limitations and so to set them free to solve their actual problems. An example of this:

A young woman has been left by her partner. Unless she can win him back, she can only accept this. She needs her energy to solve all the problems that have arisen. She must find work; she must be available as a loving mother for her children. In short, she must start building a new and valuable life.

The good news is that, once one accepts one's limitations, one becomes aware of the opportunities that come with them. For every door that closes, another opens:

- When one is 70, one cannot run as fast as when one was 20; on the other hand, at 20, one has no grandchildren to play with;
- Blind people can't see, but they hear better and their sense of touch is more acute;
- Misfortunes that a couple overcome together strengthen their love;
- What doesn't kill you makes you stronger;
- Wisdom is born out of suffering.

Thus one can say that what solutions are to problems, opportunities are to limitations.

The Uncommitted Relationship

The second question we can ask ourselves is: Does the client ask for our help? If not, therapist and client are in an uncommitted relationship. A client may have a lot of problems to solve and limitations to accept, but he or she has not asked the therapist for help. The client has somehow been sent, mandated, brought in by the police or by relatives, but he or she isn't in therapy of his or her own choosing. The client doesn't want any help, or doesn't want it from this therapist, this clinic, or this agency.

In a few cases, it may be the therapist who doesn't want to help this particular client. Clients may be aggressive or abusive and may frighten a therapist who works alone. A male client may sexually harass a female therapist. Or a case may simply seem too complicated.

Whatever the reason, therapists have the right to refer to someone else a client whom they feel they cannot work with.

Examples of Clients Who Enter into an Uncommitted Relationship

Alcoholics and Drug Addicts

About a third of all clients who are referred to an alcohol and drug treatment agency do not commit themselves at the outset. For example, an alcoholic may say that they have no alcohol problem; they just want to get their driving license back. More specifically, a man whose wife is concerned about the amount he is drinking may bring him in. He doesn't see any problem and certainly doesn't want any treatment. This client's position is: "Everything's fine with me, but my wife insists that I come to see you."

Not only alcoholics and drug addicts adopt this stance. Many adolescents come because their parents told them to. In addition, mandated clients who were given the choice between therapy and serving time in prison are rarely very motivated to do anything more than just sit there.

Psychosomatic Clients

Psychosomatic clients who come with physical complaints (headaches, migraine, backache, digestive troubles, sleeping problems, etc.) and are blind to the psychological part in the etiology of their symptoms just want drugs, physiotherapy, or whatever other somatic treatment. They want no psychotherapeutic treatment or counseling.

In most cases, these clients are sent by a somatic physician (family doctor, dermatologist, cardiologist, orthopedic surgeon, etc.) who made all necessary investigations and "found nothing." So "it's in the head." The clients don't agree. They know what they feel: physical pain. They must have a somatic illness, but the physician just didn't find out yet what it is.

How Do These Clients React to Therapy?

They react to our proposals as tourists do when do walk past a shop window: they look at our offerings and they aren't interested. They don't question their behavior, so why should they want to change it? They give us no mandate.

> Clients who don't want to be helped quite naturally resist our well-meaning efforts to help them. The more we try, the more resistance we arouse.

As therapists, we become frustrated and angry. We tend to blame the client for his or her lack of cooperation, forgetting the therapist's part in creating resistance. The relationship between client and therapist becomes tiresome. Hopefully, the client will go to someone else. If not (because he or she is mandated, etc.), we will draw back and pare down our empathy and engagement in order to avoid more frustration.

Why Do They Reject Our Help?

In SFCST, we hold the view that those clients who do not ask for help need it all the same—but most of them are convinced that there is no solution for their problems, that they can't change their habits. They cannot imagine that they can get help and support. Many feel incapable; others mistrust us. They also may be afraid of our diagnosis or of our judgment. If they are alcoholics or drug addicts, they have tried to stop and they didn't succeed. Their past with its procession of errors and failures has blinded them: Like those entering Dante's hell, they have abandoned all hope.

Many have withdrawn into the fortress of denial and refuse to acknowledge to themselves as well as to others what problems their behavior causes.

Therapeutic Strategies in an Uncommitted Relationship

I will now present different strategies that can be used in the case of an uncommitted relationship.

Show Interest and Respect

We can start by accepting the client's refusal and by reacting with a positive and interested attitude.

> *If the therapist shows interest in the client's life, skills, accomplishments, and successes, she or he creates a context in which the idea of asking for help can come up.*

This climate of respect, esteem, and trust comes up when we show our clients that we respect and appreciate them in every possible aspect of their life.

We begin by showing ourselves benevolent with regard to the problem that occasioned the consultation. Then we demonstrate our interest in different aspects of the client's private and professional life. This transforms a client who heaps failure upon failure into a client who also has succeeded in many ways and who has already tackled a quantity of problems.

The next example shows

* How we can make positive comments on general aspects of the client's life and in so doing clearly show our esteem;
* How a context is created in which the problem can be addressed in such a way that the client doesn't feel forced to block the interview.

You are a general practitioner. The O'Donnell family is on your list; you have been their family doctor for years and they trust you.

Jack O'Donnell comes to your office. Fifteen minutes before, immediately after he left his house, his wife has called and told you that you should tell Jack that he must stop drinking.

Jack complains about stomach pain. He looks very stressed. When you examine him, you notice that the gastric region is very sensitive and that his breath smells of alcohol.

He only wants something to cure his stomach. When you ask him, he says that he doesn't drink a lot, only a few glasses with his friends after work.

You have known him for a long time and you know it is pointless to tell him that his excessive drinking causes his stomach trouble. He will simply deny it. It is also useless to tell him that his wife thinks he drinks too much. This would only lead to a quarrel between them. Experience has taught you that confronting him with warnings or advice about alcohol will not work. This will induce resistance, which is the opposite of what you want to achieve.

Now, you are also the doctor for Jack's mother and you know that he visits her regularly in the retirement home. The old lady worries much about her son. You tell him he really is an exemplary son: "I went to see your mother three days ago. She told me that your frequent visits do her a lot of good. She was quite proud to tell me that your boss likes the work you do and that a friend can always count on you when he needs help. You are a big support for her."

In this way, you show that you hold Jack in high esteem, and you create a context in which it is more likely that the next announcement will be accepted: "I know that you think that you do not drink too much. And the fact is that you rarely or never get drunk. But I am convinced that your stomach can't tolerate so much beer. I can prescribe something for you and I will do so. But if you really want your stomachaches to disappear, I'm convinced that you must drink less beer."

Clients will be more ready to trust an expert who supports them and who recognizes their qualities—not only the qualities that will be useful to solve their problems, but also their general qualities as a human being. A conversation about a client's general skills and achievements (professional activities, social commitment, family involvement, sporting activities, readiness to help friends, etc.) gives the opportunity to forge an alliance that makes it easier for the client to collaborate on solving problems instead of denying them.

Describe Disaster Scenarios

A second strategy consists in describing alternative disaster scenarios. The therapist talks about similar cases that are much more dramatic than what the client describes. Compared to these stories, his or her problematic behavior looks less terrible. He or she has succeeded in avoiding the pitfalls, the mistakes, and disappointments that befell the people in the story, and thus appears as a competent and responsible person. Following are two examples of this technique.

Example 1: To a depressed man who suffered serious financial setbacks the therapist says that he has shown great courage. The therapist tells him about another client who had similar problems and took to drink, which led to divorce. This client succeeded in limiting the damage. He did everything he could to protect his wife and children.

Example 2: The therapist gives the example of another client to an alcoholic who has never used physical violence against his wife and children, even when he was very drunk. The other drinker had destroyed all the furniture in a fit of drunken anger; his wife had to flee to a shelter. In this way, the therapist shows that he understands the current client's problems and that he or she sees their positive as well as their negative sides. For the moment, he or she avoids addressing the problem directly: The client shows that he doesn't want to engage himself in therapy and the therapist respects this attitude.

Consider the Referent as the Client

In a third strategy, the therapist considers as the real client not the client him- or herself, but the person or persons who ask for help for the client. For example, if a woman comes asking for help for her husband who is a drug addict, the therapist may choose to enroll her as a co-therapist and counsel and supervise her. This strategy is consistent with the systemic idea that whoever changes the rules (the interactional habits) of the system, the others (in this case the husband) are bound to change too. It is also an application of the solution-focused idea that therapy happens at home, not during the therapy sessions.

The referent (the wife in this case) asks for help. She is motivated; she wishes that something would change. If we can get her to change her reaction to the problem, the client hopefully will change something in his own behavior, in his unwanted habits. Fish, Weakland, and Segal (1982, p. 42) say in this connection: "With few exceptions the problem is maintained and aggravated by the specific interactions between the client and the other persons who are involved in the problem" (p. 42).

The client's family members have been trying to solve the problem. Their efforts have not met with success, otherwise they wouldn't have come to see us.

For example, we need to recognize everything the mother has done for her anorexic daughter in order to get her to eat more. However, all the suggestions, the punishments, and the tasty dishes she has cooked specially for her have led her to eat even less.

To take another example, a husband whose wife is an alcoholic has gotten angry; he has implored her to stop drinking; he has tried to be gentle; he has scolded her; and he has appealed to her motherly feelings. He has locked the liquor in cupboards in the cellar; he has emptied the bottles in the sink. Finally, he has turned away from her. Now she feels misunderstood and abandoned. In guilt and despair, she turns to the only friend who is left to her: the bottle. With the referent, here the husband, one can examine which solutions he has tried out that have led to at least a partial or temporary success. One can suggest new tactics, not as solutions, but as experiments and as the basis of an observation task (e.g., how the wife reacts if the husband changes his reaction in the proposed way). From a systemic viewpoint, the husband changes his side of the interactional habits (i.e., the rules of the system). In response, the wife may change her behavior or perhaps she may admit that she needs help.

Another possibility is, in conversations with the client, to use a relationship between the client and a third party. Their intentions can be put in a positive light:

• They are concerned about the client's welfare and about his or her future.
• They show their love by trying to help him or her to avoid serious consequences (dismissal, imprisonment, divorce, etc.).

If the client accepts this view, one can congratulate him or her with the close attachment between him or her and the third person.

In the instance of a married couple, one can emphasize that they are "a good team that has stuck together in good and bad times and who have gone a long way with each other."

One can also try to discuss with the client what the third person wants. Sometimes this brings the client to talk of his or her own goals in order to distinguish them from those of the other.

Of course these strategies only work if the client can suppose that the third party has positive intentions.

Make an Alliance with the Client to Help Her or Him to Satisfy the Referent

If the client does not agree with the referent, one can fall back on a fourth strategy. For example, "What can you (or we) do, so that X is satisfied and gets off your back?" "What would you (or we) have to do so that X does not require you to come here any more?" One example of this is the following.

An adolescent who smokes cannabis regularly has put his parents in such a state of worry that his mother makes a daily search of his room. They want the therapist to make him stop consuming drugs. He has no intention of doing so. What stirs his interest however is the following question: "Would you like us to look together what can be done to calm down your mother enough so that she respects your privacy again?"

Help the Client to Recognize Our Expertise

Some clients want to get help for their complaints, but they are convinced that we are not the right persons to help them. In this case we must at first accept the client's viewpoint on his or her problems, and afterwards enlarge his or her array of semantic choices. This situation is often found with psychosomatic complaints. The client accepts only an organic cause, while it is clear for the therapist that psychological factors play a role, as shown in the following example.

Stephen, 14 years old, complains about palpitations and retrosternal pain. He often feels as if suffocating. He has briefly lost consciousness three or four times. Stephen as well as his parents are convinced that these symptoms are the mark of a serious, perhaps even of a highly dangerous disease, and that there is an organic cause to them. They ask for help, but for a somatic illness. Their view of the problem is monosemic, one-sided. There can only be one explanation: a somatic disease.

This view about the symptoms can only lead to one possible attitude: More, other, and better somatic investigations must be made that will finally lead to the correct diagnosis. If all these investigations prove fruitless, the doctors' expertise will be in doubt, not the client's one-sided views.

If we try to convince these clients that they are wrong, we will usually only succeed in strengthening their rigidity. In regard to the previous example, it is more efficient to first agree with the fact that Stephen really feels all his complaints, that the somatic symptoms are really there. The somatic investigations that have been done already are discussed and perhaps other ones may be ordered. Once it is clear that we have taken their views seriously, a context of mutual respect can appear: As the therapist respects the views of Stephen and his parents, they can consent to listen to the therapist's ideas. From there we can proceed to the idea that body and mind are one, or at the very least that they influence each other. It then becomes easier to suggest alternative viewpoints.

Polysemy (a variety of complementary views) can emerge. The client and his parents may listen with interest when the therapist expresses a more complex psychosomatic view that combines somatic and psychological explanations. Now we can integrate Stephen's complaints in a larger frame and explain the physiological consequences of stress, tension, and fear.

It is important not to press clients into abandoning their views; they can keep them and integrate them in a broader vision. We can explain the psycho-physiological mechanisms of hyperventilation. We can speak about ortho- and parasympathetic stress mechanisms or about the biological aspects of depression. Once the client admits that psychological factors can influence physiological symptoms, the way is free for examining possible psychological causes of stress, tension, and anxiety.

The Searching Relationship

Helping Clients to Use Their Strengths

In a searching relationship, the therapist and the clients co-construct a context in which the clients will be able to use their resources and their skills to develop habits that correspond to their existential choices and to live the life they want to live.

> If the clients ask for help out of their trouble, the next question is: Do they show themselves ready to work for themselves, or do they expect someone else (e.g. the therapist) to do the work for them?

If the answer to this question is no, we talk about a searching relationship. This is characterized by the fact that the clients genuinely search for help, but do not see that they will have to do the work for themselves. They put their problems and difficulties on the table and expect that the therapist (or someone else such as a spouse or a parent) will solve them. Or they offer so much or so little information that no clear and common goal can be agreed upon. Directly or indirectly, they make it clear that we cannot count too much on them. They expect to be helped, not to have to help themselves. They honestly look for help and for change, but they don't look where they can find the answers: within themselves.

The therapist's task will be to help them in specifying their goals so that they conform to the norms that I have described, and to establish a cooperative relationship in which they will use their resources and skills to achieve them.

We can distinguish three subcategories of the searching relationship: "vague" clients (so called by Steve de Shazer), clients who think they are powerless to help themselves, and clients who want others to change.

"Vague" Clients

A client complains about feeling depressed, tired, without energy, and weak. What "weak" exactly means remains unclear. Sometimes it's a little like nausea, or a dizziness, maybe giddiness, but not quite, well, a weakness mostly, more or less, and so on.

Other clients talk like a waterfall, so that the poor therapist can't succeed in saying a single word. These clients draw a totally confused picture of their situation. They complain of so many difficulties, mixed with theories about the origin and the interconnection of their problems, that a cat couldn't find her own kittens in the resulting chaos. Minor and major problems are tossed on a heap; what might be done remains completely unclear.

For example, a woman starts by complaining for 20 minutes about her husband. The therapist states that she obviously has marital problems. The client answers: "Oh, if it was only that."

Next she complains for a quarter of an hour about their children. The therapist says: "Obviously, you have many problems in your family."

The client again answers: "Oh, if it was only that."

She goes on about other complaints, about colleagues who ignore her and friends who don't understand her, so that the therapist, struggling to remain afloat in this cataract, has no idea about where to start. There is too much and at the same time too little information.

Clients Who Think They Are Powerless

Some clients feel overwhelmed and powerless against their problems. "It" (for example, the addiction) is stronger than they are. They give all power to the therapist and expect her or him to cure them, as if she or he were a surgeon: "If you could please remove my problem, I would be so grateful." They ask for help and at the same time show that they themselves can do nothing. They do not see how they could possibly help themselves.

In solution-focused therapy, however, we work together with the client. We help them to use their own skills and resources to achieve their own goals and to develop new habits—so we cannot help them in the way they wish.

ADDICTED CLIENTS

If these clients ask for our help at all, they start therapy in a searching relationship. They would like to stop smoking, drinking, gambling, or putting needles into their veins. But their best intentions melt like snow in the sun as soon as the opportunity to consume arises. Only one thing is certain: The addiction is stronger than their wish to be good. Afterwards, they often they feel so guilty that they need to put the blame on someone else: A woman drinks because her husband neglects her; a man drinks because all his friends do it.

OBSESSIVE-COMPULSIVE CLIENTS

These clients often expect a kind of instant help from the therapist. With a magic wand the therapist should whisk all their problems away. They cannot control their obsessive thoughts and compulsive behavior: They feel unable to endure the feelings of unrest and anxiety that take hold of them if they try to resist.

BROODING CLIENTS

Then there are the clients who always keep brooding over the same gloomy thoughts, who always have the same depressing and anxious feelings. Simple solutions (for example to turn their attention to something else) they reject as not being helpful: The black thoughts force themselves on them; they have already tried everything and nothing has helped.

Many clients feel they have no energy. They cannot resist this. They would want to, but "it" is stronger than their will. They have given up on themselves and their possibilities. Most depressed clients are like this.

Clients Who Want Others to Change

This is the rule with couples and in parents-adolescents therapy. The other should behave differently; they should stop with their nonsense. If they do, the problem is solved—or so each client believes. The therapist is assigned the task to change the other.

As in the uncommitted relationship, the principle of reciprocity applies. It is not just clients who may be searching for a solution outside of themselves. The therapist can also adopt a searching attitude. She or he may be pushed or seduced into trying to solve the clients' problems for them. In doing so, she or he sets the therapy goals, forgetting that one can never change someone else: One can only help the other to change. Client and therapist together search for a solution where it cannot be found because only the therapeutic work that the client does is really useful.

What can be done? How can we get clients to take charge of their own therapy?

However we proceed, whatever the strategy we use, it should lead to defining clear and attainable goals that the client and the therapist can agree on.

From the start we must adopt a respectful, positive, and sympathetic attitude in order to discover and support the positive forces, the skills, and the resources of the client.

Remember, this is about the optative: what kind of life does the client want? And how can their existential choices be incarnated into habits?

There are two main strategies into which the different interventions can be classified:

1. Orientation towards the present: What do clients already do here and now that they want to do (and think, and feel)?
2. Orientation towards the future: What do clients want? What would their life look like if it was just as they want it to be?

Orientation towards the Present

The therapist can help clients to find out how they want to live by asking them questions about a preferred future, or he or she can do so by helping them look at what they consider satisfactory right now, in their life as it is now. These are the kind of questions that help clients to clarify their existential choices:

- What good habits do the clients practice already?
- What good aspects are there inside the bad habits?
- What variations exist within the unwanted habits?
- What exceptions are there to the client's thesis that he or she cannot do anything?

Several techniques can be used to help the clients find out what they are doing right, according to their own norms. First, there are the Three Questions for a Good Life, which are for the orientation towards the present what the Miracle Question is for the orientation toward the future: the royal road to the good life.

A few words about how I and my colleagues came to formulate these questions: At St. John's Hospital in Bruges, from 1984 onwards, we have been offering our alcoholic clients a choice between two options: total abstinence or controlled drinking. They chose according to their own preferences and those of their relatives, and in consideration of what they thought they were capable of doing. This was about existential choices: They were talking about their relationships with themselves, with their relatives, and with reality in general. This part of the therapeutic conversations generally posed no problem: They wanted to be better parents, spouses, colleagues, and so on, and they more or less knew what to do to achieve this.

We then discussed strategy: What could they do not to drink, or not to drink more than a reasonable amount? How were they already doing this on days where they were drinking less? What else could they do to succeed? What helped not to drink the first glass or not to continue after they drank one? What did they do when they had drunk too much in spite of their best intentions?

Follow-up studies at one year, two years, and four years after treatment all showed more or less the same results: 45% to 50% did not drink anymore, 25% to 30% were drinking in a controlled way. Approximately 25% experienced bad results: Some had died, while some continued drinking excessively.

Around 1990, we decided to have a closer look at what distinguished the failed population from those who were successful. These were the hyper-chronic, revolving-door clients, serial relapsers. These clients were those who were admitted time and time again in a bad somatic state, who were not interested in psychotherapeutic help, who solemnly promised they would never drink again and who relapsed as soon as they were discharged, only to be readmitted a few months later.

It appeared that two characteristics distinguished this group from the others.

1.   The great majority lived alone and had difficulty doing their daily chores (washing themselves, cleaning up, taking care of their clothes, and so on).
2.   There was no way to discuss strategies with them to avoid relapse. To each question ("What could you do not to drink the first glass?" "If you did drink a first glass, what could you do not to go on?") they answered by keeping silent, or with the phrase "I will not drink anymore" repeated like a mantra.

When one asked the Miracle Question or the Best Hopes Question, no answer came.

Then a third point became clear: These clients did not suffer from amnesia in the way a Korsakow patient does. They could say, for instance, what they had for breakfast. The indicative of the past tense also was still there. However, it seemed they could not no longer learn from what happened to them, in the good as in the bad sense. They floated through their existence in a kind of eternal present, without a past that made sense and without a future that they could wish for.

It now became understandable that they neglected their daily chores and that they relapsed without thinking. The daily choices ("What shall I do now?") that normally derive from the existential choices ("What kind of person do I want to be?") were disconnected from them. The psychological functions that were no longer active belong to the prefrontal cortex. This part of the brain (Elkhonon Goldberg called it the *executive brain*; Goldberg, 2001) is responsible for our goals (and therefore for our existential choices), and for critically judging how well we have attained them. In other words: "What do I want to do?" and "Can I be satisfied with what I have done?.

I was reading Epicure at the time. Most of Epicure's writings are lost to us, but enough survives to give us a general idea of his thinking. For him, philosophy was useless if it did not help us to be happy. His conditions for happiness were two:

1.   We can be happy if we do things that we are satisfied with (that is, if we practice habits that are congruent with our personal morals and our existential choices).
2.   We can be happy if we can be content with what we have.

It seemed to me that this was precisely what these clients lacked: they had lost their existential perspective. In response I formulated the Three Questions for a Good Life:

1.   What have I done that I am happy with? (That I am satisfied with?)
2.   What has someone else done that I am happy with, or that I am grateful for? And; Did I react in a positive way (i.e., in such a way that this person might do something like that again)?
3.   What do I see around me—what do I hear, feel, smell, taste—that I am happy with or grateful for?

The Three Questions proved to be a hit. We had them printed on little cards and clients snapped them up, posted them on their refrigerators, reflected two or three minutes on them and felt good.

Chronic clients improved: Not only those serially relapsing alcoholics that first caught our attention, but also chronic clients of all kinds, somatic, psycho-somatic, and psychological. They did not necessarily shed all their symptoms, but their quality of life improved, their self-efficiency grew, they came to feel better and to be more agreeable to live with.

Here we have another instance of "solution talk" being more efficient than "problem talk." The optative is what it is all about: how the clients want to live, what strengths they can muster to live that desired and satisfying life.

Let us now examine several possibilities for therapists to turn their clients' heads in the direction of their goals and get them moving.

General Resources

We can look for general skills and resources. We can inquire about the client's professional achievements, about what is going well in their relationships. We can talk about how the clients, in spite of their complaints, have succeeded in going on working, in building a career, in maintaining the same friendships over the years, in remaining true to the same partner, in educating their children, in acquiring their own house, and so on.

Skills the Clients Already Have

The therapist can make *positive comments about the choices that the clients have already made,* for example, how they succeed in making their problems less bad than they could have been, how they limit the damages. Here are two examples of this kind of positive comment.

Example 1: A client drinks up to two bottles of wine per day, starting at dinner. He explains that he honestly would like to do something about this, that he even would like to stop completely, but it will be terribly difficult and he even thinks he will never succeed because his wife also drinks. It will be impossible for him to resist the craving he feels when he sees her getting drunk before his eyes.

He also believes that as a building contractor he cannot refuse to drink with his customers. It helps in concluding a sale.

Then he says that he used to drink two or more whiskies before dinner. He has stopped this; in fact, he has stopped drinking all spirits. In addition, he drinks only in the evening and only wine.

The therapist can praise him for the partial control he already exercises and point out that he has found in himself the resources to achieve this success. She or he can also show empathy for the difficult times he has gone through. In this way she or he values his skills and helps him realize that he is already going in the right direction. His self-confidence goes up; he will be able to fall back on it in the difficult moments that lay before him.

Example 2: A heavy smoker says that she has not succeeded in stopping in spite of repeated attempts. She tried to smoke light cigarettes; she has switched to small cigars; she started rolling her own cigarettes, one at a time. This helped to cut down on daily consumption. She has succeeded in not smoking for up to two hours if the circumstances are right—for example, during meetings.

Here too, one can praise the client for what she has achieved already. More likely than not, she will reject our praise and reply that one may not smoke during meetings anyway, and that in spite of all, she still smokes a lot. But she cannot deny that she respects the non-smoking rule and that she often doesn't smoke for two hours on end. The next question can be whether she can think of situations in which she could smoke but would feel reluctant to do so and whether she could use this reluctance to succeed in quitting altogether.

These strategies are part of a general strategy that we use with the addicted. What we try to do is to restore their freedom of choice. Every smoker knows how difficult it is to cut down gradually on the number of cigarettes that he or she smokes. By far the simplest solution is to stop completely. But this puts the smoker in a dilemma, a binary choice: Stop completely or remain addicted. This, however, is a choice between good and bad, so it's not really a choice. Our strategy starts out by offering the smoker a middle course: He or she can abstain under certain circumstances and smoke under other circumstances. Of course it is difficult to abstain again and again, the more so when there is little external pressure. To stop completely is easier in the long term. *Once clients start to feel free to choose, the choice of abstinence is theirs and, when they make it, they adhere much better to it.*

Looking for Alternatives and Exceptions

A very useful strategy consists in *looking for fluctuations and alternatives within the problematic habits*: In solution-focused terms, these are exceptions to the problems. The previous examples both are illustrative of this. With good reason, de Shazer calls the search for exceptions one of his most important techniques (de Shazer, 1988, p. 131).

Exceptions, however incomplete and insufficient they may be, are solutions that are there already. They are proof of the fact that the client is still able to make choices and that he or she has the skills he needs to implement them—the proof, in other words, that the client factors are already there. It's up to us to stimulate them.

There are no symptoms that never fluctuate in their strength or duration, none that are not absent from time to time—even if they appear so frequently that it looks as if they always are there. Following is an instance of this, and of the Ericksonian of "utilization": using whatever the client brings to help them get better.

> A bulimic young woman, who is also a devout Catholic, says that she cannot resist the temptation to stuff herself every evening when she comes home from work. When she passes the bakery she must go in, buy some pastries, and devour them on the spot. Once only she has succeeded in waiting a little: She was late and from the neighboring church the bells had announced Mass. She went into the church: "Of course I waited till after Mass to eat my pastries."
>
> The therapist tells her that, as the urge is so strong, she can continue for the moment to have her bulimic episodes, only maybe she could try to make them less compelling. To achieve this, every evening, after buying her pastries, she could enter into the church and do her evening prayers for five to thirty minutes, depending on which is stronger: Her love of pastries or her love of God.

Clients who brood all day interrupt their black thoughts to answer the telephone, to open the front door, to turn off the gas when the kettle whistles, to give a doll to a crying child, or even to watch an exciting soap opera on television.

Exceptions can be total or partial. When a depressed housewife forgets to brood during the soap opera or during a neighbor's visit, the exception is total. Variations in the intensity of the depressed feelings form partial exceptions.

Clients in a searching relationship are not always ready to admit these fluctuations. They fear that, if they did so, their suffering would not be taken seriously enough. For this reason, we must proceed carefully and caringly; a useful technique is to give an observation task and have the clients rate their symptoms on a scale every evening. Another technique is to ask first for the most difficult episodes since the last visit, and only then ask about the better moments.

ONCE THE EXCEPTIONS ARE DESCRIBED, CLIENT AND THERAPIST MUST
EXPLORE HOW THEY COME ABOUT

Exceptions can occur spontaneously, without visible reason. Clients have no idea how they could reproduce them. They feel they do not control them, and neither can they explain them. One day just is better than the other, without discernible reason.

Exceptions can give the impression that they are completely dependent on context. The bulimic woman doesn't eat in church. A depressed client tells us that he feels less down when his daughter brings his granddaughter for the day. A hallucinating client does not listen to the voices that insult him when he chats on the Internet with a group of ecologist friends.

Exceptions can also be consciously produced by the client. Depressed clients benefit from physical activity. Phobics feel less anxious in the company of family members.

WHAT STRATEGY ONE CHOOSES DEPEND ON THESE DIFFERENT MODALITIES

If exceptions can be produced consciously, the client may agree with the proposition that he or she can introduce alternatives in his or her habits: He or she already does so. We can compliment the client, encourage him or her to continue, and together see whether he or she could extend those skills to other areas. If the client agrees, he or she moves from a searching to an experts' relationship.

When exceptions appear to be dependent on the context, we can discuss with the client if and how those circumstances can be reproduced. If the client can reproduce the context, he or she will notice that he or she is able to influence his symptoms. I have shown this with the God-fearing bulimic. The depressed grandfather can have his grandchild staying with him more often, or perhaps even take care of other children.

One can aim directly at the oikos and help clients to produce new positive contexts. Many tasks that Milton Erickson gave can be understood in this way. He very rightly took the view that being too interested in one's gloomy thoughts and feelings, too introspective, only aggravates a depressed condition—so he sent his clients to ascend Squaw Peak early in the morning to admire the sunrise over the Arizona desert, or he sent them to the botanical garden in Phoenix to discover the rich variety of desert plants.

In the famous case of the "African Violet Queen," described here, Erickson applied two strategies: He strengthened an existing exception and established a context in which new exceptions could arise.

The nephew of a depressed and completely isolated widow asks Erickson to visit his aunt at home. The house where she lives is dark and gloomy. Only in the veranda does he find signs of a brighter life: Here the lady grows flowers, and in particular some lovely African violets. One can breed these in large numbers by putting leaves in the soil and allowing them to take root.

Erickson utilizes the lady's green thumb to help her to find new friends and break out of her isolation. He asks her to give a pot of her pretty violets to every young mother who has given birth in the nearby maternity clinic. She soon becomes a joyfully expected visitor; when she dies, she has become so popular that the local newspaper reports: "The Milwaukee African violet queen has died. Thousands mourn her."

Loosing Up Black-and-White Thinking

There are several ways to soften many clients' tendency to think in yes-or-no, black-and-white thinking (e.g., using scales). Here is an unobtrusive way in which the therapist first joins the client and then, without the client noticing, starts turning him or her in the desired direction.

One can start by literally repeating the client's complaints:

CLIENT: "I feel so tired."
THERAPIST: "You feel so tired."
CLIENT: "I can't get up in the morning."
THERAPIST: "You can't get up in the morning."

One can even exaggerate a little:

CLIENT: "I feel so tired."
THERAPIST: "You feel so terribly tired."

After a few exchanges like this, one can start to intersperse nuanced repetitions:

THERAPIST: "When do you finally succeed in getting up?"
CLIENT: "I never get up before eleven."
THERAPIST: "You hardly ever get up before eleven."

If one takes care to alternate straight and nuanced repetitions, the client rarely objects. In fact, he or she even rarely notices the alterations. Without noticing it, he or she has started admitting that there are exceptions, and that he or she has some skills left.

The First Session Formula Task

This task aims to turn the client's attention to what goes well in his or her life, that is, his or her strengths, achievements, and skills. Steve de Shazer and the Milwaukee team thought up this task and for some time gave it systematically at the end of each first session, hence the name: First Session Formula Task.

"Between now and next time we meet, we would like you to observe, so that you can describe to us next time, what happens in your family that you want to continue to have happen" (de Shazer, 1985).

If one fears that this task would be too incongruent with a problem-filled first session, one can give the following rationale: "Today you have told to me about your problems and how heavily they weigh on you. You have come to try and do something about them by means of a psychotherapy. I agree to try to help you. Now, psychotherapy by necessity is an enterprise of change. If at the end of the therapy nothing has changed, nothing would have improved in your life; this could hardly be called a successful outcome. Nonetheless, I would not want something to change that you wouldn't like changed. I wouldn't like us to throw the baby out with the bathwater and to induce changes in your life that you would later regret. Therefore, I would be glad if you paid attention from now to the next appointment to everything that happens in your life that you would like to keep as it is. This may be about quite small and simple things: the music you like to listen to, games you like to play with your children. All kinds of things that you like in your family, at work, in your leisure hours—and also the values that are important to you. For example, pay attention to when you say to yourself, 'This is the way I behave as a (husband, wife, mother, grandmother, friend, and so on) and I would like this to remain the way it is.' Would you agree to pay attention to this?"

Clients come to therapy in order to make a change. However, they often are apprehensive because they don't know what to expect. Most obsessive-compulsive clients abhor any change, however much they also long to be released from their troubles. Chronic clients cannot return to their state before their illness: This belongs to a phase in their life that is long gone. They are afraid of the unknown that awaits them.

If we appreciate this difficulty and aim not only to change the unwanted aspects of their life, but also to maintain the valuable aspects, these clients give us more of their confidence, they put their trust in us, and they cooperate.

What's New?

Finally, there are quite a few clients who, although they still remain in a searching relationship, start to show signs that they might agree to cooperate in an active way. For example, they already feel a little better since they phoned for their first appointment. They ascribe this to chance or to someone else's help, not to themselves, but their attention has already been directed to what has improved. One can help these clients to observe and appreciate small changes:

> "If you agree, you could perhaps take a few minutes in the evening to think about everything that has happened during the day that you would like to continue, everything that you would like to happen again. You might even discover something new that you like. It can be something quite small, something unimportant in itself, but that makes your life a little more pleasant, like a nice bath, a good talk with a friend, whatever. It would be interesting to make a brief note of these little things so as not to forget them. Next time we can come back to it."

This formulation suggests "spontaneous" changes, requires no active decision to "do something," and induces little resistance. Even if in the evening the client doesn't want to do the task, just thinking about it starts it up: The pink polka-dot elephant paradox works in a therapeutic way.

In the session following the First Session Formula Task, it is useful to ask about the results. Usually these are not very spectacular and the answers are quite banal: For example, a man would like to keep his job, to continue living in the house he lives in, and to continue enjoying the little nice things that happen every day. Even so, something useful arises out of this task.

Clients who had a vague, imprecise or chaotic demand for help can describe their problems more precisely and, more importantly, they can formulate their goals much more clearly. They can better define what they would like to change and what they want to keep.

Clients who engaged in a searching relationship and who paralyzed themselves in regard to their self-helping skills become more active. They wanted more satisfactory habits but they recoiled before the abyss of the unknown. Now they find reassurance in a therapeutic relationship that aims at change, but also at stability and continuance. They can give their trust to somebody who does not want to drag them into an adventure, someone who will serve them as a companion, even when the goal is not yet fully clear. The therapist will not lead them into dangerous water. It is the concern to protect their achievements that leads them into resistance: They are afraid to walk on the way to change, but they gladly consent to be led by a careful therapist.

The tasks of just focusing on what should be maintained and of looking out for what is new and better are suitable for all clients who enter into a searching relationship, even if they show little readiness to work for themselves. To start with, the clients don't have to change anything about their problems; their attention is gently deflected away from them and is turned towards their resources, skills, and achievements. To describe the problems precisely becomes unimportant.

Here is a quote from de Shazer (1985) on the relationship between problems and solutions: "'Problem' is just one of the many ways such events can be labeled and understood. It is a gestalt with solution being the ground to the figure of the problem. Without the idea that problems can be solved, what are called problems in the psychotherapy world would become just 'facts of life'" or unfortunate occurrences that could not be avoided and/or changed."

Using Scales

Most clients incline to black-white, present-absent, binary ways of thinking about their reality. If they did not, their problems would never have become as intractable as they are. For them, the symptoms are there or they aren't. Half a solution is no solution. You have this problem or you don't.

AN INTRODUCTION TO SCALES

A scale helps clients to think about solutions in a nuanced and gradual way.

One variant of a pathological habit is less bad than another. A small step in the right direction is, well, a little step already—and many small steps take one just as far as a big step.

Many clients are loath to make the effort needed to reach their goal. They have tried many times and they failed again and again. Now molehills look like mountains. Every relapse, however small, takes their courage away.

Scales help clients to see that a small setback doesn't mean that one must begin again from the start: One can build on partial successes, and one can pass a test without receiving the highest mark.

Scales help clients to choose how quickly and how much they want to change, and which efforts they want to make. Sometimes also they can weigh in what measure they prefer to endure the pain that the problem brings or to make the effort to work on it. "Scales are a useful technique to make complex aspect of the clients' life more concrete for therapist and client" (De Jong & Berg, 1998, p. 108).

Working with scales does not have any disadvantages. With children or oligophrenics who do not understand numbers, one can work with a laughing ☺ and a crying ☹ face. For the few clients who are allergic to numbers one can use a visual-analog scale:

− _____ +

If a client steadfastly refuses to work with scales, in general there is some other problem. Perhaps their goals were not taken into account enough and for the moment they are still in an uncommitted relationship. Perhaps it is not clear to them yet what they want to change and what they want to maintain. It is also possible that it is the therapist who does not feel at ease with scaling and with numbers. Sometimes an understanding client then comes to his or her aid.

In order to avoid confusing the client, it is advisable to work with scales in which 10 is always better than 0. If one wants to use a symptom scale (such as an anxiety scale or a pain scale), one can define 0 as "an anxiety that is so terrible that you say: I endure this no minute longer" or "the worst fear you ever had" and 10 as "free from anxiety" or "so little fear that you think: This is good enough." One can also work with a negative scale, from −10 (the worst) to 0 (absence of the symptom), or a scale of 0 (no symptom) to 100 (maximum of the symptom).

The figures on a scale are not real numbers. They are metaphors, like the figures on a thermometer. Just like 30 is not ten times hotter than 3, 8 is not twice as good as 4: 4 stands for "It could be worse, but there is still a lot to do," and 8 stands for: "We're almost there."

What counts is not the exact number, but the relationship between this number and other numbers, in particular where the clients situated themselves in the last session and where they put themselves now. The following case description is an illustration of this.

Laura is an obsessive-compulsive client. Before she goes to bed, she walks three times around her house to confirm that all doors and windows are closed and bolted, and that all buttons, faucets, and switches are off. When she wants to wash laundry, she asks her husband to pour the washing powder into the machine and to select the program. To the Miracle Question she answers that she "would trust her own eyes." On a scale from 0 to 10 where 0 stands for the worst time in the last six months, and 10 for how things would be after the miracle, she puts herself at 3. Before, even three rounds didn't calm her enough to fall asleep. She sometimes asked her husband to check everything a fourth time. She never needs this any more, and now she sleeps much better.

It is clear that the number 3 has no objective character. At another moment Laura might have answered 2 or 4. If one would have asked her husband and if he would also have answered 3, this would not have been Laura's 3. *The metaphor "3" is brought by the client into therapy and is at the same time a statement and a commitment.* "I am at 3" means: "At this moment in our therapeutic relationship, I take it upon myself to put myself at 3. I do what is needed to be at 3. I also undertake to cooperate with you. I am willing to cooperate up to level 3. I make the choice to be at 3."

The number 3 has no static meaning but a dynamic one: "Look, I am moving already, I have already started changing something, I already stand at 3."

When the therapist asks Laura: "What is in this 3? What is it that allows you to say you are at 3? What is the difference between 0 and 3?" she gives a specific description of the partial goals that she has reached already, of the skills she has shown, of how her habits have started changing already. With her answer Laura also gives the mandate that she will share with the therapist. Therefore, it is good to investigate exactly what changes she has already committed herself to: "What else is there in this 3? And what else?" The more elements that Laura indicates, the more details she supplies, the more she commits herself to cooperate.

As always, here too the principle applies that all the answers clients give are good ones. If Laura gives the merit of her improvement to someone else, the therapist simply goes on questioning, for example:

LAURA: "What is also in this 3 is that my husband helps me so much."
THERAPIST: "And how exactly do you use the help of your husband? Give me an example where your husband has helped you yesterday or the day before and how you have reacted to what he did in such a way that it really was helping you."

If a client talks about one aspect only of the new habits that are appearing, we can make the logos-pathos-ethos-in-oikos gestalt more complete, which will make it more stable. For example, in Laura's case:

LAURA: "I feel more at ease."

THERAPIST: "And what do you do if you feel more at ease?" Or: "What are your thoughts when you feel more at ease?" Or: "And do you feel more at ease all the time and everywhere, or are there certain situations in which you feel more at ease?"

Next, one has a choice between two questions:

• "What do you believe is needed for you to stay on n (in the case of Laura: on 3)?"
• "What do you believe is needed for you to be able to say: 'I am at $n + \frac{1}{2}$ (or $n + 1$)' (with Laura: on 3 $\frac{1}{2}$ or 4)?

It probably makes little difference which of the two questions we choose. The client's answer of the client will be about the same. The first question is better adapted to clients who do not show themselves eager as yet to become very active, the second one if they accept the fact that they will have to work if they want to get better. Another formulation for the first question, that could be given as an observation task, could be: "So now you are at 3. Now in the next days, it's quite possible that at some time you feel you have gone down to 2, or even to 1. Life is like that. Now when you have been at 2 or 1, and then you come up to 3 again, if you could note how you have done that? That would interest me tremendously."

In Laura's case, the therapist hesitates: Laura obviously expects the therapist to help her to get better, but obsessive-compulsive clients distrust any change. So the therapist opts for a tactic that combines continuity with change:

THERAPIST: "What you think that it would take for you to remain at 3 till our next appointment? Maybe you might even tell me there have been moments at 4. What would it take for that?"

LAURA: "If I could wash my laundry without any help from my husband."

THERAPIST (is glad about so much enthusiasm but is afraid that the hurdle will be too high and that the client could fail): "Don't you think that would be more than 4?"

LAURA: "Yes, perhaps."

THERAPIST: "So what would be just 4, just the smallest possible step in the right direction?"

LAURA (after some reflection): "Perhaps if I could pour the washing powder and set the program with my husband watching, so that I'm sure that I'm not doing it wrong."

THERAPIST (tries to put the bar even lower and to excuse failures in advance): "Wonderful! If you could do this just the once and even if you don't succeed the other times, this would be wonderful already!"

Where can one use scales? Probably in anything that has to do with therapy (and education, and coaching, in fact in anything that has to do with change).

The most universally applicable scale is a progress scale in which the client defines a goal and the scale indicates how far he or she has come.

How can one define 0 and 10? Examples of 0:

- "The worst it has been during the last six months."
- "The way it was before you arranged for the appointment."
- "The moment in which you attempted suicide."
- "A moment in which you have thought: 'I cannot endure this one moment longer.'"
- "The moment in which you were told about the death of your husband."
- (During a hospitalization) "The condition you were in before you came here."

Examples of 10:

- "When you have reached the point where you can say, 'If my life goes on like this, maybe it's not perfect, but it can stay like that.'"
- (In connection with the Miracle Question) "How it would be after the miracle happened."
- "If you could say you can live with your difficulties."
- "When the problems for which you are here will have disappeared."
- "When you can say, 'Of course, every day life serves us a fresh helping of problems, but I can manage.'"

In Laura's case I have shown how I have proceeded:

- The client gives a rating: Laura says 3.
- The therapist asks what is in this number, and what else, and what else.
- All answers are considered resources, achievements, and skills and appropriate compliments are given.
- Now the therapist asks either how this condition can be maintained or what could be the next small step.
- An observation task follows (explicitly or implicitly) from the answer.

Instead of asking during the session what the next small step would look like, one can give this question as a homework task, after the "what elses" have been exhausted:

> "If you agree, I would like to suggest that you take five minutes every evening to look over your day and ask yourself how you have been up and down on this scale. There will likely be moments where you were down to 2, but then there will be others where you pulled yourself up again and you came to 3 or even to 4. What would interest me very much is, when you rise to 3 again or even to 4, what you have done there, what has happened there. How did you do it? Or if someone helped you, how did you

use that help? Perhaps you could make a brief note of it so that you don't forget it, and next time we can talk about it."

This technique is particularly useful if time is up and we must conclude the session, or if the answers to the scales question have been hard to get.

A scale of hope for change can also be useful, as described here:

- "If 0 stands for 'I have no hope that I will ever solve my problems,' and 10 stands for 'I am sure that I somehow will find a solution,' how much confidence do you have that you will succeed?" And: "What gives you this confidence?" And: "What would have to happen so that you can become a little more confident?"
- "If 0 stands for 'I have no hope that I will ever reach my goal,' and 10 stands for 'I am sure that I will succeed,' how much hope do you have? And: "What allows you to put yourself at this number?" And: "What would you have to do to get just one point higher?"
- "If 0 stands for 'I am sure that I will never stop my bad habits, and that I can never become the person I want to be,' and 10 stands for 'I am sure that I will succeed,' how much confidence do you have on this scale?" And: "What allows you to put yourself at this number?" And: "What would you have to do to get just one point higher?"

If a client answers 5, for example, he or she suggests that he or she has a 50% chance of succeeding.

One can let a motivation scale follow on the hope scale:

- "If 0 stands for 'I don't have the smallest urge to do even the smallest thing to reach my goal,' and at 10 you would say 'I would do everything possible,' where would you rate yourself?" And: "What allows you to put yourself at this number?" And: "What would you have to do to get just one point higher?"
- "If 0 stands for 'I have no energy for it,' and 10 for 'I will exert myself with all my force,' where would you put yourself?" And: "What allows you to put yourself at this number?" And: "What would you have to do to get just one point higher?"

In his or her answer the client indicates how much he or she is ready to do what it takes. A client who answers 1 or 2 in fact is stating that the therapeutic relationship is at the uncommitted stage. It is better not to give this client any homework. If one feels one cannot do otherwise, then give nothing more active than an observation task offered without any obligation.

If the client rates him- or herself at 8 or 9, he or she is entering into a consulting or an experts' relationship. The client takes the initiative to work hard. One can give this client to-do tasks, even difficult ones like a "benevolent ordeal" (Haley, 1973). To the question of what is in their 8 or 9, clients often answer by talking about their values and their existential choices. This helps them to better succeed in adjusting their ethos and ETHOS while developing new habits.

Occasionally the motivation scale can be delicate to handle. If, for example, in marital therapy one spouse rates his or her motivation at 7 and the other rates motivation at 2, this can be the expression of a real difference between them. But sometimes it is only the expression of a momentary annoyance about something that has just been said. However, when the numbers are stated, they acquire an appearance of (pseudo) objectivity and afterwards they stand in the way of progress. For this reason it is better to use the scale only when one can suppose that both answers will be in the high numbers.

A coping scale such as the following is useful with depressed, discouraged, and complaining clients:

> "You are going through a terrible period in your life. I'm surprised that you still cope as you do. On a scale from −10 to 0, with −10 the worst it has been during the last six months and 0 where your problems are solved enough so that at last you could breathe again, where would you rate yourself now?" And: "What allows you to put yourself at this number?" And: "What would you have to do to get just one point higher?"

The therapist recognizes how heavy the weight is that clients have to carry. However, in the same movement she or he also turns their attention to their resources: They have survived; they have held out however bad the problems were; they have succeeded in limiting the damage.

The negative numbers in this scale fit better with the clients' pessimistic existential attitude: It is more acceptable to come back to 0 than to have to climb up to 10.

Relational scales can be used when working with couples and families:

- "If 0 stands for 'If this goes on for one day more, tomorrow I go to the lawyer,' and 10 stands for 'Well, our relationship is not so bad after all. If it goes on like this can we have still have a nice time together,' how would you rate your relationship" And: "What allows you to put your relationship at this number?" And: "What would you have to do to get just one point higher?"
- "If 0 stands for the absolute most abysmal point in your relationship, and 10 stands for 'It is all right again, we need no more therapy. We can solve our differences,' how would you rate your relationship" And: "What allows you to put your relationship at this number?" And: "What would you have to do to get just one point higher?"
- (Between parents and children): "If 0 stands for 'My parents still live in the Middle Ages,' and 'Tomorrow our son must go to the Borstal (a juvenile detention facility),' and 10 stands for 'We often have differences in opinion, but we can solve them together,' where would you put your relationship?

And: "What allows you to put yourself at this number?" And: "What would you have to do to get just one point higher?"

Everybody positions themselves on the scale. The numbers are nearly always different; an interesting discussion follows about the difference between the 4 of the wife and the 7 of the husband, for example. When the husband has given a 7 to his view of the possibilities in their relationship, and if one then asks what gives him so much hope and what his wife contributes to this number, his answers will be compliments to his wife. After this, one can ask of the wife what her husband does that still makes her put the relationship at 4. Her answers will be compliments to him. An example:

Simon is 70 years old and asks to consult because of a depression. He wants to commit suicide; he sees no reason to go on living. His life is an utter failure. He is an incorrigible gambler. He had stopped, but six months ago the game devil caught hold of him again. His wife Hannah has discovered his relapse; she also knows the size of his gambling debts. He stopped gambling again two weeks ago and only now he clearly recognizes that he has destroyed everything. His wife is the single person who is still important to him. Because of the danger of suicide, the therapist proposes to see them both as quickly as possible. They come the next day.

First the therapist joins Hannah. She uses the opportunity to make a catalogue of her grievances against her husband. After she has unburdened herself of her complaints it becomes possible to talk about something else. The therapist asks her to rate their relationship. Hannah rates it at 2. In this 2 are the good moments they have shared and the moments in which her husband has supported her when she was in trouble. To get to 3, she would have to be able to trust her husband again. Thereupon the therapist suggests a scale of trust.

He asks Simon how much trust he believes that his wife still has in him. Simon says 0. He is surprised when his wife says 1. She values the fact that both have come together to see the therapist. In order to get to 2, her husband would have to show her the statements of his bank account, so that she can follow the transactions. Both have separate bank accounts and until now her husband, out of shame, has refused to let her see his account. She says that this would improve not only her trust, but the whole of their relationship. Simon agrees to do what she asks.

Simon rates their relationship at 3. He loves his wife. She has always been a perfect wife to him, he says. All their problems are his fault. He has made a lot of mistakes. At 4, his wife would scold him less often. But Hannah answers that she could only do this if she had more trust in him. She speaks again about her hopelessness and her disappointments. She is afraid of the future. Now she talks about herself and her fears, and she stops blaming him. Now her husband can listen to her. The therapist compliments them both about this. He asks Simon to pay attention to what he will be doing every day to help his wife to trust him more.

There are also any number of ad hoc scales adapted to the clients' different problems, goals, and skills.

Observation Tasks

In these tasks the client the observes the problem sequences in their different aspects: under which circumstances the problems appear, what happens when they are there, and how they come to an end; what variations are present already, and what control the client already exerts.

Observation tasks are a staple of solution-focused cognitive therapy. In other therapy forms observation tasks mainly serve to get a clearer sight of the problem. Here their purpose is rather to look at the clients' skills, achievements, and resources. The clients observe what they are doing well already, in other words, how they are already doing their self-therapy. The focus is on the exceptions, the variations in the problem habits, and on the end of the symptom sequence, that is, on the amount of control the clients already exercise.

Observation tasks can (and often do) follow a scaling question:

- "May I ask you to pay attention until our next appointment to the occasions where you are little bit higher, one point or half a point higher on the scale. If you could observe what exactly happens at that moment, what you and maybe the others do, how that makes you feel, what thoughts come up."

Or:

- "I would like to suggest to take five minutes every evening—or if you prefer every second evening—to look over your day and see whether there have been moments where you were a little bit higher, one or perhaps even two points higher on the scale, and to pay attention to what has happened: what you have done, what your wife (husband, etc.) has contributed to this small step forward. How did you feel, and what did you think about it?"

Or:

- "I would like to suggest something that may be helpful. There will be moments when things are worse again and when you will slide down a

little on the scale. Life is like that; sometimes it gets really tough. But after
that, there will be moments when you come back on the scale to where you
stand now, maybe even moments where you climb a little higher, where
you succeed in something you didn't expect. If you could look and perhaps
write down in a few words what happened when you went up on the scale
again, what you did, how others helped you, what you were feeling, and
what you thought about it, that would interest me greatly."

Different observation tasks can give insight into the modalities of problematic
habits: how they start, how they end, how they vary.

Let us take as a first example an observation task for alcoholics. I use two
forms here. On the first the client notes the moments in which he or she has
felt some degree of craving, but did not drink (Figure 8.1). These are complete
exceptions, moments in which the problematic behavior was not produced.

If you didn't drink   Craving Diary

Name : ....   Week from .... to.......

DAY	HOUR	INTENSITY OF CRAVING 0-100	WHERE	WITH WHOM	WHAT FEELING	HOW DID IT STOP?	HOW DIFFICULT WAS IT? 0-100
Mo							
Tu							
We							
Th							
Fr							
Sa							
Su							

Figure 8.1 Craving Diary

On the second form the client records the occasions when he or she has drunk (Figure 8.2). The occasions where he or she has lost control entirely are noted as well as the moments where he or she has been drinking less than usual. These last are partial exceptions; they are instances where control was exercised up to a point.

Let us look at the different columns in these two forms.

1. Day: All days of the week are taken into account, the successful as well as the unsuccessful ones.
2. Hour: Some clients start in the morning and drink for the entire day. Other heavy drinkers never drink during working hours on weekdays and they start after work. This can be seen (and commented upon) as a form of partial control.
3. In Figure 8.1 the intensity of craving is recorded: the stronger the craving, the more the merit of the client who has resisted. In Figure 8.2, how much

If you have been drinking   Alcohol Diary

Name : ....   Week from .... to ......

DAY	HOUR	WHAT	HOW MUCH	WHERE	WITH WHOM	WHAT FEELING	HOW DID YOU STOP?	REMARKS
Mo								
Tu								
We								
Th								
Fr								
Sa								
Su								

Figure 8.2 Alcohol Diary

alcohol is consumed is recorded in units of alcohol (1 unit = 0.34 fl. oz.). The exact number is not very important. If the client has been drinking a lot, he or she may have forgotten how much was drunk, or he or she may lie. The client has been drinking too much at any rate. The important entries are the exceptions, the occasions when the client drank less than usual: How did he or she do that?

4.   Where? With whom? These columns address the circumstances, the oikos in which the symptomatic behavior happens: Is the client alone or in the company of friends when he or she has a craving or even starts drinking? Does he or she drink at home, during a meal, or in a bar? Changes in context can often be rather easily arranged.

5.   What feeling? What emotions, what pathos, has led to the craving or behavior: Was the client simply thirsty? Did he or she want a fresh beer on a hot day or a glass of red wine with the cheese? Was he or she at someone else's home and felt he couldn't decline? Was he or she nervous, stressed out, lonely, or depressed? Alcohol abuse is often not only an addiction and a habit, but also a solution for other problems. It may be necessary to address these.

6.   And then the most important column: How did the client succeed in stopping the drinking behavior (Figure 8.2)? What has he or she done to stop after n glasses? Or, in Figure 8.1: How did the craving subside without the client drinking any alcohol?

Generally, some of the answers are not usable: The client has stopped drinking because he or she has fallen asleep, or was so drunk that he or she remembers nothing. Other answers offer no solution in themselves but can be a good starting point for discussion: For example, the client had wine with dinner. The bottle was empty, and he or she stopped drinking. Did the client open another bottle? If no, why not? How did he or she succeed in that?

A client has left the bar and his friends when the card game was over. How did he succeed in not staying in the bar where the landlord is such a good friend?

Another client drinks only during the days in which she has what she calls her "terrors," that is, her recollections of the sexual abuse that she suffered. On these days she goes to the shop and buys two bottles of wine, which she drinks one after the other. When her daughter comes home from school, she finds her mother sleeping and she has to do the household chores. The client feels extremely guilty about this. Now, why does she buy only two bottles and not three? If she already limits herself to two bottles, could she perhaps on coming home pour half a bottle in the sink and drink only one bottle and a half? Or after the first bottle, could she go to bed and try to sleep? Or perhaps drink a little slower and, in the meanwhile, do the household chores? She has a close friend, the only one to whom she has confided her past. Could she call this friend before opening the first bottle and talk to her in order to feel less lonely?

We can distinguish two types of questions in these examples.

First we have questions like, "How did you succeed in doing this?"

The therapist aims to put to put into doubt the clients' conviction that they are powerless and irresponsible, that they lack willpower and strength of character: The clients are already practicing partial control, even if they and their relatives do not see it in this way. The aim of the treatment is then to help them improve this control. The clients already have some skills and resources; it will be easier for them to use these rather than to follow a pre-established protocol that calls for acquiring new ones.

It is not a problem if—as is very often the case—clients have no answer to the question: "How did you do it?" The important thing is first of all that they have received an indirect compliment to their self-efficiency, and second that their attention is focused on skills rather than on imperfections.

Second, we have questions that suggest a possible change in the behavior, the ethos, namely in either the ending of the symptom sequences, or in the oikos, the context in which they arise: "What would happen if you . . .?" It is not necessary that the clients act on these suggestions. If they choose to, why not? But it is more important that they are inspired to try out new approaches to their problems, that they focus on the changes for the better and that they become aware of the fact that they can choose. For this reason it is useful to offer several, not just one, suggestions and/or homework tasks they can choose from.

Returning to Figure 8.1, in the last column clients can write any remarks they wish to make. This again gives the opportunity to compliment them on their successes and their progress.

Almost all symptoms can be documented by means of an observation task. (Ready-to-print examples of all the forms discussed in this chapter can be downloaded from korzybski-international.com and drisebaert.org.)

For instance, the form for bulimia shows the following:

- In the first column, clients note all the instances where they could have succumbed to a bulimic attack, whether they did have one or not.
- In the second, they note the circumstances (i.e., place, time, and so on).
- In the third, they note the nature and intensity of their unwanted feelings (craving, hunger, anger, loneliness, etc.) on a scale of 0 to 100.
- In the fourth, they record what they did (bulimic behavior or something else).
- In the fifth, if they had a bulimic episode, they note how strong this was (100 = the strongest attack they ever had).
- In the sixth they describe how the symptom sequence came to an end.
- In the seventh, they reflect on how successful what they did (giving in to bulimia, or something else) was in reducing their unwanted feelings.

It often appears that a bulimic attack doesn't produce better results than another behavior or technique. Realizing this helps the client to remain motivated when the craving is strong.

A form for anxiety and panic consists of seven columns, as described here.

- In the first column, clients note the date or the day of the week.
- In the second, they record the time.
- In the third, they record the subject of the fear, what they were afraid of.
- The fourth lists who was there with the clients.
- In the fifth, clients note the intensity of the fear or panic on a scale from 0 to 100.
- In the sixth, they describe the method they used to control their fear.
- The seventh documents the results: How effective was the method chosen to calm down the anxiety? (Scale of 0–10)

Partners who fight a lot could use a double form. The first part of the form is for those occasions when the clients could have picked a fight but didn't, the second for when they had a fight.

- In the first column, clients note the time when a fight could have erupted but was avoided (first form), or when a fight did happen (second form).
- In the second, they describe the circumstances.
- In the third, they describe the nature of the emotions (e.g., irritation at unwanted behavior, annoyance at not feeling understood, feeling a lack of respect, etc.).
- In the fourth, they rate the intensity of the feeling on a scale from 0 to 100.
- In the fifth, they describe the occasion, the direct event that elicited the feeling.
- In the sixth column, in the first form they document what they did instead of fighting; in the second form they describe how violent the fight was on a scale from 0 to 100.
- In the seventh column, in both forms, they note how satisfying was the result. (Scale of 0–10)
- In the eighth column, in the first form, they note what happened afterwards; in the second form they describe how the fight came to an end.

One last example is an observation form for self-mutilation. Most of these clients are convinced that harming themselves is the only effective method of fighting against unbearable mental suffering (such as a flashback to a traumatic past): The physical pain supersedes the mental anguish.

- In the first column, clients note the time when the urge to harm themselves came up.
- In the second, clients note the circumstances (where were they, were they alone or not, did something happen that provoked the urge, etc.) .
- In the third, they note the nature of the emotion that led to the self-mutilation.
- In the fourth, they rate the intensity of this emotion on a scale of 0 to 100).
- In the fifth, they note whether they self-mutilated and if so, how deep was the cut or the burning.

- In the sixth, they note what they did differently if they did not self-mutilate.
- In the seventh, they note how successful the chosen method was (self-mutilation or something else, e.g., a technique like 54321).
- In the eighth, they note what they did afterwards.

In most cases, after a short time a client discovers that the intensity of the mental anguish does not correlate directly with mutilation: at times, the suffering was very intense and the client has succeeded in controlling it in another way; at other times, the emotion was not so intense and nevertheless the client has self-mutilated. The client also finds out that the other methods that she or he uses to counter the painful fascination are not less successful than mutilating. Now the client starts to doubt that self-mutilation is necessary and unavoidable, so she or he often quite rapidly stops hurting her- or himself.

The most helpful instances usually are the moments where the symptom context (the circumstances where the problem habit is produced) was there but the symptoms did not appear. For example, the alcoholic was in a pub and drank a soda; a domestic quarrel threatened to erupt, but the partners agreed to come back to it at a quieter moment. Instead of the symptom behavior, "the client does something else" (de Shazer, 1985). Here a new interactional chain is set in motion, out of which a new habit can arise.

Sometimes observation tasks acquire their therapeutic effectiveness through the attention that the clients have given to their problem. Alcoholics occasionally are surprised when they notice how much alcohol they actually have been drinking in one week. This helps them to pull themselves together and enter into an experts' relationship with the therapist.

One last remark: Observation tasks always are also indirect symptom prescriptions. The symptom must be produced if one wants to observe it. Very rarely this leads to the paradoxical result that the symptom behavior stops being produced. An example of this is a couple who often got into quite aggressive fights, although they loved each other very much and didn't want to quarrel. Paying attention to the very first interactions that started the quarrels led to raising their creativity in inventing alternative solutions. In a short time they succeeded in drastically reducing the frequency of their fights.

Prediction Tasks

In a prediction task clients try in the morning (or the previous evening) to forecast what their day will probably look like.

From a solution-focused point of view changes in the symptom behavior fundamentally must be considered as attempts at a solution, as a conscious or unconscious choice in favor of an alternative for the symptoms. Many clients however see this differently. They do not feel they have made a choice. In their eyes, changes appear arbitrarily and by chance, without any decision they made. To them, the thought, for example, that they could choose between having and not having a panic attack appears as preposterous. The therapist unsuccessfully tries to explain that symptoms are linked to a context, and that one can try to control the symptoms by changing the context. They cannot accept this at all: In their experience the fears emerge out of nowhere. They feel powerless; they feel they can do nothing at all to solve their problems.

At first sight the idea that they could forecast the intensity and the frequency of their symptoms seems absurd to them. How can one predict the unpredictable? Nevertheless, we do things like this every day when, for example, we decide in the morning not to take an umbrella for the day, or when we play the lotto. We forecast that today it will not rain, or that some lucky day we will choose the correct numbers.

In a similar way, we can ask clients (and/or family members) to forecast their feelings and their behavior. They can choose whether they do this on the previous evening or in the morning, if they do it on a daily basis, every other day or on days determined by tossing a coin.

The subject of the prediction may be the intensity of the symptoms as well as their frequency, how much control the clients will exercise and/or—if we use a scale—how the clients will rate themselves.

The therapist stresses that this is not about intentions (what do I want to do), but only about predictions (what I think will probably happen). Most clients however feel a natural inclination to make the prediction come true. Now we have a mixed congruent and paradoxical situation: permissive symptom prescription and stimulation of symptom control. One can strengthen this contradiction somewhat:

> "You have made the prediction in the morning and in the evening you will look to what extent you were right. Now let's say that on a scale from 0 to 10 you have forecast that you will reach 6. In the evening you find out that your prediction was correct or close to it: that is, you rate yourself at 6, or maybe at 5 or at 7. In that case, I would like to suggest that you give yourself a small reward. But attention! You do not reward yourself if you have reached 8 or 9. The reward applies to your cleverness and your self-knowledge when making the prediction. Anyway, the joy of having succeeded in reaching 9 or 10 will be a reward in itself."

Here follows an example:

Kate is a cleanliness freak. She vacuums twice a day and cleans the bathroom in the morning and in the evening. The table is cleared and washed up while her husband and children have the last bite still in their mouths. The atmosphere gets more and more tense, and her compulsive behavior is less and less tolerated.

Kate wants to change, but she doesn't know how. At first, the therapist tries to look whether she would agree to start with the washing up: Could she wait a little after dinner before clearing away the plates? But Kate has not come for such banal suggestions. She says it is stronger than herself: If it was that simple, she wouldn't need any therapy.

Then the therapist suggests choosing every day one of her "obsessions"—vacuuming, washing up the dishes, or whatever. She doesn't have to plan to do this activity less "obsessively," and she certainly must not change anything at all to the rest of the household chores. But she could try to make a prediction for the task she has selected: on a scale of self-restraint, where 0 would stand for a degree of cleanliness of which even Mr. Clean would be jealous and 10 stands for not cleaner than the average between three of her friends who clean well (without exaggerating).

If Kate finds out in the evening that she has not deviated more than one point from her prediction, she has won and she may reward herself with something that either she herself or the whole family will enjoy.

Kate is in a searching relationship with the therapist: "I cannot change, it is stronger than me." She refuses direct and congruent advice. The therapist uses a combined strategy to try and weaken this "resistance":

- Kate doesn't have to change anything; she just selects one item every day that she might perhaps change.
- She must not plan to change even this, just try to make a prediction.
- She determines her goal by making a comparison with three friends; this point is not discussed with the therapist.
- She must not reach this goal.
- Nothing is imposed on her, there are only predictions and observations.
- Everything is formulated permissively, but at each stage, moments of choice are inserted, putting in question her conviction that she cannot change.
- All changes that happen will appear to have come out of her own initiative, and can be commented upon at the next appointment.

This example also shows that, like an observation task, a prediction task contains an element of indirect symptom prescription: To achieve the predicted number, clients must produce and control the symptom at the same time. They have to voluntarily produce the symptoms, the emotions, the thoughts, and the behavior that they think of as involuntary. As the promoters of paradoxical therapy have shown (Selvini-Palazzoli et al., 1975; Weeks and l'Abate, 2001), one possibility for getting out of this paradox is to move into a meta position and to ask oneself: "What do I really want?"

Orientation towards the Future: The Miracle Question

The Miracle Question was developed by Steve de Shazer and Insoo Kim Berg at the Brief Family Therapy Institute in Milwaukee. It is probably the most helpful of all future-oriented techniques.

The Miracle Question gives the best results if the sequence described in this section is observed.

Introduction: Yes-Set

A Yes-Set is an Ericksonian technique in which the therapist starts with a series of truisms: assertions and questions with which the client can only agree. The Yes-Set fosters compliance.

THERAPIST: "Can I ask you a strange question?"
CLIENT: "Yes."
THERAPIST: "We're sitting here, it's a quarter past three now. When we are finished here, you will leave, you will do whatever you have to do, and then you will go home. In the evening you will have dinner, and then you will do whatever you do after dinner, watch TV or do something else, and then you will go to bed."

It should be noted that for a well-constructed Yes-Set, it is necessary that all the therapist's assertions can be confirmed only by the client. If the therapist just said: "After dinner you will watch TV," a client could ask himself whether he or she really wants to watch TV this evening and the Yes-Set would be interrupted. But here, as the therapist makes several banal statements in a row, the client starts to wonder when this strange question will be coming and can only agree with everything the therapist says. When the next statement comes—containing the Miracle Question—chances are that the client will agree again.

The Miracle Question

I will now provide a few options for asking this question.

Therapist: "Let's suppose that miracles can happen. And while you sleep a miracle happens. The result of this miracle is that the problems that you are here for are gone." (Another formulation: "that you can cope with the problems that brought you here." Or: "that you can say to yourself, 'Maybe this isn't paradise on earth, but if things go on like this, that's all right with me, I'm satisfied.'") "So tomorrow morning when you wake up the miracle has happened. Only you know nothing about it because you were sleeping. But then you will start noticing it. You will notice: 'This and this is so different, a miracle must have happened.' So how do you notice that the miracle has happened? And what else? And what else? And how will your husband (wife, children, etc.) notice it?"

If one wishes, one can stimulate the clients' creativity by creating a fairy-tale–like atmosphere, like so:

> THERAPIST: "What is your first name?
> CLIENT: "Anne."
> THERAPIST: "OK. Let's suppose that in the Catholics' heaven Saint Anne is sitting there while you sleep, and she is singing the eternal praise of God. She has been doing this day and night. Tonight she gets a little bored and she thinks: 'Why don't I do a miracle, just to keep in practice.' So she looks down and she sees you lying there, and she thinks: "Aha, there's an Anne! She is one of mine." She does a miracle on your person as you lie there asleep. And in the morning you wake up . . ."
> OR WITH CHILDREN: "While you sleep a gentle fairy comes and sits next to your bed. She looks at you lying there and she thinks: "I'm in the mood for miracles, I'll just do a quick one." She touches your shoulder with her magic wand and—abracadabra! The miracle has happened."

The Answer

In their answers clients describe how they want their life to be. Certain elements describe the absence of their problems; others don't have a lot to do with them: The class of solutions often does not have a lot to do with the class of problems.

For example, let's continue with Anne:

Anne is 45 years old and depressed. She has no energy; she cannot do her household chores anymore. She has a good job as an administrative secretary but she has been on sick leave for six weeks. Her sleep is bad and tormented by nightmares. She has no appetite but she hasn't lost weight: She eats lots of chocolates.

She feels lonely and abandoned. Her two sons are away at college and she sees them only twice a month. She misses them very much. Her husband is serially unfaithful; she has just learned that he has a new girlfriend, a young saleswoman. Anne feels old, not up to the competition. Four months ago she had a short affair herself with an old friend to whom she had cried her heart out. She broke off the affair because "she is not that kind of woman." If her sons had heard of it, she would have died of shame.

To the Miracle Question she answers:

"I would not be so tired when I wake up."

THERAPIST: "You would not be so tired when you wake up. So how would you feel that would be different?"
CLIENT: "Well, I would feel that I had a good rest. I would have slept well."
THERAPIST: "You would have slept well. And what would you do then, after you wake up and you feel that you had a good rest?"

The therapist repeats what the client says. When she hears it from someone else, it acquires more reality value. All answers are good, but negative answers need to be completed by positive ones because these direct the client's look toward the life they want to live.

CLIENT: "I would have a nice hot bath with a beautiful scent."
THERAPIST: "You would have a nice hot bath with a beautiful scent. And what would this feel like?"

The therapist helps the client to describe the state after the miracle in terms of a new habit (pathos, "rested"→ ethos, "have a bath"→ pathos, "feel like"), for example:

CLIENT: "It would be heaven."
THERAPIST: "Like heaven. And then? What would come after that?"
CLIENT: "Then I would have breakfast with my husband, and he would show more interest in me than in his newspaper."
THERAPIST: "How would he show his interest?"
CLIENT: "Oh, nothing special. He would ask how I had slept. Perhaps he would even give me a kiss when he came down."
THERAPIST (ENTHUSIASTIC): "He would give you a kiss? And how would you react to that?"

CLIENT: "Ah, it would be so beautiful. In himself he is a nice husband, you know, if he only . . ."
THERAPIST: "So you come down, you feel rested, you smell good after your bath, and then your husband comes down and kisses you—"
CLIENT: "No, actually, he would be down before me if I have taken a bath. He would have made coffee; he often does in the morning."
THERAPIST: "Oh. So you come down, feeling rested, smelling good, coffee is ready, and your husband kisses you. It would be beautiful if your husband gave you a kiss. Tell me, does it still happen occasionally that your husband gives you a kiss?"

The therapist follows closely the client's description of the state after the miracle. While repeating, he switches between the conditional and the indicative: this makes the description, that is already very concrete, even more realistic: It almost feels as if it is happening already.

CLIENT: "Yes, he does when he comes home, and also in the morning, in fact, if I do not look like a scarecrow. But then I can't help thinking of this hussy—"

The therapist investigates whether small parts of the miracle are not already happening. He also tries to construct short wished-for interactional sequences. He has not asked the question yet how she would react to a kiss, so he does now:

THERAPIST: "Now if, after the miracle happened, he kisses you, how would you react?"
CLIENT: "I would think only of us. I would act as if she didn't exist. I would kiss him and cuddle him a little bit—"
THERAPIST: "Would this be nice?"
CLIENT: "Yes, absolutely!"
THERAPIST: "And what else would be different when the miracle has happened? What else would happen?"
CLIENT: "What else . . . oh, one of my sons would ring me. And I would not eat so much chocolate. And I would put flowers on the table and cook a proper meal; I would enjoy it again."
THERAPIST: "That would be nice! What would you be cooking there?"

In itself it obviously is totally unimportant what the client will cook. The therapist only tries to help the client to picture the desired scene as realistically as possible by asking for specific details. He could have asked which flowers Anne would like to put on the table, or what her son would be saying when he called.

CLIENT: "Oh, I do not know yet . . . Asparagus perhaps, it is the season, and I haven't cooked any yet this year."

THERAPIST: "You would like asparagus. And would you do anything else when the miracle has happened?"

CLIENT: "Yes . . . Of course I would have to go to work again . . ., but perhaps not immediately. I would like to stay at home a little bit and work in the garden."

THERAPIST: "Yes, you would keep it quiet to begin with, stay at home and work in the garden. What would you do there? Mow the lawn? Weed the flowerbeds?"

CLIENT: "Not the lawn, that is for my husband. But weed, yes, and transplant. And pick flowers for the house. The peonies are blossoming now, and they are beautiful."

Now the therapist must decide whether the description of the desired condition is sufficiently complete and detailed, and whether it contains enough realistic elements that can serve as partial goals. Then he can choose whether he immediately proposes a scale or whether he first explores whether parts of the miracle have already occurred, perhaps during the last weeks. Because Anne has already indicated that this is the case, it looks as if this is the best choice.

First, however, a few remarks:

1. Parts of the answer to the Miracle Question refer to the absence of the client's problems ("not tired"). Others describe the recovery of old elements and even the forming of new elements of the desired reality. These have to do with regained dignity and better self-esteem, with existential choices and individual ethics, and with loving interactions with the client's relatives and friends.

2. The map is not the territory (Bateson, 1972; Korzybski, 1933): In the landscape of our problematic reality we try to find our way by looking at the problems ("I want to avoid this roadblock and nevertheless I keep running into it, I want to walk around this marsh and each time I fall into it"). With a future projection, the client is lifted out of the problem landscape and put down in the solution landscape. The map of the desired landscape is

drawn by asking questions about specific details and by completing the gestalt of the new habits: the thoughts, feelings, behaviors, and circumstances. Short interactional sequences are described: "I want to go this way. I want to sit down in this garden and see that it is good."

3. Open questions with a positive formulation turn the client in the direction of solutions ("What would you notice? What would you feel? What would you do?"). The therapist supplies the questions, while the client supplies the content. Closed questions ("Would you mow the lawn? Would you weed the flowerbeds?") are not put to suggest any solutions, but to stimulate the client's creativity and to introduce a context of choice. When asking closed questions, at least two choices should always be offered.

4. Clients sometimes give utopian answers to the Miracle Question. Overnight an amputated leg has grown back; the child that died has risen from the grave; in the morning the philandering husband lies next to the client and kisses her awake. The prodigal son comes home and the fattened calf is killed. No problem! If this gets too much for the therapist, he or she can say something such as "You know, nowadays everything goes down the drain. Even miracles are not what they used to be. What if only a small miracle had happened?" However, usually it is enough just to ask: "What else would be different if the miracle had happened? And what else? And what else?" Most clients quickly come to feasible, realistic answers—and if they don't, also no problem. The therapist simply does a scale with 10 standing for the unattainable ideal and the client will say at what point on the scale he or she will be satisfied.

5. A difficulty can arise if the client sees someone else as being changed by the miracle ("He would be more interested in me than in his newspaper"). In this case, the therapist helps the client to construct a desired interactional sequence. ("How would you react to that? And how would he then react to what you do?")

Sometimes, something unrealistic is expected from someone else, as in the following example.

A 28-year-old man, a teacher, has an affair with a colleague. Both are married. They move in together, but after a short time the girlfriend returns to her handicapped husband because she feels guilty about abandoning him. Now the teacher lives alone. He feels lonely and wants to go back to his wife. She does not refuse him, but wants some time to think it over.

This annoys the client. He explains that now he has understood that he has never really loved the other woman. In fact, he says, there was only a sexual attraction. The more he thinks about it, the more it is clear to him that he has always loved his wife and only her. Unfortunately, in saying so, he forgets that he has explained exactly the opposite to his wife a few months ago. At the time, he told her that he had discovered that he never loved her, and that he had found out what true love meant with his girlfriend.

Now he does not understand why his wife takes so seriously what was simply an error on his part.

As an answer to the Miracle Question he says his wife would agree that they live together again. Then all his problems would be solved. Now he is at 0 on the scale; if his wife said yes, he would be at 10.

He sees no possible intermediate stages.

The therapist now formulates the scales question in a different way: at 0 he would have no hope of going home, and with 10 the miracle would still have happened.

Now he puts himself at 4: He believes that his wife's main objection is removed, since he no longer lives with another woman. The initiative did not come from him, but, well, nevertheless, couldn't his wife be a little more flexible? Then the therapist asks him whether perhaps his wife could have other reasons that speak against his return. Although he sees none, he promises to ask his wife and to take her answer into account.

There follows a phase in the treatment in which he learns to cooperate with his wife, to respect her wishes, and to gradually become less dependent on her. After four months the treatment is concluded. They live together; both agree that they are more open, more authentic and more respectful in their relationship. Maybe, the wife says, the crisis was necessary.

BACK TO REALITY

Once the landscape of the life the clients want is mapped in enough realistic detail, the therapist can go different ways.

For example, the therapist could ask a scaling question: "If 0 stands for the worst it has been during the last six months (or: how things were when you called to arrange the appointment, etc.), and 10 stands for how things are after the miracle, where would you put yourself as you are now on a scale like that?" If Anne were asked this question, she would put herself at 1. The therapist could counter with: "At 1. And what allows you to say that you are at 1, and not at 2 or at 1/2?" The therapist would continue this line of questioning, as described in the chapter on scales (pp. 107–115).

It is very important to go on asking "And what else?" till clients run out of steam. This makes it clear to clients that they have skills and resources: However small, a part of the way to the preferred future has already been completed. Certain clients in a searching relationship have no idea how they can work on their problems, so it is natural that they expect the therapist to do all the work.

Describing what part of their miracle clients are already doing makes them aware that, one small step after another, they are going in the right direction: They are not helpless.

The therapist could also ask whether parts of the miracle are present already.

> Therapist: "Have there perhaps been moments in the last few weeks where something has happened already from what we have been talking about now?"

After the clients answer a (permissively formulated) task can follow:

> "Would you agree to regularly pay attention whether this happens again, or maybe something else that could also be part of the miracle?"

The therapist can also suggest as a task parts of the description that have not happened yet. She or he can formulate it as a simple observation task:

> Therapist: "Would you be willing, in the evening, to look back on your day and see where you were on the scale, and if you were on more than n (1, in Anne's case), whether something happened from what you have been saying about the miracle."

Or as a prediction task:

> "You could toss a coin, in the evening for example, and if it's heads, you try to predict if somewhere during the next day you will do some little thing that was in your miracle. You choose something hat you would really like to do or something that seems useful. If it's tails, you are free, you can do what you want."

> Or: "Perhaps you could try every morning to predict whether you will do something from what you have described," and so on.

Still another possibility is to suggest to try to act as if the miracle had happened (A Do-as-If Task).

Do-as-If Tasks make sense, for example, when clients are convinced that their feelings would have to change before they can do even a small step in the direction of their goals. One cannot force oneself to feel better or to desire to something. To change a habit directly from the pathos, the emotional side, is difficult. It is easier to behave in a different way than to feel differently. If the attention is then focused on one's own creativity and on the reactions of others, and if the changes must be tried out in certain moments only, then most clients show no resistance: They start carrying out small behavioral changes that, with some luck, can lead to a positive chain of actions and reaction.

Do-as-If Tasks can be applied in a particularly interesting way when treating a child. One asks the child to select two days in every week when he or she will try to do everything just as if the miracle had happened. Under no condition should the days be revealed to his or her parents. Then the father and mother must try to find out, independently from each other, which days the child has selected. They take note of it and do not talk to each other about it. If they wish, they can also judge the behavior of the child every day on a scale from 0 to 10, also without discussing it.

At the next appointment, they share what they have noted down. What almost always appears is that the parents have got it right on some days and wrong on others: For example, the father thought that the child has done as if the miracle had happened on Tuesday and Thursday. However, the child had chosen Monday and Thursday. Then what happened on Tuesday? Did a miracle really happen on that day?

The Letter from the Future

This technique from Yvonne Dolan (Dolan, 1991) can offer an alternative to the Miracle Question. Clients imagine themselves journeying into the future, as far away as they feel they need to solve their current problems. On this trip through time, they take with them someone who is close, a family member or a good friend whom they can trust and in whom they can confide. When they have arrived, they write to this loved and trusted person a letter in which they describe in detail how they are doing now (in the preferred future) and what they have done to get there. They choose an ordinary day to describe: what they do, how they feel, their thoughts and convictions, the relationships they are engaged in, what they have learned from their problems, and who has helped them and how.

The Older and Wiser You

This is another method of Yvonne Dolan's where clients consult with a future version of themselves, which she calls "The Older and Wiser You." Here is the set of questions that the therapist should ask:

Therapist: "Imagine that many years have passed, and you are an older, wiser version of yourself. You still enjoy a good health, you still look good and still have all your wits with you."

"If you look back at your life, what advice would you like to give to this younger X (client's name)?"

"If you look back on your life, what do you like most in the life that
   you have lived?"
"Is there something that you would rather have done less of?"
"Is there something what you would rather have done more of?"
"What do you hope that your children (grandchildren, etc.) will be
   glad to remember from their life with you?"
"On a scale from 0 to 10, how much is there already in your life as it
   is now that corresponds with these ideas?"
"What would be the smallest step to go up just a little bit on this
   scale?"

An interesting, slightly more hypnotic variant of this technique consists in
giving the task to the client to go for a walk somewhere where she will not be
disturbed. During this walk she will imagine that the older and wiser her is
walking at her side. The client will talk about her problems and the older and
wiser her will give her advice. Clients who have some experience with autohyp-
nosis often report that these walks have are inspiring. Some clients make a habit
out of it: from time to time, when they want to reflect on a problem that has
come up, they go and have a walk with their older and wiser self.

A Day in Your Life, One Year After

The task I call "A Day in Your Life, One Year After" can be useful for people
who have to make a choice that will affect their life in an important way. The
following example concerns a man who is deciding whether to leave his wife
and children and move in with his new girlfriend.

"A task that I think would be useful to you would be that you take a
sheet of paper and you write a description, as a reporter would write
an article for a newspaper, in which you describe in detail a day in
your life one year after you have decided to move in with your girlfriend. You can choose a weekday or a day in a weekend, according
to what gives you the most to think about, but you should take into
consideration all the consequences of your choice: Where are your
children? How much do you see them? How did they react to your
decision? How does your girlfriend manage with them? Also consider the financial consequences. In addition, describe which of your
friends are still friends with you and which ones are on your wife's
side, and so on.
   "Two days after this, write a new report, but this time describing a
day in your life one year after you would have chosen to stay with your

family. Include all the consequences: Did you break of all relations with your girlfriend or are you still seeing her from time to time? How are you getting on with your wife and your children?

Your descriptions should be quite detailed and at least two pages each."

This task is useful in two cases:

- If a client is in doubt and cannot make up his or her mind between different possibilities: The task helps him or her to think clearly about the consequences of each choice.
- If one has the impression that the client is going to make a decision without giving enough thought to the probable or even necessary consequences of his or her choice

For example, this task was useful in the following situation.

A 45-year-old man, an industrialist, stands before a heart-rending choice, worthy of a Greek tragedy.

He has hired a young woman as a marketing manager. Professionally, she is brilliant; as a woman, she is extremely attractive. He has fallen head over heels in love with her and the attraction is mutual.

He has only one desire: to go and live with the love of his life. Nobody, he forcefully asserts, can deny him the right to do this. But he doubts and hesitates: he has a 6-year-old daughter and a 4-year-old son whom he loves with all his heart. The thought that he would see them only during visiting weekends seems unbearable. There is another problem: his father has left him to manage the family business, but he has kept all the shares and he is very strict in questions of morality. There is a very real possibility that the client and his love would find themselves out of work. He has no qualifications; he never thought that he would need them.

His wife considers her rival a gold digger and demands that he dismiss her immediately. His answer to this is to threaten to kill himself.

His family doctor has hospitalized him with a diagnosis of a suicidal depression. This has given him some time to think things over, but at discharge he will have to make a decision. The nursing team is split in two: one side wants to appeal to his sense of morality and hold him to his duty. The others think that it is up to him and only him to make such a vital choice.

As a compromise the team proposes that he complete the "A day in your life, one year after" task with three different options. In the first version he has decided to live with his lover; he has been fired by his father and sees his children every second weekend. In the second version he has chosen to stay with his family; he has dismissed his girlfriend and has no more contact with her. In the third version he goes on seeing his lover in secret.

He sweats water and blood during the task, but he does it with the courage that comes with despair. With a broken heart he chooses his duty and financial security. He helps his girlfriend to find a new job and pays her a big severance. She soon finds consolation and comfort in the arms of a dashing young man.

The Five-Year-Plan

The Five-Year-Plan is useful with clients for whom it is difficult to develop a long-term vision. They live from one day to the other; they often change their opinions; and they rarely finish what they have started. They either complain about a lack of willpower or about Murphy's law that overwhelms them and that makes all their initiatives trickle away in the sand.

In the Five-Year-Plan clients are instructed to divide a big sheet of paper into columns, one for each of their goals. These goals can be personal, relational, professional, financial, or whatever other pursuits they are interested in. They then draw horizontal lines to create six rows of cells in this chart.

In the top row of cells they write down where they would like to stand in five years for each separate goal. In the second row comes what they need to have achieved in three years if they are to accomplish what they want in five years. The remaining rows of cells list what they have to have done in two years, in one year, in six months, and what they have to start to do right now.

The Five-Year Plan helps the clients to set down realistic aims that are compatible with each other, and to accomplish this in a reasonable amount of time.

The Spiritual Testament

This is a projection into the future that helps clients to reflect on their existential choices and their personal ethics. Here is the sequence of questions the therapist asks:

"May I ask you, at some time between now and our next appointment, to think about the following questions:

At the end of our life, we all die. You too will die one day. Now let's suppose that some of your family members are still alive when you die.

- Which memories of you would you like that your wife/ husband keeps and cherishes?
- And which image of you would you like your children to keep?
- And your grandchildren?
- And your friends? Your neighbors? Etc."

The Consulting Relationship

Clients in a consulting relationship want to be helped. They also realize that they cannot remain passive and that they will have to handle their problems themselves.

In the Bruges Model, we assume that in themselves (or in their environment, in their systems) clients have the resources they need to solve their problems, that is, to change themselves and their habits in the desired direction. The problem, however, is that clients often do not know how to make use of their resources in a helpful way. For example: When I bend my arm, the extensor muscles have to relax; when I stretch it, the flexor muscles relax. We all know how to let go and relax our muscles. Now the proprioceptive perception of relaxed muscles reduces anxiety to such a large extent that it is hardly possible to feel anxious while having relaxed muscles and a relaxed respiration. Unfortunately, phobic clients do not know how to force their muscles to relax during an anxiety attack.

In a consulting relationship, the client is willing to purchase our expertise. A consultant brings no new resources to a company but helps the personnel to acquire skills and methods by which they can make better use of their existing resources. In the same way, in a consulting relationship, the therapist helps the clients to develop techniques with which they can make better use of their resources.

One could say that clients in a consulting relationship lack resources of a second order: the knowledge and the skills necessary to apply their resources in the situation where they need them.

All the techniques and interventions that have been described for the searching relationship can be used: They stimulate the client's self-efficacy and self-management. One could say that from a solution-focused perspective it can be considered as a technical error to propose a technique as a solution to a problem. Techniques should be seen as tools to help the clients realize that they are able to control their symptoms, to solve their problems, and to accept their limitations. Once this has become clear, they can put our techniques in the trash bin and develop their own methods. A solution that the clients have found by themselves will enhance their self-efficacy. One they have learned from us will do so much less.

What follows is a selection of possible interventions. Different schools of psychotherapy all have developed interesting and often very efficient techniques.

In my selection, I have privileged methods that are simple to use. Readers who are expert in another form of therapy will doubtlessly find ways to adapt some of their most cherished procedures in a solution-focused way. The important thing here is to remember that the goals of therapy are the clients' goals and that therapists do not offer solutions: They help the clients to access and implement their own.

Some interventions aim to change habits mainly by entering through the logos aspect, others through the pathos, the ethos, or the oikos. I have tried to classify methods by their main point of entry. This classification is not important in itself. In fact, most interventions access more than one side of the habit gestalt.

Logos

Let us start with a few interventions that are mainly aimed at the logos.

Many symptom habits are maintained by unwanted chains of thoughts: Clients keep worrying about the same things and unwanted thoughts keep popping up. The contents are depressive, self-deprecating, or anxious. The corresponding emotions accompany them; they re-enforce each other.

Many clients recognize the irrational character of these worries and try not to think about them. They feel much relieved when they succeed in changing the current of their thoughts. They are happy to try any method that holds a promise of success.

Others feel justified in thinking their problematic thoughts. Clients subject to panic attacks see their fears proved right time after time. Hypochondriacs are convinced they have an illness that nobody finds; their bodily complaints are sufficient proof. Clients with melancholia (the deepest form of depression) are absolutely sure that their total ruin is imminent. These clients are still in a searching relationship with the therapist. One cannot expect them to collaborate actively. It is better to hold off on the methods that follow until a consulting relationship has been developed. If clients insist so much on getting advice that one feels one cannot hold back, one can at least "package" the technique one proposes as an experiment to be tried in the course of an observation task. For example:

> "Whether you are right or wrong with these thoughts is one thing. What is sure is that they make you suffer. And you will probably agree with me when I say that it doesn't help you any better if you are busy with them for five hours or if it's just half an hour. You just suffer more. So I would like to propose that you try out a couple of methods that can help you to take some control of your thoughts and to see what happens if you succeed in doing that: Do you feel different? Do you do something else? What other thoughts come up? You can tell me about this next time we meet."

We can distinguish two groups of techniques: those that aim to interrupt unwanted thoughts and those that turn the attention to something else.

Thought Interruption

THE THOUGHT STOP

Here follows a short description of this widely used technique. A more complete description can be found in Neenan and Dryden (2000).

After agreeing with the client what thought he or she wants to address, the client is asked to close his or her eyes and to concentrate on the unwanted thoughts. The client can signal to the therapist that the thought is present and strong by nodding his or her head, lifting a finger, or simply by saying so. The therapist then shouts "Stop!" and claps his or her hands. Normally, the client will be startled, will open his or her eyes and concede that the unwanted thought has momentarily disappeared. The procedure is repeated a few times, then the client gets the instruction to practice at home: At first he or she will retire several times per day, evoke the unwanted thought, then shout "Stop!" while clapping hands or banging a fist on a table or making whatever noise he or she prefers. Afterwards, he or she can visualize an open and shouting mouth, or a red traffic light, or whatever metaphor or symbol seems suitable.

The client is instructed to practice often and to use the technique every time unwanted thoughts come up. These will probably increase in frequency in the first two or three days, then rapidly decrease and become easier to control.

THE LAST FIVE MINUTES

Many clients have been trying without success to avoid unwanted thoughts. They have fallen victim to the paradox of the yellow polka-dot elephant on roller skates. The therapist explains that because of this paradox, people think about something every time they try not to think about it. It is a little easier to postpone a thought than to not think it, and if one knows one doesn't have to wait too long before coming back to it, it gets even easier. One way to do this is by using a technique that puts a limit on the time spent with unwanted thoughts: the Last Five Minutes. Every time clients realize they are thinking unwanted thoughts, they look at their watch. If the time is between five minutes to the hour and the hour (e.g., between 9:55 and 10:00) or between five minutes to the half hour and the half hour (e.g., between 9:25 and 9:30) they can worry to their heart's content, till the hour (or the half hour) strikes. In the other 25 minutes they should try to switch their attention to something else; they can promise themselves to come back to the unwanted thought during the next "last five minutes." Of course, if by then they have forgotten or do not wish to worry anymore, that is OK. For clients for whom the contents of their thoughts are important even if they do not want to worry about them all day, it is useful to add the Worrying Diary task to the Last Five Minutes.

THE WORRYING DIARY

This method is used primarily in conjunction with the Last Five Minutes or another of the techniques that aim to interrupt or deflect unwanted thoughts.

Clients who want to spend some time reflecting on their problems without being invaded by them can do so with this method.

Clients sit down with a notebook and write down all the worrisome thoughts that have occurred to them. This can last for a quarter of an hour or longer if necessary. They can do so as often as they want—once or twice a day or every two days, as they wish.

Writing down their thoughts helps the clients to bring more order to them and to differentiate between more and less important issues. In addition, reading what they have written three or four weeks ago often helps to put things into perspective.

A variant is the Worrying Walk. Here, clients briefly jot down the various contents of their problem thoughts. They then take a walk, during which they alternately concentrate on one item in the list, then switch and interest themselves in the environment: what flowers are in bloom, what birds are whistling, and so on. Then they return to the list and consider the following item, then again switch their attention to the environment. In this way they can exercise alternately concentrating on and switching off their problems.

THE WORRYING CHAIR

This technique aims at changing the situation in which the symptom sequence is allowed; it works by changing the oikos rather than the logos. I put it here because it can be useful to propose it together with the Last Five Minutes and the Worrying Diary as three techniques that limit symptom production. Clients can try them out at the same time to see which one suits them.

Clients allow themselves to worry only in a very specific situation, namely in a chair that is now devoted to this task. Whenever they find themselves having unwanted thoughts, they try to concentrate on something else, such as on the task or chore they are doing, or they can use 54321, or whatever method they prefer. If they don't succeed (or if they want to go on thinking about the problem) they go and sit in their Worrying Chair. There they do nothing but concentrate on the unwanted thoughts: knitting, watching television, reading, solving crossword puzzles, whatever else they might want to do has to be postponed. There is one exception only: They can use the time they spend in the chair to write their Worrying Diary.

When they have had enough of sitting there, they can get up and concentrate on something else, for example, they can do a household chore with mindful attention.

The fact that apart from the Worrying Chair, the rest of the house becomes a worry-free zone is greatly appreciated by some clients. A drawback is that it can hardly be done anywhere but at home.

Deflecting Attention

This group of techniques goes a little further than the preceding ones in that an alternative content is offered by the technique.

The Therapeutic Double Bind

Intellectuals and other complicated clients like the elegance of this technique, which was invented by Milton Erickson. As was often the case with Erickson, he gave several definitions of therapeutic double binds. I and my colleagues use this in our practice: a method by which the clients either keep the symptom under control, or if they let it happen, set themselves a sanction that is in itself a good thing. The upshot is that they do well—or they do well.

This technique distinguishes itself from other methods of symptom control that are usual in CBT by the following characteristics:

- Allowing the unwanted thoughts, feelings, and behavior leads to a reward rather than a punishment. This induces in the client a paradoxical relationship towards the problem habit: It becomes unwanted (in itself) and wanted (as a condition for the reward). The client reacts to this paradox by going into a (auto-reflexive) meta position: "Now, what do I really want?"
- The technique itself delivers agreeable and positive content that is used to replace unwanted thoughts and emotions.
- The unwanted habit becomes "infected" by the agreeable, trivial, or joyful nature of the sanction. This loosens the rigidity of the habit and makes the technique helpful even if the client does not apply it very faithfully.

In the following example, these points are illustrated.

A 40-year-old female client spent the whole day deprecating herself: "You've got teeth like a horse and a nose like a donkey; you can't cook; you never do anything right;" and so on. The therapist explained that, in her opinion, she was not a very good friend to herself. A good friend would tell her without embellishments what she thought about her; she would criticize her where appropriate, but she would also recognize the efforts she made and would appreciate what she accomplished even if it was not 100% successful. The therapist asked if she would agree for her to help her to become a better friend to herself. She then asked her how she could do herself a small favor if she became a good friend to herself. The client answered that she liked chocolates.

The therapist then proposed a double-bind experiment. On one hand, every evening the client would briefly review her day and look out for instances where she had been a good friend to herself. On the other hand, she would try to dam up that tiresome flood of self-criticism. To this end she would buy a box of excellent chocolates. She would try to concentrate on something else every time she criticized herself, no matter whether she thought she was right or she might be wrong. If she didn't succeed in diverting her attention, she would eat a chocolate and allow herself to enjoy it.

At first, the client thought this was not such a good idea. She thought she would put on a lot of weight from the many pounds of chocolates she would have to eat. But she agreed to give it a try with just one box and see what happened.

Two weeks later, she reported an unexpectedly successful outcome. In the first couple of days, as soon as she realized she was criticizing herself, the pleasure of a good chocolate and the fear for her weight immediately chased away the unwanted thought. After two days, she had started to be glad when she "sinned" and could get her "penitence." On the fourth day, at one point she had such a craving for a chocolate that she went to look in a mirror and told herself: "You look awful!" The she laughed out aloud.

She had also started to talk to herself as a good friend would. When she had to make a decision she would ask herself: "What would my friend say I should do?" This made her much less dependent on her husband, which in turn led to a few small fights—but in general both were very happy with her increased independence and her better mood.

Clients decide how they will recompense themselves (chocolates, cookies, cigarettes, etc.). If they have no vice, they can save money to buy something that otherwise would be too expensive: a trip to the city, a chic handbag, an expensive perfume. Or they can save for a present for their partner, or to go to a nice restaurant together, and so on. If they choose to save, it is a good idea to physically put the money in a piggy bank, or move it from one pocket to another, or make a note on a piece of paper.

Here are a few more examples of the double-bind technique.

- A young woman was plagued by the fear she might suddenly commit suicide by jumping in front of a passing truck or by throwing herself through a window (She was not suicidal; these were intrusive and unwanted thoughts.) She also was a moderate smoker. She committed to smoking a cigarette as soon as possible every time this happened. The triviality of the sanction contaminated the symptom and made it less compelling and less terrifying. When she also started to try and think of her compulsion every time she wanted to smoke, the unwanted thoughts stopped.

- An agoraphobic mother collected points every time she felt afraid of going out to shop. At 100 points she baked a cake for her children. Their enthusiasm made her feel less guilty and less depressed.

- A man's wife had left him. He took to pitying himself and to drinking in the evening to console himself. He agreed with his therapist that while having compassion for himself was all right, self-pity was not. Every time he caught himself at it, he would collect a point; five points equaled a drink in the evening. He negotiated that he could have two drinks for free; anything more would come out of saving points. As a result, he started drinking much less and took his life in his own hands.

Mindful Attention to the Five Senses

One of the simplest ways to deflect attention from one's inner monsters is by paying close attention to whatever one is doing and to what one's senses are feeding into one's brain. There is only so much room on the screen of conscience.

For example, when a phobic woman learns to concentrate on the hair color and cut of the four people before her in the queue, whether the color seems natural or whether it came out of a bottle, whether the hair has a coarse or a fine structure, whether it looks dry or well-nourished, and so, then the person in front of that, and so on to the clerk himself, if she then counts the number of bread loaves on the upper shelf, then on the second, and so on, there is not much room left for her fears. Neither is there if she concentrates on the color and texture of the peel of the potato she is peeling, how thin she can make the peel, how easily the knife slices through the flesh, and so on.

When walking in a street, the client can focus on successive red (or green, or blue) objects and notice the shades of red. Or she can listen to the different noises, concentrating on the noise one car makes, then another, and on the twittering of birds. Or she can feel the contact of her feet in her shoes with the pavement, or on the graceful, relaxed way her muscles move. Her fears will probably go on lurking at the back of her mind, but they will not be able to overwhelm her, and she will start to feel back in control.

The following methods require more time than the preceding two. Therefore they are less adapted to cut short single thoughts than to influence an unwanted stream of thoughts or a depressed mood.

The Good Message with the Non-dominant Hand

In the Good Message with the Non-dominant Hand by Yvonne Dolan (1988) the therapist tells clients they will need a piece of paper, a pencil, and another piece of paper on which they have written a positive message to themselves— something like "I always do my best to be a good parent to my children" and so on. This message should be 10 to 15 words long.

When clients are plagued by unwanted thoughts and feelings, they should copy this positive message with their non-dominant hand, taking care to make the letters as beautiful as possible. The therapist explains that they will need something between 3 and 5 minutes to copy the message and that during this time they will be occupied with writing as beautifully as possible, while at the background of consciousness the contents of the good message will be present, so there will be little room for the unwanted thoughts. When they have finished copying, they can of course start worrying again—or they may prefer to do something more useful.

The techniques I have described up to now are not meant to solve the clients' problems. Their only purpose is to provide a simple way to bring their thoughts under control. Clients seldom use them over a long time. As soon as the client realizes that they can control their thoughts, they no longer need them or they develop a method of their own. The next method however is so effective that many clients keep using it for a long time.

54321

This technique was invented by Betty Erickson, Milton Erickson's wife, and popularized by Yvonne Dolan.

The therapist asks clients to look attentively (mindfully) at five objects and to describe them aloud so the therapist can control if they are paying enough attention. Then the therapist asks clients to listen to (and describe) five sounds they hear; then to pay attention to five bodily sensations; then to four objects, four sounds, and four sensations; then to three objects, three sounds, and three sensations; then to two objects, two sounds, and two sensations; and finally to one object, one sound, and one sensation.

A great advantage to this method is that it can be used anywhere and under all circumstances: There are always things to see, sounds to hear, and sensations to feel.

54321 can be used as a relaxation method if clients sit or lay down in a comfortable position. Clients who are trance-sensitive should stretch after 54321 and walk around for half a minute. These clients should make use of the technique with care if they have to drive a car or operate a machine.

The technique can be used as a sleep induction method, in which case a few adaptations are necessary. For the visual part, clients can represent to themselves objects in a place they like, such as their living room, a garden, a mountain path, and so on. In general, there are few sounds in the bedroom: one's own respiration (one can count the expirations) and maybe that of one's partner. Of course, there are any number of proprioceptive sensations.

An adaptation by Yvonne Dolan is 54321 Plus (Dolan, 1991): Clients alternate between visual, auditive, and proprioceptive sensations where they are, and these sensations (which they represent themselves with closed eyes) in a safe, comfortable, and/or cozy place.

I have developed one last version of the technique: 54321 with Acceptance, Joy, or Gratitude. For each object, sound, or bodily sensation, clients ask themselves: Can I be glad about this? Can I be grateful? Or can I just accept it as it is? For example, I see my cup of coffee and I'm grateful to the person who made it. I see velvet red gloxinias flowering on the windowsill and I'm glad about them. I hear a jackhammer in the street and I don't like that sound, but I tell myself that there is work out there that has to be done and I accept it.

This version is quite useful with light to moderate depression. In severe depression clients may find it helpful if they add, "If I were feeling better, I think I could be grateful or glad about this, or I might be able to accept it. Right now I cannot feel joy or gratitude or even acceptance, but I can think about these feelings."

Ethos (Behavior and Existential Choices)

The good message with the left hand, the therapeutic double bind and the versions of 54321 do not limit themselves to interrupting unwanted thoughts. They also offer positive content. They help clients to divert their attention away from what they do not want and to what they do well already and what they want to do well in their life: to their skills, their resources, and their existential choices.

ethos (BEHAVIOR)

The next two methods are mainly directed to the ethos as behavior.

Not Thinking about Something

The therapist gives a task where a client should go on a two-hour walk. During the first hour he or she can think about whatever comes to mind. During the second hour they *cannot* think about something that the therapist determines. This concerns a suggestion that the therapist does not want to make directly because the client would most probably reject it. For an example of this technique, review the following case study.

A 40-year-old man came into therapy after a serious suicide attempt. He considered his whole life a failure. A third and last child, he had been much protected by his mother and considered to be somatically and mentally weak by his father, who had been a self-made man and owner of two factories. After his death, the client's two elder brothers had succeeded their father in running the factories; for him, a sinecure had been reserved, a small department where he earned good money and had as good as no responsibilities to bear. He had married a very successful scientist who was vastly his superior academically and intellectually.

The therapist saw him as a gentle, sensitive, and artistically gifted man whose talents had never been fostered. His history showed that his mother had had similar talents to his and that his father had greatly admired her for this. The client had rebuilt and refurbished his house with great taste. Also, his little department was running perfectly.

The therapist told him that a walk in the morning is an excellent antidepressant. He might try to walk twice a week for two hours; in the first hour, he could let his thoughts wander where they wished, but in the second hour he was to concentrate on the beauty of the flowers and the plants on the wayside, he might even take a botanical handbook to look up their names. It was of paramount importance that during this second hour, he should not think about the things he had done so far that his father would have been happy about (or maybe even proud of) if he had still been alive.

It took some patience on the therapist's part to convince the client to go for a walk early in the morning. He preferred to stay in bed a little longer. However, he had to lose weight. With some reluctance he agreed to do the task.

One month later, he started an antique shop as a part-time activity. Six months later, his eldest brother suffered a heart attack. The client took over as a CEO on an interim basis. He did so well that his brother went into retirement and let him go on running the business. He did this very successfully for two years, then sold out for a huge price to a multinational and devoted himself to his antique shop and his collection.

The suggestion not to think about what his father would appreciate in the client as he is now implies that the therapist believes there are reasons that the father would have approved of him. Because of the yellow polka-dot elephant paradox, the client cannot help but having instances of this popping up all the time while he tries to do the task, and as he has to chase them from his mind, he doesn't have the time to rationally contradict them: There is no time for critical dialectics. This creates the opportunity for existential re-orientation.

In addition, chance gave the client a strong push in the back. As the saying goes, be prepared when opportunity knocks at your door. In this case, the client was ready.

The Guardian Angel

There are two versions of this technique: a non-hypnotic version devised by Yvonne Dolan (1988), and a hypnotic adaptation of this by myself.

The hypnotic version can be done during a session, after which clients, if they wish, could do it at home as an auto-hypnotic exercise. The therapist explains that he or she wants to help the client to find within themselves the strength, the resources, and the qualities they will need to solve his or her problems and to change his or her habits.

> "If you agree, I would like to propose this exercise with your guardian angel. Let's assume there are guardian angels and we all have one. Please close your eyes and imagine your guardian angel sitting on your right shoulder. He's always been there but you have never noticed because angels have no weight. But he sits there and he knows you through and through: He has known you since you were born. He often talks to you and gives you good advice, but you have never heard it: Angels have no voice. But when you have good ideas and comforting thoughts, or when you feel inspired, it may well be that your guardian angel is whispering in your ear.
>
> "So I would like to propose, now that you are sitting there so quietly, and you can sit there as calmly as you want to, to let your thoughts float freely around, not to search. Just let rise by itself what you need, waiting for your guardian angel's whispers. You do not hear your guardian angel, but you can let the thought about the strength you need and that is in you arise, and wait until your guardian angel—who knows you through and through—lets a good quality you have come up in your mind. Let your mind float freely, and when the good thought, that good quality, is there, you can open your eyes."

The therapist waits until the client opens his or her eyes and then asks what name could be given to the quality. Suppose he or she says "joy."

> "Joy. Please close your eyes and go back in time, in the recent past, until a moment comes up where you felt that joy. Take your time, and when such a moment is there, you can show it to me by simply nodding your head."

When the client has nodded his or her head:

> "Right. You are in this situation of joy. Please look around you: Who is there with you? . . . What are you doing? . . . Look at the colors in this situation of joy. . . . And maybe while you are in this joy there are a few

words, a sentence that sums up this situation of joy . . . maybe there are words like that, maybe not . . . and while you stay in this joy you can let this feeling of joy flow through your whole body . . . everywhere . . . it is your joy . . . (The therapist waits for about 45 seconds.) And while your joy flows through your whole body, there may be a place somewhere in your body where you feel your joy even better than elsewhere . . . Take your time and when you're ready, you can open your eyes."

If necessary, the same induction can be repeated once or twice with the guardian angel suggesting a second, a third quality. These are anchored in the same way.

One can leave it at that. The exercise was suggested in the context of the clients' problems; the suggestion is implicit that the clients can address these with the qualities that came up. Or one can give an observation task where the clients regularly look at their day: Where have I used these qualities? A third option is to, during the session, help clients to integrate the suggested quality into the problematic situation. Let us keep the quality of joy for the sake of this example:

"If you wish, we can now complete the exercise by helping you to take your joy into a situation where your problem was present (Replace the formulation "Where your problem was present" with a description of the problem: "Where you were afraid, where you felt sad, etc."). You can close your eyes and go back to such a situation in your recent past. When you have a situation like that, you can nod your head.

(Client nods). "Right. Look where you are, who is with you, what you are doing. And look at the colors in this situation where it's hard for you . . . Try to feel your (sadness, fear, anger, etc., whatever the bad feeling the client is complaining of) as strongly as possible . . . OK. Now open your eyes . . . On a scale of 0 to 100, where 0 stands for no (sadness, fear, anger, etc.) and 100 stands for the worst (sadness, fear, anger, etc.) that you ever experienced, where would your feelings be now?

(The client gives a number). "OK. So now let's get back to your joy, and you can go back to the situation where you felt this joy, your joy, and briefly look again where you are . . . what you are doing . . . the colors . . . and concentrate on your joy, where you feel it strongest in your body . . . and keep that, keep feeling this joy, there where you feel it strongest, and take it into the situation of (sadness, fear, anger, etc.) . . . You can keep your joy inside you, there where it's strongest, and take it with you . . . because it's your joy . . . and go on feeling your joy there inside you in the situation of (sadness, fear, anger, etc.) . . . and see what happens when you're there and your joy stays inside you . . . see what is different . . .

"OK. You can come back again. Open your eyes. How high would you rate your (sadness, fear, anger, etc.) now on that scale?" (Hopefully the client gives a lower number than the first time). "Right. Now what you can do is this, you can do this exercise a few times at home, and when you feel you have mastered it, then you can try and do it in a situation when your (sadness, fear, anger, etc.) arises."

Confrontational and Paradoxical Interventions

In the 1930s, Frank Dunlap (1928, 1930) and Viktor Frankl (1960) were the first to develop paradoxical procedures wherein clients were asked to exacerbate their symptoms instead of avoiding them. In Frankl's Paradoxical Intention procedure, for example, a girl who suffered from erythrophobia when addressing someone to whom she felt inferior was told to say to herself: "I want my face to be as red as possible, as red as a tomato, as red as the cloth the torero holds out for the bull." Likewise, a man who trembled when people looked at his hands had to try to tremble as hard as possible. A variant that addressed sexual problems was that a man with impotence shouldn't care about his erection but concentrate exclusively on his lover and only try to give her as much pleasure as possible.

The rationale for these methods came from the paradox of forced spontaneity: One cannot produce at will automatic neuro-vegetative processes like blushing, sweating, or trembling. These are elicited by the fear that they may come up. It is difficult to will and fear something at the same time, so the symptom disappears (when the technique works). In the sexual version: One cannot willingly produce a spontaneous behavior, which is what a man does when he wills an erection. Concentrating on his lover's pleasure not only makes for better sex, but also creates the condition for the spontaneous behavior that is an erection.

The Achilles heel of these early confrontational methods lay in the difficulty to motivate the client to try to apply long enough a method in which they didn't believe. They have a historical importance in that (together with Milton Erickson's symptom prescription techniques) they paved the way for the paradoxical methods of the Milan school and the MRI in Palo Alto, as well as for Frank Farrelli's provocative therapy and for the confrontational techniques in CBT. These last undoubtedly count among the most successful procedures in therapy, but they are not so commonly used in SFCST for practical reasons:

- Single sessions can last for up to two hours, sometimes more; for many therapists, this not easy to schedule.
- Some of the techniques are felt as traumatic by the clients.
- The clients must unambiguously stand in a consulting relationship to the therapist. As long as they remain in a searching relationship ("It's stronger than me") they refuse to engage in the procedure or, worse, they drop out of therapy.

More "gentle" techniques can help clients who hesitate to engage actively in therapy (who are still with one leg in a searching relationship) to cross the threshold and take their change in their own hands. The following sections describe a few techniques that clients don't find too difficult.

Write, Read, and Burn

Steve de Shazer and Insoo Kim Berg developed this simple method for bringing intrusive thoughts and images under control: The clients should retire to a place where they will not be disturbed. There they write down their unwanted thoughts, feelings and images. They can also draw them or do whatever makes it easier to clearly express themselves. They then read their notes to a person whom they trust, if available, or to themselves. Finally, they tear the paper apart and burn it.

This task is best combined with a technique that links to positive contents, such as the Three Questions for a Good Life, the Miracle Question, the Guardian Angel, or 54321 with Acceptance, Joy, or Gratitude.

The Three Pictures

For this technique from Yvonne Dolan (1988) clients provide themselves with paper, colored pencils, and whatever other material they want to use to draw or paint a picture. They then create three pictures:

1. A picture of the thoughts, feelings, behaviors, and images that are connected to unwanted thoughts;
2. An image showing what they would like to do instead of the unwanted habit;
3. A picture symbolizing the way in which they go from the first to the second condition.

After this, they can talk about the three pictures with a trusted person or speak about them aloud to themselves. Finally, they tear up and burn the first picture.

Panic in the Bathroom

In this procedure, adapted from a technique invented by Aline Vecchiali-Roux (personal communication), clients train themselves to concentrate on their anxious thoughts, to elicit feelings of fear and panic, and then to switch them off. This should be proposed only after clients have learned to relax and control their breathing.

In the morning, the clients get up half an hour before the rest of the household. They retire to a place where they will not be disturbed, such as the bathroom. They take things that will help them to concentrate their attention, such as crossword puzzles, a laptop game, cross-stitch needlework, and so on. They then spend five minutes trying to evoke all the fearful things that could happen during the day to come. They should pay close attention to the bodily manifestations of their fears and even try to stimulate them. However, they can continue breathing calmly.

After five minutes, they break off the exercise and concentrate on the crossword puzzle or whatever they brought along. After five minutes of that, they try again to evoke their fears about the day to come. If five minutes is not long enough to work up a good anxiety, they can stretch the confrontation to ten minutes. As soon as they think they are ready for it, they can insert into the representation of the phobic scene the diverting techniques they will use in vivo: describing the hair of the woman in front of them in the queue, counting the packets of chewing gum on the counter, and so on.

As one can see, this technique amounts to a limited confrontation in sensu combined with an exercise in controlling the unwanted feelings and a paradoxical effort to will spontaneous manifestations.

With this kind of techniques, it is useful for the therapist to enquire in detail about the successes the client obtained, and to qualify the failures as only to be expected.

Do Something Else

From chaos theory one knows the proposition that the flutter of a butterfly's wings can cause a tornado hundreds of miles away. A very small change in the sequence of a client's problem habit can be the beginning of a more radical change.

Luckily, fluttering butterflies rarely have an impact on weather conditions, and snowballs seldom cause avalanches. For that to happen, preexisting instability must be important. All the same, it can be useful to insert small changes between the links of the symptom sequence. Small alternatives are introduced into the problem habit, so small that the clients do not object to them, even if the habits are fully automatized and rigidified. With obsessive-compulsive habits, bulimia, and dependencies in particular, small changes can be introduced that elicit no resistance, but that change the context just enough so that the clients get the feeling they have some control over their habits after all, and so feel emboldened to make bigger changes. With many small steps one can go a long way, as shown in these examples.

> • A middle-aged couple said they were drinking half a bottle of whisky and a bottle of wine each and they wanted to do something about it. They owned a small factory. The wife would get up at 4:00 A.M. and supervise the morning shift; at noon they lunched together, and the husband took over for the afternoon shift from 1:00 to 8:00 P.M. The first habit they wanted to tackle

was the two double whiskies they both drank before lunch. When they came back two weeks later, the husband was down to half a bottle of wine in the evening and no spirits. The wife said that she felt she needed her whisky at noon to relax, although she knew that she must stop it. The therapist said that he could propose something that might help her, only it would cost a little money. She said she was ready to give it a try. The therapist then told her to pour herself her normal measure, then pour half of it in the sink, then drink the other half, pour herself another measure, pour half of it away and drink the other half and so on until she had drunk her usual amount. She soon followed her husband's example and started successfully to control her drinking.

- A grossly overweight client was eating huge amounts of food at each meal. The therapist suggested that she serve herself a plateful that she considered a normal meal. After eating this, she would go to another room and watch television, read a book, or do whatever she fancied for a quarter of an hour. Then she would come back to the dining room and eat as much as she wanted. As expected, a feeling of satiety started to develop and after a few weeks she was able to eat sensibly, which, in combination with an exercise program, helped her to lose weight.
- A bulimic client passed a bakery on her way back from work. Every evening she bought 15 doughnuts to eat for her dinner. Looking for resources, the therapist found out that she lived on the first floor of a house with a small garden and a shed where she parked her bicycle. She wanted to do some exercise but she had time for this only in the evening, and after she had eaten her doughnuts she lacked the stamina to do it. The therapist asked her if she would agree to try out a method that would make her do a little exercise, not too much, and maybe reduce her doughnut consumption. She agreed to try it out. The therapist then proposed that for one week she would take three doughnuts up to her flat and eat them, leaving the rest in the shed with her bicycle. After eating the first three, she would go back for three more, and so on, until she had eaten them all. The following week she would take only two doughnuts at a time, and during a third week only one. She came back to report laughingly that she had failed at her task. In the third week, she had stopped going back to the shed after ten doughnuts. The rest didn't seem worth the effort. Now she bought only ten. She suggested that she would cut back

to nine doughnuts, then to eight, and so on, when she felt ready for it. The therapist agreed.

- A mother had lost her 5-year-old child and was still in deep mourning four years later. She was brought by her husband, who complained that she didn't properly care for him and their other two children. She was not interested in any therapy that would help her to mourn less, but she agreed that she should somewhat change her attitude towards her family—though she didn't see how she would be able to do that (therapeutic relationship between uncommitted and searching). The therapist learned that she had a fixed routine every morning: After the children had gone to school and her husband to work, she would go to the cemetery and spend half an hour there, then to mass, then to the supermarket. The therapist suggested that she change the sequence of these activities at random: one day mass would come first, then the supermarket, then the cemetery; the following day the supermarket would be first, then mass, then the cemetery, and so on. In addition, the therapist suggested that her dead son could help her in relation to her family: As she talked with his spirit every day before his tomb, she could ask him what he thought she had done well the day before for her husband and her other sons. Maybe he would even have suggestions for her on what to do during the day to come. This helped her to accept that change was possible and even desirable and also wholly compatible with her love for her lost child.

The Expert Relationship

The expert relationship is all about self-management and self-efficacy. The therapist acts as a supervisor to clients who devise and implement their own therapy.

In the expert relationship, clients formulate a workable request for help. They show themselves willing to do their share of the therapeutic work. They set clear and achievable goals, and they have not only the resources but also the skills they need to change their habits effectively. They are the experts on their own life, on what they want, and how they can make it happen. The therapist is an expert in general but focuses on procedures and methods. Therapy becomes a conversation between experts.

In most cases, the therapist's task will be to make use of his or her general knowledge to accompany clients in developing an effective strategy.

Often it is sufficient to focus on variations in the habits that were there before therapy, or that come up during therapy. For intelligent and creative therapists there is a danger here. The changes and the solutions that the clients make are generally preferable to those that the therapist comes up with, because they foster the clients' self-efficacy. We had just devised an elegant, subtle, and inventive task! The client's solution seems trivial by comparison. Too bad! We must shelve our superior knowledge and use modesty and restraint. When clients are making progress toward their goals, we should accompany them only from behind, so as not to get in their way.

What is talked about during therapy now consists of what is better, how did the clients accomplish this, what does this show about their strengths and their possibilities, and what needs to happen next.

When the therapist now asks: "What is there that still has to change before you can say you no longer need me?" the answer may come: "Nothing really, I think I can go on by myself now." At this point the therapy is done.

At this stage, time and again it happens that the therapist still sees problems that he or she is not convinced that the clients can solve on their own. In short, the therapist would like to help when no more help is asked for. Again: modesty and restraint! It is rarely a good idea to suggest to clients that they are less capable than they think themselves. One small exception to this rule is that in ambulatory therapy, research has shown that clients make most progress in the first six sessions. It has also shown that just one to three sessions more help to stabilize the changes. So if clients are content with the progress they made in four to six sessions, it may be a good idea to see them for one or two sessions more. These findings are to be expected from the theory of habits: As clients develop new and more satisfying habits, these need to be made automatic and to come up in preference to the unwanted ones; just wait one or two sessions more (i.e., two to four weeks) and they will be more safely anchored in the brain.

At this stage, one can point out a paradox in the therapeutic relationship. As long as clients are in an uncommitted relationship and do not ask for help, no therapy should be done: What should be done is to create a context in which a request for help may come up. In the searching relationship, in which clients do not show themselves ready to work on their therapeutic goals, the therapist should not attempt to do the therapeutic work in their stead, but only try to create a context in which clients will agree to work on their therapeutic goals. In the consulting relationship, the therapist does not do any therapy; he or she only tries to help clients to develop the skills that are necessary for therapy. Finally, in the expert relationship, the therapist also restrains from doing therapy: The clients do that themselves. The whole art of the therapist, therefore, is never to do any therapy as such, but to limit him- or herself to be the context and the tool for the clients with which they can make their own therapy.

Note

1. This was clear to the BFTC group, but unfortunately the choice of the words led practitioners to understand them as categories that clients belonged to.

Part III

Placebo Factors

9 Hope, Confidence, Allegiance

Jerome Frank's study of placebo factors in *Persuasion and Healing*, his seminal work (Frank & Frank, 1961), led him to define them as composed of hope and allegiance. In this study, the first major one to pick up the thread that Saul Rosenzweig had started, Frank compared not only the major (then existing) schools of psychotherapy, but also healings by sorcerers and quacks, and "miracles" in Lourdes and similar places. He confirmed Rosenzweig's Dodo Verdict and elaborated on it, founding the modern science of comparative psychotherapy. He found, among other insights, that in all these disparate forms of healing, the same placebo factors as in pharmacotherapy were active, both with the therapist and with the clients: hope that this treatment will work for this client; confidence that the diagnosis and the treatment method are right; and allegiance to the school of therapy the therapist belongs to.

Hope and Confidence

The English word *hope* has the same etymology as the verb *to hop*: The image that springs to mind is that of children hopping in the expectation of a treat. Hope makes us confident that change is possible, that good things can happen, that we can attain our goals, that we will be able to live as we wish to live. We are not sure yet; things may still go wrong, but we expect them to go right.

Hope is always hope for something: "Faith is not a preoccupation with the object of the faith. Fear, nostalgia and hope, to the contrary, are always turned toward their object" (Wittgenstein, 1989).

In hope we are turned toward the future. The "preferred future" is the condition we hope for. The optative expresses itself in satisfaction and gratefulness when we look at the past and the present, and in hope when we look to the future.

Maybe a human being cannot live without at least a sprinkle of hope: How should a human being behave, about whom one would say: he never hopes?— The first answer is "I don't know." What I could say is how a human being should act who never longs for something; or who never is glad about something; or who never is scared, or who fears nothing (Wittgenstein, 1989).

Hope is potent. Many grandmothers, most hands-on workers in suicide prevention (e.g., Ackerman, 1994; Quinnett, 2000, p. 205), and especially the real experts—our clients—have always known that "even a single molecule of hope" (Quinnett, 2000, p. 205) could make a real difference (Fiske, 2008).

Hope can be tainted with the fear that the hoped-for condition never happens—or it may betray us, as Nietzsche wrote in his discussion of Pandora's box (in which, after all the plagues had flown out, only hope remained): "Zeus namely wanted that Man, however tormented by the other evils, would not throw away life, but would go on letting himself be tormented by ever new ailments. That is why he gives Hope to Man: in truth, she is the worst of all evils, because she makes the agony go on and on" (Nietzsche, 1967).

With Faith and Charity, Hope is one of the three major virtues (and mercies) in the Christian faith, the one that, according to Martin Luther, epitomizes it.

Whatever Nietzsche may have thought, hope is essential to the idea of human existence as an endeavor: "What is necessary is to learn to hope. Hope does not renounce, it is in love with success instead of failure" (Bloch, 1985). For Bloch, hope is always an expectation of what is possible. If not, it becomes false hope—an illusion or a utopia.

Research has confirmed Frank's views about the importance of hope for a successful therapy, whatever the therapeutic school. Clients need to work on recovering or developing good habits; hope of attaining their goals is the strongest motivation possible.

So here are some of the most effective ways of fostering hope and confidence:

- Expressing, verbally and non-verbally, hope that clients will succeed. As Fiske notes (2008): "Positive treatment outcomes are more likely when clients perceive that their therapists have hope for them (Bachelor, 1991). This finding does not mean that we should meet every new client with a hearty 'I'm hopeful about you!' It does suggest, however, that we have an explicit responsibility as helpers to do whatever is necessary to keep our own hopes alive."
- Searching for partial solutions, exceptions, and resources in clients and in their environment.
- Searching for skills, good habits that the clients practice in other contexts than the problematic situations.
- Looking at past successes and accomplishments.
- Asking about pre-session change: If there is already some change for the better, however small that may be, it is proven that change is possible.
- Asking the Three Questions for a Good Life: a focus on what goes well in the client's life gives confidence that the wished-for existence is possible.
- Scales of confidence: "If 10 stands for "I'm sure I will succeed," and 0 stand for "I'm certain I will not get any better," where would you stand now? And what allows you to say you are at *n*?"
- Setting a homework task of looking at what happened every time the clients went up a little on their scale, even if they went down before going up again.

- And last but not least, eliciting client feedback within questions like "Is this helpful, what we're doing now?" and eminently, through the ORS and the SRS, that foster a sense of shared responsibility and shared efficacy: "Together we can do it."

Allegiance

If the therapist and/or client are convinced that this therapeutic procedure is the right one for this client and this problem, the results will be better than if they are doubtful.

This contaminates the Dodo Verdict with a small paradox: "All therapy models have equally good results, except my model, which is better than the others. And this is true for every therapy model."

Bibliography and Works Cited

Ackerman, N. (1994). *The psychodynamics of family life.* Jason Aronson, Lanham MD.

Ambühl, B. & Schiepek, G. (1994). Soteria-ein integratives Behandlungskonzept für Menschen mit psychotischen Störungen. In: Hütterer-Kirsch, R. (Ed.): *Psychotherapie mit psychotischen Menschen.* Springer, Berlin.

Andersen, T. (1991). *The reflecting team: Dialogues and dialogues about dialogues.* W.W. Norton, New York.

Anderson, H. & Goolishan, H. (1992). The client is the expert: A not-knowing approach to therapy. In: Namee, S. & Gergen, S.J. (Eds.): *Therapy as social construction.* Sage, London.

Aristotle. (1926). *Ars Rhetorica.* Loeb Classical Library, Harvard University Press, Cambridge, MA.

Aristotle. (1952). *Ethica Nicomachea.* Loeb Classical Library, Harvard University Press, Cambridge, MA.

Augustine. (1989). *Confessions.* Loeb Classical Library, Harvard University Press, Cambridge, MA.

Ausloos, G. (1995). *La compétence des familles: Temps, chaos, processus.* Erès, Ramonville-Saint-Agne, France.

Austin, J.L. (1962). *How to do things with words.* Oxford University Press, London.

Bachelor, A. (1991). Comparison and relationship to outcome of diverse dimensions of the helping alliance as seen by client and therapist. *Psychotherapy, 28,* 534–549.

Bandler, R. & Grinder, J. (1979). *Frogs into princes.* Real People Press, Moab, UT.

Bandura, A. (1969). *Principles of behavior modification.* Holt, Rinehart & Winston, New York.

Bandura, A. (1977). Self—efficacy: Toward a unifying theory of behavioural change. *Psychological Review,* 84 (2), 191–215.

Bannink, F. (2010). *1001 solution-focused questions* (2nd revised ed.). W.W. Norton, New York.

Bannink, F. (2012). *Practicing positive CBT: From reducing distress to building success.* Wiley-Blackwell, Chichester, UK.

Bateson, G. (1972). *Steps to an ecology of mind.* Paladin Books, London.

Bateson, G. (1975). The birth of a matrix. In: Berger, M.M. (Ed.): *Beyond the double bind.* Brunner/Mazel, New York.

Bateson, G. (1979). *Mind and nature: A necessary unity.* Wildwood House, London.

Batra, A., Wassmann, R. & Buchkremer, G. (Eds.) (2000). *Verhaltenstherapie: Grundlagen - methoden - grenzgebiete.* Thieme, Stuttgart, Germany.

Bauer, J. (2006). *Warum Ich fühle, was du fühlst: Intuitive Kommunikation und das Geheimnis der Spielgelneuronen.* Hoffmann & Campe, Hambourg.

Beck, A. (1976). *Cognitive therapy and the emotional disorders.* International University Press, New York.

Beck, A. & Freeman, A. et al. (1989). *Cognitive therapy of personality disorders.* Guilford Press, New York.

Beck, A., Rush, A.J., Shaw, B.E. & Emery, G. (1979). *Cognitive therapy of depression.* Guilford Press, New York.

Beck, A., Wright, F.D., Newman, C.F. & Liese, B.S. (1993). *Cognitive therapy of substance abuse.* Guilford Press, New York.

Berg, I.K. (1991). *Family preservation: A brief therapy workbook.* BT Press, London.

Berg, I.K. (1992). A wolf in disguise is not a grandmother. *Journal of Systemic Therapies,* 13 (1), 13–14.

Berg, I.K. & De Jong, P. (1996). Solution-building conversations: Co-constructing a sense of competency with clients. *Families in Society: The Journal of Contemporary Human Services,* 6 (77), 376–391.

Berg, I.K. & Dolan, Y. (2001). *Tales of solutions.* W.W. Norton, New York.

Berg, I.K. & Kelly, S. (2000). *Building solutions in child protective services.* W.W. Norton, New York.

Berg, I.K. & Miller, S. (1992). *Working with the problem drinker.* W.W. Norton, New York.

Berg, I.K. & Reuss, N. (1998). *Solutions step by step: A substance abuse treatment manual.* W.W. Norton, New York.

Beyebach, M. (2006). *24 Ideas para una psicoterapia breve.* Herder, Barcelona.

Beyebach, M. & Herrera de Vega, M. (2011). *200 tareas en terapia breve.* Herder, Barcelona.

Binswanger, L. (1962). *Grundformen und Erkenntnis menschlichen Daseins.* Reinhardt, München.

Binswanger, L. (1965). *Wahn: Beiträge zu seiner phänomenologischen und daseinsanalytischen Erforschung.* Günther Neske, Pfullingen, Germany.

Blanchard, K. & Johnson, S. (2011). *The one-minute manager.* Harper, New York.

Bloch, E. (1985). *Werkausgabe, Band 5: Das Prinzip Hoffnung.* Suhrkamp, Frankfurt a.M.

Boszormenyi-Nagy, I. & Spark, G. (1973). *Invisible loyalties.* Harper & Row, New York.

Brantley, J. (2003). *Calming your anxious mind.* New Harbinger Publications, Oakland, CA.

Bruner, J. (1986). *Actual minds, possible worlds.* Harvard University Press, Cambridge, MA.

Cade, B. & O'Hanlon, W. (1993). *A brief guide to brief therapy.* W.W. Norton, New York.

Carnegie, D. (1993). *How to win friends and influence people* (1st ed. 1936). Cedar, London.

Cellerier, G. & Real del Sarte, O. (2010). *Le couple coopère-t-il? Perspectives Piagéticiennes et systémiques.* Erès, Ramonville-Saint-Agne, France.

Ciompi, L. (1982). *Affektlogik.* Klett-Cotta, Stuttgart.

Comte-Sponville, A. (1995). *Petit traité des grandes vertus.* Presses Universitaires de France, Paris.

Csikszentmihalyi, M. (2002). *Flow* (1st ed. 1988). Rider, London.

Damasio, A. (1994). *Descartes' error: Emotion, reason and the human brain.* Putnam, New York.

Damasio, A. (2000). *The feeling of what happens: Body, emotion and the making of consciousness.* Vintage, London.

Damasio, A. (2004). *Looking for Spinoza.* Vintage, London.

De Jong, P. & Berg, I.K. (1998). *Interviewing for solutions.* Brooks & Cole, Pacific Grove, CA.

de Shazer, S. (1978). Brief hypnotherapy of two sexual dysfunctions: The crystal ball technique. *The American Journal of Clinical Hypnosis,* 20 (3), 239–250.

de Shazer, S. (1979). Brief therapy with families. *The American Journal of Family Therapy*, 7 (2), 83–95.

de Shazer, S. (1982). *Patterns of brief family therapy*. Guilford Press, New York.

de Shazer, S. (1984). The death of resistance. *Family Process*, 23, 11–21.

de Shazer, S. (1985). *Keys to solutions in brief therapy*. W.W. Norton, New York.

de Shazer, S. (1988). *Clues: Investigating solutions in brief therapy*. W.W. Norton, New York.

de Shazer, S. (1991). *Putting difference to work*. W.W. Norton, New York.

de Shazer, S. (1994). *Words originally were magic*. W.W. Norton, New York.

de Shazer, S., Dolan, Y., Korman, H., Trepper, T., McCollum, E., & Berg, I.K. (2007). *More than miracles*. Routledge, New York.

Detienne, M. & Vernant, J.P. (1978). *Les ruses de l'intelligence: La mètis des Grecs*. Flammarion, Paris.

Dilthey, W. (1984). *Das Wesen der Philosophie*. Reclam, Stuttgart.

Diogenes Laertius. (1925). *Lives of eminent philosophers: Book 10: Epicure*. Loeb Classical Library, Harvard University Press, Cambridge, MA.

Dolan, Y. (1985). *A path with a heart: Ericksonian utilisation with resistant and chronic clients*. Brunner/Mazel, New York.

Dolan, Y. (1991). *Resolving sexual abuse*. W.W. Norton, New York.

Dolan, Y. (2000). *Beyond survival*. (Original title: Living Well is the Best Revenge). BT Press, London.

Dolan, Y. & Pichot, T. (2003). *Solution-focused brief therapy: Its effective use in agency settings*. Haworth Clinical Press, Binghamton, NY.

Doutrelugne, Y. & Cottencin, O. (2005). *Thérapie brève: Principes et outils pratiques*. Masson, Paris.

Doutrelugne, Y. & Cottencin, O. (Eds.) (2009). *Thérapie brève: Situations cliniques*. Masson, Paris.

Duncan, B., Hubble, M. & Miller, S. (1997). *Psychotherapy with "impossible" cases*. W.W. Norton, New York.

Duncan, B., Miller, S., Wampold, B. & Hubble, M. (2010). *The heart and soul of change* (2nd ed.). APA., New York.

Dunlap, K. (1928). A revision of the fundamental law of habit formation. *Science*, 57, 360.

Dunlap, K. (1930). Repetition in the breaking of habits. *Scientific Monthly*, 30, 66.

Durrant, M. (1993). *Residential treatment: A cooperative, competency-based approach to therapy and program design*. W.W. Norton, New York.

Eberling, W. & Hargens, J. (Eds.) (1996). *Einfach, kurz und gut: Zur Praxis der lösungsorientierten Kurzzeittherapie*. Modernes Lernen, Dortmund.

Ellis, A. (1962). *Reason and emotion in psychotherapy*. Lyle Stuart, New York.

Ellis, A. (1977). *Rational-emotive therapy*. Magination Press, American Psychological Association, New York.

Emerson, R.W. (1842). *Selected journals, 1820–1842*. Library of America, New York.

Erickson, M. (1980). *Collected papers*. (Rossi, E.L., Ed.). Irvington, New York.

Erickson, B.A. & Keeney, B. (2006). *Milton H. Erickson, M.D.: An American healer*. Crown House Publishing, Carmarthen, UK.

Farelly, F. & Brandsma, J. (1974). *Provocative therapy*. Meta Publications, Cupertino, CA.

Festinger, L. (1957). *A theory of cognitive dissonance*. Stanford University Press, Stanford, CA.

Fiedler, P. (2000). *Integrative Psychotherapie bei Persönlichkeitsstörungen*. Hogrefe, Göttingen.

Fisch, R., Weakland, J. & Segal, L. (1982). *Tactics of change*. Jossey-Bass, San Fransisco, CA.

Fiske, H. (2008). *Hope in action: Solution-focused conversations about suicide.* Routledge, New York.

Fliegel, S., Groeger, M., Künzel, R., Schulte, D. & Sorgatz, H. (1998). *Verhaltensthera-peutische Standardmethoden: Ein Übungsbuch* (4th ed.). Julius Beltz, Weinheim Germany.

Frank, J. & Frank, J. (1961). *Persuasion and healing.* Johns Hopkins University Press, Baltimore, MD.

Frankl, V. (1960). Paradoxical intention: A logotherapeutic technique. *American Journal of Psychotherapy,* 14, 520.

Frankl, V. (1985). *Der Mensch vor der Frage nach dem Sinn.* Piper, München.

Frankl, V. (1999). *Theorie und Therapie der Neurosen* (1st ed. 1956). UTB, Stuttgart.

Franklin, C., Trepper, T., McCollum, E. & Gingerich, W. (2011). *Solution-focused brief therapy: A handbook of evidence-based practice.* Oxford University Press, New York.

Friedman, S. (Ed.) (1995). *The reflecting team in action: Collaborative practice in family therapy.* Guilford Press, New York.

Furman, B. (1998). *It's never too late to have a happy childhood: From adversity to resilience.* BT Press, London.

Furman, B. & Ahola, T. (1992). *Solution talk: Hosting therapeutic conversations.* W.W. Norton, New York.

Fürstenau, P. (1992). *Entwicklungsförderung durch Therapie.* Pfeiffer, München.

Gergen, J. (1991). *The saturated self: Dilemmas of identity in contemporary life.* Basic Books, New York.

Gergen, J. (2001). *Social construction in context.* Sage, London.

Gilligan, S. (1987). *Therapeutic trances: The cooperation principle in ericksonian therapy.* Brunner/Mazel, New York.

Gilligan, S. & Price, R. (Eds.) (1992). *Therapeutic conversations.* W.W. Norton, New York.

Gingerich, W. & Eisengart, S. (2000). Solution-focused brief therapy: A review of the outcome research. *Family Process,* 39, 477–498.

Girard, R. (1978). *Les choses cachées depuis la fondation du monde.* Grasset, Paris.

Goldberg, E. (2001). *The executive brain: Frontal lobes and the civilized mind.* Oxford University Press, New York, USA.

Goldfried, M. & Davison, G. (1976). *Clinical behavior therapy.* Holt, Rinehart & Winston, New York.

Goldstein, A.P. (1973). *Structured learning therapy.* Academic Press, New York.

Goldstein, K. (1934). *Der Aufbau des Organismus.* Martinus Nijhoff, Den Haag.

Goleman, D. (2004). *Emotional intelligence & working with emotional intelligence.* Bloomsbury, London.

Gordon, D. & Myers-Anderson, M. (1981). *Phoenix: Therapeutic patterns of Milton Erickson.* Meta Publications, Cupertino, CA.

Gourevitsch, A. (1973). *Les catégories de la culture médiévale.* Gallimard, Paris.

Grawe, K. (1998). *Psychologische Therapie.* Hogrefe, Göttingen.

Grawe, K. (2004). *Neuropsychotherapie.* Hogrefe, Göttingen.

Grawe, K., Donati, R. & Bernauer, F. (1994). *Psychotherapie im Wandel: Von der Konfession zur Profession.* Hogrefe, Göttingen.

Groopman, J. (2005). *The anatomy of hope.* Simon & Schuster, London.

Hafkenscheid, A., Duncan, B. & Miller, S. (2010). The Outcome and Session Rating Scales: A cross-cultural examination of the psychometric properties of the Dutch translation. *Journal of Brief Therapy,* 7 (1 & 2), 1–12.

Haley, J. (1963). *Strategies of psychotherapy.* Grune & Stratton, New York.

Haley, J. (1973). *Uncommon therapy: The psychiatric techniques of Milton H. Erickson, M.D.* Norton, New York.

Haley, J. (1976). *Problem solving therapy*. Harper & Row, New York.

Haley, J. (1984). *Ordeal therapy*. Jossey-Bass, San Fransisco, CA.

Haley, J. (1985). *Conversations with Milton H. Erickson, M.D. parts 1, 2 & 3*. Triangle Press, New York.

Hansch, D. (1997). *Psychosynergetik: Die fraktale Evolution des Psychischen. Grundlagen einer allgemeinen Psychotherapie*. Westdeutscher Verlag, Opladen, Germany.

Hargens, J. (2000). *Bitte nicht helfen!* (2nd ed.). Carl Auer, Heidelberg.

Hautzinger, M. (Ed.) (1998). *Kognitive Verhaltenstherapie bei psychischen Störungen*. Psychologie Verlags Union, Weinheim, Allemagne.

Hendrick, S. (2007). *Un modèle de thérapie brève systémique*. Erès, Ramonville-Saint-Agne, France.

Hendrick, S., Isebaert, L. & Dolan, Y. (2011). Solution focused therapy in drinking problems. In: Franklin, C. & Thomas, F. (Eds.): *Solution-focused brief therapy*. Oxford University Press, New York.

Hoyt, M. (1996). Solution building and language games: A conversation with Steve de Shazer. In: Hoyt, M. (Ed.): *Constructive therapies 2*. Guilford Press, New York.

Hubble, M., Duncan, B. & Miller, S. (Eds.) (1999). *The heart and soul of change* (1st ed.). American Psychological Association, Washington.

Husserl, E. (1969). *Philosophie als strenge Wissenschaft*. Vittorio Klostermann, Frankfurt a.M.

Isebaert, L. (1997). Der lösungsorientierte Ansatz in Europa. In: Hesse, J. (Ed.): *Systemisch-lösungsorientierte Kurzzeittherapie*. Vandenhoeck & Ruprecht, Göttingen, Germany.

Isebaert, L. (1998). Das Brügger Modell. In: Dörring-Meyer, H. (Ed.): *Lösungsorientierung/ Ressourcenorientierung*. Vandenhoeck & Ruprecht, Göttingen, Germany.

Isebaert, L. (2002). Het brugse model. In: Rijnders, P. (Ed.): *Kortdurend Behandelen in de Praktijk*. Bohn Stafleu van Loghum, Houten, Netherlands.

Isebaert, L. (2004). *Kurzzeittherapie: Ein praktisches Handbuch. Die gesundheitsorientierte kognitive Therapie*. Thieme, Stuttgart, Germany.

Isebaert, L. (2007). *Praktijkboek oplossingsgerichte cognitieve therapie*. De Tijdstroom, Utrecht, Netherlands.

Isebaert, L. (2009). Thérapie brève de l'abus et de la dépendance alcoolique. In: Doutrelugne, Y. & Cottencin, O. (Eds.): *Thérapie brève: Situations cliniques*. Masson, Paris.

Isebaert, L. & Cabié, M.C. (1997). *Pour une thérapie brève: Le libre choix du patient comme éthique en psychothérapie*. Erès, Ramonville-Saint-Agne, France.

Isebaert, L. & Dumoulin, J.P. (2000). *Drink Wijzer*. Van Haelewyck, Leuven, Belgium.

Jackson, P. & McKergow, M. (2002). *The solution focus: The simple way to positive change*. Nicholas Brearly, London.

Jellinek, E. (1960). *The disease concept of alcoholism*. Hillhouse Press, Highland Park, NJ.

Kabat-Zin, J. (1991). *Full catastrophe living*. Dell, New York.

Kandel, E. & Hawkins, R. (1999). The biological basis of learning and individuality. In: *The scientific American book of the brain*. Lyons Press, Guilford, CT.

Kandel, E., Schwartz, J. & Jessel, T. (Eds.) (2000). *Principles of neural science*. McGraw Hill, New York.

Kanfer, F.H. & Goldstein, A.P. (Eds.) (1975). *Helping people change*. Pergamon Press, New York.

Keeney, B. (1983). *Aesthetics of change*. Guilford Press, New York.

Keeney, B. & Erickson, B.A. (2006). *Milton H. Erickson, M.D.: An American healer*. Ringing Rocks Press, Philadelphia.

Körkel, J. (Ed.) (1988). *Der Rückfall des Suchtkranken: Eine Flucht in die Sucht?* Springer, Berlin.

Körkel, J. (2003). Rückfall und Rückfallprävention bei Alkoholabhängigkeit. In: Steingass, H.P. (Ed.): *Chronisch mehrfach beeinträchtigte Abhängige*. Neuland, Geesthacht, Allemagne.

Korzybski, A. (1921). *Manhood of humanity: The science and art of human engineering*. E.P. Dutton, New York.

Korzybski, A. (1933). *Science and sanity*. Non-Aristotelian Library, Lakeville, CT, USA.

Lambert, M. (2013). *Bergin and Garfield's handbook of psychotherapy and behavior change*. John Wiley & Sons, Hoboken, NJ.

Lammers, C.L. (2007). *Emotionsbezogene Psychotherapie*. Schattauer, Stuttgart.

Lazarus, A. (1972). *Behavior therapy and beyond*. McGraw-Hill, New York.

Lazarus, A. (1976). *Multi-modal behaviour therapy*. Springer, New York.

Lazarus, A. (1981). *The practice of multi-modal therapy*. McGraw-Hill, Highstown.

Linden, M. & Lautzinger, M. (2000). *Verhaltenstherapiemanual* (4th ed.). Springer, Berlin.

Linehan, M. (1993a). *Cognitive-behavioural treatment of borderline personality disorder*. Guilford, New York.

Linehan, M. (1993b). *Skills training manual for treating borderline personality disorder*. Guilford Press, New York.

Lipchik, E. (Ed.) (1988). *Interviewing*. Aspen, Rockville, MD.

Lipchik, E. (2002). *Beyond technique in solution-focused therapy*. Guilford, New York.

Lowe, R. (2004). *Family therapy: A constructive framework*. Sage, London.

Ludewig, K. (1992). *Systemische Therapie: Grundlagen klinischer Theorie und Praxis*. Klett-Cotta, Stuttgart.

Lyubomirsky, S. (2010). *The how of happiness*. Little, Brown, London.

Madanès, C. (1991). *Strategic family therapy*. Jossey-Bass, San Francisco, CA

Madanès, C. (2014). Soft shock therapy. *Psychotherapy Networker*, 38 (2), 38.

Maercker, A. (Ed.) (1997). *Therapie der posttraumatischen Belastungsstörungen*. Springer, Berlin.

Margraf, J. (Ed.) (2000). *Lehrbuch der Verhaltenstherapie, Band 1 & 2* (2te Auflage). Springer, Berlin.

Marlatt, G.A. & Gordon, J.R. (Eds.) (1985). *Relapse prevention: Maintenance strategies in the treatment of affective disorders*. Guilford Press, New York.

Meichenbaum, D. (1977). *Cognitive-behaviour modification*. Plenum Press, New York.

Miller, G. (1997). *Becoming miracle workers: Language and meaning in brief therapy*. Aldine De Gruyter, New York.

Miller, G. & de Shazer, S. (1998). Have you heard the latest rumor about . . .? Solution-focused therapy as a rumor. *Family Process*, 37 (3), 363–377.

Miller, S., Hubble, M. & Duncan, B. (Eds.) (2003). *Handbook of solution-focused brief therapy* (1st ed. 1991). Jossey-Bass, San Fransisco, CA.

Minkovski, E. (1968). *Le temps vécu* (1st ed. 1933). Delachaux & Niestlé, Neuchâtel.

Minuchin, S. (1974). *Families and family therapy*. Harvard University Press, Cambridge, MA.

Minuchin, S. & Fischman, H.C. (1981). *Family therapy techniques*. Harvard University Press, Cambridge, MA.

Neenan, M. & Dryden, W. (2014). *Cognitive behavior therapy: 100 key points and techniques*. Routledge, New York.

Neill, J. & Kniskern, D. (1982). *From psyche to system: The evolving therapy of Carl Whitaker*. Guilford Press, New York.

Nelson, T. (Ed.) (2005). *Education and training in solution-focused brief therapy*. Haworth Press, Binghamton, NY.

Nelson, T. & Thomas, F. (Eds.) (2007). *Handbook of solution-focused brief therapy: Clinical applications*. Haworth Press, Binghamton, NY.

Nietzsche, F. (1873). *Schopenhauer as educator*. In: *Werke in zwei Bänden*. Carl Hanser Verlag, Munich.

Nietzsche, F. (1967). Menschliches, Allzumenschliches. In: *Werke in zwei Bänden*. C. Hanser, Munich.

Norcross, J.C. (Ed.) (1986). *Handbook of electic psychotherapy*. Brunner/Mazel, New York.

O'Connell, B. (1998). Solution-focused therapy. Sage, London.

O'Hanlon, W.H. (1987). *Taproots: Underlying principles of Milton Erickson's therapy and hypnosis*. W.W. Norton, New York.

O'Hanlon, W.H. & Weiner-Davis, M. (1989). *In search for solutions*. W.W. Norton, New York.

O'Hanlon, W.H. & Wilk, J. (1987). *Shifting contexts*. Guilford Press, New York.

Oughourlian, J.M. (2013). *Notre Troisième Cerveau*. Albin Michel, Paris.

Pichot, T. & Dolan, Y. (2003). *Solution-focused brief therapy: Its effective use in agency settings*. Haworth, New York.

Prochaska, J.O., Norcross, J.C. & Di Clemente, C.C. (1994). *Changing for good*. Morrow, New York.

Quick, E. (2008). *Doing what works in brief therapy: A strategic solution-focused approach* (2nd ed.). Academic Press, Elsevier, San Diego, CA.

Quick, E. (2012). *Core competencies in the solution-focused and strategic therapies: Becoming a highly proficient solution-focused and strategic therapist*. Routledge, New York.

Quick, E. (2013). *Solution focused anxiety management*. Academic Press, Elsevier, San Diego, CA.

Quinnett, P. (2000). *Suicide: The forever decision. Crossroad Publishing*. Spring Valley, NY.

Rabkin, R. (1977). *Strategic psychotherapy*. Basic Books, New York.

Ratner, H., George, E. & Iveson, C. (2012). *Solution-focused brief therapy: 100 key points and techniques*. Routledge, New York.

Reiter, L. & Ahlers, C. (Eds.) (1991). *Systemisches Denken und therapeutischer Prozess*. Springer, Berlin.

Retzer, A. (Ed.) (1991). *Die Behandlung psychotischen Verhaltens*. Carl Auer, Heidelberg, Allemagne.

Rittermann, M. (1983). *Using hypnosis in family therapy*. Jossey-Bass, San Fransisco, CA.

Rogers, C. (1951). *Client-centred therapy*. Houghton Mifflin, Boston.

Rosen, S. (1982). *My voice will go with you: The teaching tales of Milton H. Erickson*. W.W. Norton, New York.

Rosenzweig, S. (1936). Some implicit common factors in diverse methods of psychotherapy. *American Journal of Orthopsychiatry*, 6, 412–415.

Rossi, E. (Ed.) (1980). *The collected papers of Milton H. Erickson*. Irvington, New York.

Salovey, P., Brackett, M. & Mayer, J. (2004). *Emotional intelligence: Key readings on the Mayer and Salovey Model*. Nati Professional Resources, Naples, FL.

Scheler, M. (1972). Die Idole der Selbsterkenntnis. In: Scheler, M. (Ed.): *Vom Umsturz der Werte* (1st ed. 1915). Francke, Bern CH.

Schiepek, G. (1991). *Systemtheorie der klinischen Psychologie*. Vieweg, Braunschweig, Allemagne.

Schneider, K. (1923). *Die psychopathischen Persönlichkeiten*. Deuticke, Leipzig, Allemagne.

Segal, Z. (2002). *Mindfulness-based cognitive therapy for depression*. Guilford Press, New York.

Selekman, M. (2010). *Collaborative brief therapy with children*. Routledge, New York.

Selekman, M. & Beyebach, M. (2013). *Changing self-destructive habits: Pathways to solutions with couples and families*. Routledge, New York.

Seligman, M. (1975). *Learned helplessness: On depression, development and death*. Freeman, San Fransisco.

Seligman, M. (2003). *Authentic happiness*. Nicholas Brealey, London.

Seligman, M. (2007). *What you can change and what you can't: Learning to accept who you are.* Nicholas Brealey, London.

Selvini-Palazzoli, M., Boscolo, L., Cecchin, G. & Prata, G. (1975). *Paradox and Counterparadox.* Jason Aronson, Lanham, MD.

Shapiro, F. (2001). *Eye movement desensitization and reprocessing* (2nd ed.). Guilford Press, New York.

Shaw, G.B. (1903). Man and superman. Penguin, London.

Simon, F. (1990). *Meine Psychose, mein Fahrrad und ich.* Carl Auer, Heidelberg, Allemagne.

Skinner, B.F. (1953). *Science and human behavior.* Macmillian, New York.

Sparrer, I. & Varga von Kibéd, M. (2007). *Miracle, solution and system.* Solutions Books, Oxford, UK.

Squire, R. & Kandel, E. (1999). *From mind to molecules.* Scientific American Library, New York.

Steingass, H.P. (2003). Suchtkrank, suchtkränker, am suchtkränksten. In: Steingass, H.P. (Ed.): *Chronisch mehrfach beeinträchtigte Abhängige.* Neuland, Geesthacht, Allemagne.

Streek, U. & Broda, M. (2003). Editorial, Themaheft über Zwangserkrankungen. *Psychiatrie im Dialog 3/*2003/ 4.Jg.

Talman, M. (1990). *Single session therapy.* Jossey-Bass, San Fransisco, CA.

Tavris, C. & Aronson, E. (2007). *Mistakes were made (but not by me).* Harcourt, Orlando, FL.

Trepper, T. & Barret, M.J. (1989). *The systemic treatment of incest.* Brunner/Mazel, New York.

Tschunschke, V. & Czogalik, D. (Eds.) (1990). *Psychotherapie-Welche Effekte verändern?* Springer, Berlin.

Turnell, A. & Edwards, S. (1999). *Signs of safety: A solutions and safety oriented approach to child protection.* W.W. Norton, New York.

Turnell, A. & Essex, S. (2006). *Working with "denied" child abuse: A resolutions approach.* The Open University Press, Buckingham.

Van der Hart, O. (1978). *Overgang en bestendiging.* Van Loghum Slaterus, Deventer, Netherlands.

Van der Kolk, B. (1996). *Traumatic stress: The effects of overwhelming experience on mind, body and society.* Guilford Press, New York.

Van Gennep, J. (1969). *Les rites de passage.* Mouton, La Haye, Pays-Bas.

Van Velden, K. (Ed.) (1977). *Directieve therapie, 1 & 2.* Van Loghum Slaterus, Deventer, Netherlands.

Vannier, J. (2014, 31 March). *Osservatore Romano.* The Vatican.

Varga von Kibéd, M. & Sparrer, I. (2000). *Ganz im Gegenteil.* Carl Auer, München.

Von Schlippe, A. & Schweitzer, J. (1996). *Lehrbuch der systemischen Behandlung und Beratung.* Vandenhoeck & Ruprecht, Göttingen, Germany.

Von Weizsäcker, V. (1950). *Der Gestaltkreis.* Thieme, Stuttgart, Germany.

Wampold, B. (2001). *The great psychotherapy debate.* Lawrence Erlbaum, New Jersey, USA.

Watzlawick, P., Beavin, J. & Jackson, D. (1967). *Pragmatics of human communication.* W.W. Norton, New York.

Watzlawick, P., Weakland, J. & Fisch, R. (1974). *Change: Principles of problem formation and problem resolution.* W.W. Norton, New York.

Weeks, G. & l'Abate, L (2001): *Paradoxical psychotherapy: Theory and practice with individuals, couples and families.* Routledge, NY.

Weiner-Davis, M. (1993). *Divorce busting: A revolutionary and rapid program for staying together.* Summit, New York.

Weiner-Davis, M., de Shazer, S. & Gingerich, W. (1987). Building on pre-treatment change to construct the therapeutic solution: An exploratory study. *Journal of Marital and Family Therapy*, 13, 359–363.

White, M. & Epston, D. (1990). *Narrative means to therapeutic ends*. W.W. Norton, New York.

Wittgenstein, L. (1989). *Bemerkungen über die Philosophie der Psychologie*. Werkausgabe, Band 7, Suhrkamp, Frankfurt a.M.

Wittgenstein, L. (1992). *Philosophische Untersuchungen*. Werkausgabe, Band 1, Suhrkamp, Frankfurt a.M.

Wolberg, J.L. (Ed.) (1965). *Short-term psychotherapy*. Grune & Stratton, New York.

Wolpe, J. (1969). *The practice of behaviour therapy*. Pergamon Press, New York.

Wolpe, J. & Lazarus, A. (1966). *Behaviour therapy techniques*. Pergamon Press, London.

Yapko, M. (Ed.) (1989). *Brief therapy approaches to treating anxiety and depression*. Brunner/Mazel, New York.

Zeig, J. (1980). *A teaching seminar with Milton H. Erickson*. Brunner/Mazel, New York.

Zeig, J. & Gilligan, S. (1990). *Brief therapy: Myths, methods and metaphors*. Brunner/Mazel, New York.

Index

For Product Safety Concerns and Information please contact our EU
representative GPSR@taylorandfrancis.com
Taylor & Francis Verlag GmbH, Kaufingerstraße 24, 80331 München, Germany

www.ingramcontent.com/pod-product-compliance
Lightning Source LLC
Chambersburg PA
CBHW070414270326
41926CB00014B/2812